Pro Microsoft Hyper-V 2019

Practical Guidance and Hands-On Labs

Andy Syrewicze
Richard Siddaway

Apress®

Pro Microsoft Hyper-V 2019: Practical Guidance and Hands-On Labs

Andy Syrewicze
Jenison, MI, USA

Richard Siddaway
Baston, Lincolnshire, UK

ISBN-13 (pbk): 978-1-4842-4115-8
https://doi.org/10.1007/978-1-4842-4116-5

ISBN-13 (electronic): 978-1-4842-4116-5

Library of Congress Control Number: 2018961411

Managing Director, Apress Media LLC: Welmoed Spahr
Acquisitions Editor: Joan Murray
Development Editor: Laura Berendson
Coordinating Editor: Jill Balzano

Cover image designed by Ryan McGuire

Distributed to the book trade worldwide by Springer Science+Business Media New York, 233 Spring Street, 6th Floor, New York, NY 10013. Phone 1-800-SPRINGER, fax (201) 348-4505, e-mail orders-ny@springer-sbm.com, or visit www.springeronline.com. Apress Media, LLC is a California LLC and the sole member (owner) is Springer Science+Business Media Finance Inc (SSBM Finance Inc). SSBM Finance Inc is a Delaware corporation.

For information on translations, please e-mail rights@apress.com, or visit www.apress.com/rights-permissions.

Apress titles may be purchased in bulk for academic, corporate, or promotional use. eBook versions and licenses are also available for most titles. For more information, reference our Print and eBook Bulk Sales web page at www.apress.com/bulk-sales.

Any source code or other supplementary material referenced by the authors in this book is available to readers on GitHub via the book's product page, located at www.apress.com/9781484241158. For more detailed information, please visit www.apress.com/source-code.

Printed on acid-free paper

To my wife, Crystal, and my son, Evan, for their continued love, their support of my IT community work, and, more generally, for always putting up with my shenanigans and tomfoolery.

—Andy

To the ladies of my family—June, Ann, Sarah, and my granddaughters Lauren and Hannah

Thank you for being a treasured part of my life.

—Richard

Table of Contents

About the Authors

Andy Syrewicze is based in the United States and currently has the distinct pleasure of acting as a Technical Evangelist for Altaro Software. Andy is heavily involved in the IT community, on Altaro's behalf, in several different ways, including podcasts, webinars, blogging, and public speaking. Overall, Andy has spent the last 15+ years in IT, with areas of focus including virtualization, cloud services, VMware, and the Microsoft server stack, with an emphasis on Hyper-V and clustering. Andy spends a great deal of time working with the IT community as one of Microsoft's cloud and datacenter management Most Valued Professionals (MVPs). Andy has a passion for technology and always enjoys talking about tech with peers, customers, and fellow IT pros over a cup of coffee or a cold beer.

Richard Siddaway is based in England. With more than 25 years of experience in various aspects of IT, Richard specializes in the Microsoft environment at an architectural level, especially around Active Directory (AD), Exchange, SQL Server, and infrastructure optimization.

Much of his recent experience has involved the automation, usually with PowerShell, of administrative tasks, including a client service portal for cloud-based services, AD management, and infrastructure creation.

Microsoft has recognized his technical expertise and community activities by presenting him the Microsoft MVP award over multiple years. Richard is a frequent speaker at conferences in the UK, continental Europe, and the United States. Richard has several books to his credit, covering the PowerShell language, using PowerShell to administer Windows systems, Windows Management Instrumentation (WMI), and AD.

Acknowledgments

It's always a surprise when you stop to consider the number of people it takes to actually produce a book such as this. Our names are on the cover, but there is a whole list of people who contribute behind the scenes. This is one of the best bits to write—in which we get to thank them for the hard work they've put in to this book.

First, we'd like to thank the Microsoft Hyper-V team, for the product. If they hadn't produced such a great hypervisor that people were interested in using, we'd have nothing to write about.

The members of the team Apress put together for this book have been superb: Joan Murray, Laura Berendson, and Jill Balzano.

There were a number of reviews of the manuscript during its development. The individual reviewers gave their time to read and comment on the book, and we're very grateful for their input. They helped improve the book, by making us think about their comments.

Notwithstanding the input of so many people, any errors of omission, or commission, are still ours.

Andy would like to thank Richard for always being there to lend a hand when the task list became too large and whose contributions to this text have been invaluable. This book would not have been possible without you, my friend.

Richard would specifically like to thank Andy for the opportunity to contribute to the book and for the many interesting discussions about Hyper-V and related technologies. It's been a very enjoyable experience.

Introduction

This book is designed to be a tutorial in Hyper-V administration. As such, we recommend that you read the chapters in order. You'll probably find yourself referring to earlier chapters, as you work through the book. When you've finished the book, you may find yourself referring to a chapter, to help solve a problem. That's fine. It's your book!

This book takes a task-oriented approach to Hyper-V management, and as such, you will be able to immediately apply some of the knowledge gained in the day-to-day administration of Hyper-V.

While you may feel comfortable conducting some of these tasks. We have gone out of our way to instruct you as to which tasks require extra care and attention. When it comes to infrastructure management tasks and virtualization, there may be times when you are working with some very sensitive items, such as storage, and any misconfiguration and/or incorrect setting could be potentially disastrous. We're not trying to scare you, just pointing out the actual pitfalls.

Is This Book for You?

In short, this text is designed to take a junior IT professional, who knows nothing about Hyper-V or virtualization, and bring him or her to competency.

In a few more words, one constant in the world of IT is that things are always changing. Businesses must stay competitive, which means a need for more efficiency. Many are turning to virtualization as one of these efficiencies. Most IT departments and hiring managers now require virtualization know-how as a core skill for most IT jobs. If you're a junior level IT professional looking to branch out, get a promotion, or increase your job security, this book is for you. If you're looking to change roles within your organization, the knowledge gained from this book will help. Maybe you're a developer who would like to understand more about the test environment you're working in.

Another common situation today is a merger, in which the incoming company already has some Hyper-V hosts in place. Or maybe your company has historically gone with a different vendor, such as VMware, and you're in the process of moving to Hyper-V, for its many advantages and cost savings. If you're an IT pro finding yourself in this situation, this book is for you as well!

Whatever the reason, you'll find Hyper-V to be a mature, powerful, but still-evolving technology that will aid you in your everyday work, if leveraged and utilized properly. This book will teach you the best practices for using Hyper-V on a day-to-day basis.

In order for this book to be most effective in teaching you the target material, there is a prerequisite level of knowledge required. You should have *at least* some experience in each of the following:

- The installation and configuration of Windows Server Operating Systems

- Basic AD management

- NTFS file level permissions

- IPv4 networking

- Understanding of server hardware platforms

- Basic knowledge of PowerShell

- Storage concepts, including: direct-attached storage, network-attached storage (NAS), iSCSI, NFS, and Fibre Channel

Road Map

In Chapter 1, we introduce you to Hyper-V and virtualization, setting the scene for future chapters. Chapter 2 teaches you how to configure your Hyper-V host and connect to virtual machines (VMs). You may think that odd, but we want you to be using the knowledge and skills you learn from this book as soon as possible, and once you can connect to a VM, you can use your Windows Server knowledge to administer that system.

The next set of chapters are concerned with creating and administering VMs. Starting with their creation in Chapter 3, we move on to configuring VM resources, in Chapter 4. You will learn how to manage Hyper-V Integration Services in Chapter 5. Integration services are important to get right, as they control how your VM communicates with the Hyper-V host.

Chapter 6 focuses on managing and modifying VM files. Your VM is a set of files existing on your Hyper-V host. Their location, protection, and management are vital to the well-being of your virtual environment. Chapter 7 extends your knowledge of the underlying file structure, when we consider checkpoints—a point-in-time snapshot of a VM. You'll also learn how to effectively use checkpoints and when not to use them.

If you've worked in IT for any length of time, you'll know that networking (Chapter 8) and storage (Chapter 9) are essential parts of your environment. In these two chapters, you'll learn how these aspects of your environment are virtualized and how you manage them.

Your users expect their applications to be available. In many cases this means you must implement some kind of high availability. In a Hyper-V environment, this could mean that you cluster the hosts (Chapter 10) or the VMs (Chapter 12). You also must know how to manage the clusters (Chapter 11). We recommend that you read these three chapters as a group, as they are closely related.

In Chapter 13, you'll learn how to monitor your Hyper-V hosts and the virtual machines and a little bit about capacity planning.

The next three chapters are loosely related. Chapter 14 will teach you how to migrate VMs between Hyper-V hosts. There are a number of techniques you'll learn, as well as when to use each technique. Chapter 15 extends these thoughts, by showing you how to move existing workloads to Hyper-V. Disaster recovery is an important topic for all administrators. You'll learn how to use a Hyper-V replica in Chapter 16.

There's a change of emphasis in Chapter 17, which is a bit more focused on applications. Containers have been a part of the Linux landscape for a number of years, and now they're available on Windows. The chapter will show you how to install the containers feature, as well as create and manage containers.

Chapter 18 will help those of you with large Hyper-V environments, when we look at using System Center Virtual Machine Manager.

The book closes with Chapter 19, in which we discuss ways to extend your learning. As administrators, there's always something new to learn, and we'll provide our thoughts on a number of topics you should consider.

Most of the chapters include step-by-step instructions to perform the administrative tasks under discussion. We also provide PowerShell code that will perform the task. We recommend that you learn to use the PowerShell commands, so that you can automate your tasks and so make your life easier.

Creating Your Lab Environment

There are a number of ways to create a lab environment for the practical examples in this book. The ideal way would be if you had a number of spare servers and several terabytes of storage, so you could create a lab that approached a real production environment. Most of us aren't that lucky, so we'll supply a few suggestions for a lab.

It is possible to "nest" virtualized Hyper-V instances on top of a VMware ESXi host, but quite a bit of tweaking is needed. As far as nesting Hyper-V on top of Hyper-V, it is only supported in Windows Server 2016, later versions of Windows 10, and Windows Server 2019.

You could use nested compute instances in Microsoft Azure, but keep in mind that there is a monthly cost associated with that.

If you have a bit of spare hardware that can be used for your lab environment, you'll at least want two physical hosts with a low-end NAS, or other sharable storage, to be used by them. You'll also need a gigabit switch and a couple of Ethernet cables.

You can manage most of the book with a single machine with 16GB RAM. You need to be very careful about what else is running, but it is possible to perform most of the practical work in the book. As usual, more is better!

We have assumed that you can install and configure Windows Server and install the Hyper-V feature.

CHAPTER 1

Introduction to Hyper-V

Do you remember the days of physical servers? Generally, the rule of thumb was to have one major role or application per server. That was mainly because many applications and services just did not play well together. They had to be separated, so that they couldn't fight among themselves and cause problems for users on the network. The unfortunate side effect of this practice was that all of these physical servers were, on average, utilizing 20% of their resources, meaning 80% of those resources were being wasted. We don't pour a glass of water only to drink 20% of it and waste the rest, do we? We don't live in only 20% of our homes, do we? Clearly, resource utilization in IT needed a makeover. This is where virtualization technology comes in.

Virtualization has solved our resource utilization problems, by enabling us to make more effective use of the hardware available. This means that we can now host more workloads using less space inside of our datacenters. We can dynamically move workloads from one piece of physical hardware to another, without any interruption to the running workload. We can even provide high-availability functionality to workloads using these virtualization technologies.

It's not difficult to see how virtualization is changing the IT management landscape. System administrators should now be looking to add this knowledge to their toolbox, to help them manage ever-increasing IT complexity, as virtualization continues to be a staple of IT departments everywhere.

While there are many different virtualization technologies on the market today, this book will focus on Microsoft's Hyper-V, with a primary focus on Windows Server 2019 and Windows Server 2016, with some mention of Windows Server 2012 R2.

We'll start this chapter by considering the fundamental nature of Hyper-V. We're going to be discussing Hyper-V, and virtualization in general, from the standpoint of the fictional company XYZ Corp. This will allow us to take a difficult conceptual topic—Hyper-V—and apply it to solve everyday business issues. This will make it easier to see

© Andy Syrewicze, Richard Siddaway 2018
A. Syrewicze and R. Siddaway, *Pro Microsoft Hyper-V 2019*, https://doi.org/10.1007/978-1-4842-4116-5_1

where this technology could fit in your organization. Once we understand the "why," we'll explain how this technology works from the ground up. We'll continue to build on this foundation throughout the book.

Let's dig in.

What Is Hyper-V?

Simply put, Hyper-V is a hypervisor. The problem with this answer is that it will likely lead you to the question "What is a hypervisor?" A hypervisor is a piece of software that is designed to delegate access to physical resources, such as CPU and memory, to multiple virtualized operating systems (OSs) or applications, as shown in Figure 1-1.

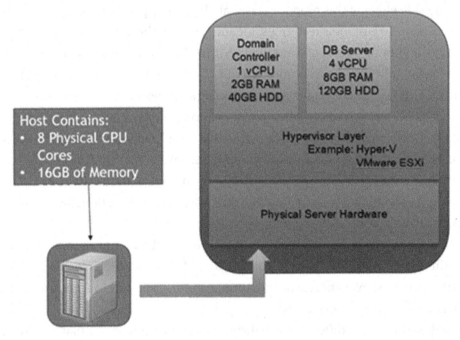

Figure 1-1. *Logical layout of a hypervisor*

In Figure 1-1, we have a physical server that contains 8 physical CPUs and 16GB of memory. The hypervisor layer gets installed directly on top of the physical hardware and acts as a broker for the resources contained in the host machine. Figure 1-1 shows that two "virtualized" servers have been created, and each is being given a portion of the host's physical resources. Each of these virtual machines (VMs) contains fully functional

OSs and will act just like physical servers on your network. They are also isolated and separated from one another, just like physical servers. This is the most basic function of a hypervisor such as Hyper-V.

The hypervisor is truly the core of any virtualization platform. Hyper-V itself performs the core functions of Microsoft's virtualization platform, but other technologies, such as System Center Virtual Machine Manager and Failover Clustering, help create a more holistic virtualization solution. We cover these technologies later in the book, after you've learned about the core functions of Hyper-V itself.

Sometimes, it's not enough just to know what a technology does. We also need to understand how it benefits us and how it can help us solve our business problems. With that in mind as you read the text, picture the fictional company XYZ Corp., which is a company with aging IT infrastructure that is badly in need of updating. As you work through the first couple of chapters, imagine this fictional company as an example of how this technology benefits you and your organization.

The Business Benefits of Hyper-V

Hypervisors have been around for some time. Widespread adoption started more than ten years ago, when IT professionals saw the inherent benefits of virtualized workloads. Some variant of VMware's ESXi product has been around for the last ten years or so, and some mainframe systems have been utilizing this type of technology since the 1980s!

Let's look at this from a business perspective, using the example of the fictional company XYZ Corp., which is approaching a hardware refresh cycle. This approach will enable you to see why the industry has transitioned to virtualized workloads.

Setting the Stage

XYZ Corp. is a company that is getting ready to make some expenditures on technology as part of a three-year refresh cycle. Its existing infrastructure has been in place for some time, and no virtualization technologies are in use today. Cost is a major concern, as well as stability. The IT department has been given a limited budget for upgrades, but several of the physical machines are out of support and warranty, and a significant investment would be needed to replace each existing physical machine with another, more current model.

The Physical Computing Model

To date, XYZ Corp. has used the older computing model of one role/function per physical server. This methodology has a number of flaws associated with it. Before we go any further, let's get a look at what it currently has. The servers and workloads owned and operated by XYZ are shown in Figure 1-2.

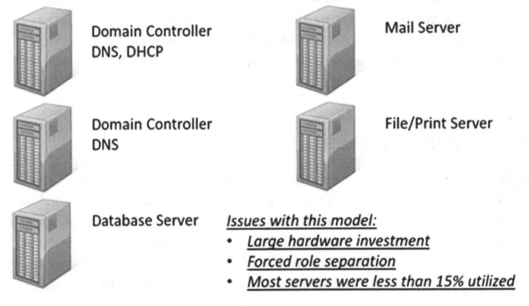

Figure 1-2. *A list of physical servers owned and operated by XYZ Corp*

Figure 1-2 shows that XYZ Corp. has five physical servers and that each server generally follows the rule of one role/feature per physical box. Sadly, this method was not conducive to efficient use of computing resources. Historically, most systems would go through life running at only 20% utilization (on average), leaving the remaining 80% of the system with nothing to do.

One role per server was never an official standard; it was an unspoken rule that most system admins adopted. In reality, there are so many bits of software on any given system that, once in a while, issues are bound to arise wherein some of that code doesn't play nicely with other code on the system. This can cause system outages or degrade performance. Downtime equals money lost to the business. The unspoken rule of one role per machine helped prevent this from occurring.

SERVER CONSOLIDATION

Before the widespread introduction of virtualization, many organizations invoked projects to reduce the number of servers in their environment. This was essentially a cost-cutting exercise, in order to free up hardware for new applications.

Consolidation projects would attempt to match workloads, to enable multiple applications to run on the same server, with varying levels of success.

If your management suggests that a server consolidation project would be a good thing to attempt, you should immediately start talking up the benefits of virtualization. Virtualization gives you the benefits of server consolidation but retains the application isolation inherent in the one-application-per-server concept.

Don't consolidate—virtualize.

The increase in cost to buy additional physical servers to fill all the roles needed on the network was an acceptable cost, because at the time, there wasn't a mainstream technology that would allow system admins to make better use of the available hardware. Nor was there any software available that would ensure the separation of workloads to prevent those situations in which two pieces of code are in conflict and create issues. Virtualization technology has now solved this computing dilemma, in the form of the hypervisor.

Making the Change to Virtualized Computing

Virtualization technology enables XYZ Corp. to purchase one or two new, powerful physical servers and place the workloads shown in Figure 1-2 into isolated "virtual" instances on top of a hypervisor running on the new equipment. More powerful servers will be more expensive than a similar though less powerful system, but reducing the number of physical servers and maintaining warranty and support on them usually allows you to have a much lower overall cost.

Table 1-1 reviews the resources that are currently in use by the physical workloads.

Table 1-1. *Total Physical Computing Resources Configured for XYZ Corp*

Workload	Number of Physical CPU Cores	Amount of Physical Memory in GB	Amount of Storage in GB
Domain Controller	2	2	80
Domain Controller	2	2	80
Database Server	4	8	300
Mail Server	4	8	300
File/Print Server	2	4	500
Total	14 CPU Cores	24 GB	1260 GB

Table 1-1 shows that the company needs significant resources. These are currently physical resources in their existing infrastructure that are underutilized. XYZ Corp. will have to do some performance checking on each of the systems, to obtain a more precise measure as to how much the systems are underutilized. Once they have the actual demand and some hard data, they can start sizing the new physical servers on which they'll be placing their hypervisors.

Note   You can use such tools as Perfmon, Task Manager, and others to discover and capture this type of information.

As an example, let's say that after examining the resource demand for each physical server, XYZ Corp. determines that the *actual* resource demand for each workload (with a little wiggle room) is as shown in Table 1-2.

Table 1-2. *Projected Resource Demand per Virtualized Workload for XYZ Corp*

Workload	Number of Physical CPU Cores	Amount of Physical Memory in GB	Amount of Storage in GB
Domain Controller	1	2	50
Domain Controller	1	1	50
Database Server	2	6	200
Mail Server	2	6	150
File/Print Server	1	2	250
Total	7 CPU Cores	17GB of RAM	700GB

Comparing Table 1-2 to Table 1-1 shows that a reduction of 7 CPU cores and 7GB of RAM are required, if the workloads are virtualized, and 560GB of storage space will be potentially released.

MORE TO LEARN

You may find that a server appears to be using a very small portion of the resources allocated to it, and you'll want to downsize the workload accordingly, once virtualized. You still need to take into account the minimum software requirements for the OS and the software running inside the virtualized OS, to maintain a supported configuration with the associated vendor.

For example, you may have a Microsoft SQL Server system that has a memory demand of 256MB of memory (unlikely, but it could happen). While you could size the workload in that manner once it's virtualized, the minimum system requirements for Microsoft SQL Server state that 1024MB of memory is the minimum required. Therefore, when sizing the memory for that workload, you wouldn't drop below 1024MB of memory for that VM.

Without getting too into the details of the sizing math at this point, taking into account the resource requirements listed in Table 1-2 and adding the resource overhead required to run Hyper-V itself, XYZ Corp. now knows how powerful of a server (or servers) to procure. These new physical server(s) will be more powerful individually than the previous five physical servers and will conduct the work that all five of them performed previously.

Additionally, it would be wise for XYZ Corp. to allocate an additional 20%–40% of resources to account for future growth. This is by no means an industry-defined standard. The needs of the organization will dictate this more than anything. Many organizations will add the maximum number of CPUs and maximize the RAM in a new virtualization host, as it's cheaper to do that than to add components at a later date. This approach ensures that there is room for future growth in the virtualized environment.

The Virtualized Computing Model

Once the new hardware is purchased and arrives, Hyper-V will be installed and the workloads migrated in their existing state into a VM, or they may be migrated in a more traditional manner, if the OS and/or installed software is being upgraded as well. During this process, XYZ Corp. can allocate each of its core computing resources (CPU, memory, storage, and networking) to each virtualized workload, using the projected resource demand they determined earlier in Table 1-2.

Once migration has been completed, each workload will be running on one of the new servers, each in its own isolated virtualized environment. In this new configuration, every entity on the XYZ Corp. network that was able to talk to the (now virtualized) workloads can still do so. *Nothing* has changed from a communications perspective. These workloads are still reachable on the network, and the end points won't even know that the workloads have been virtualized. Everything is business as usual for XYZ Corp.'s end users.

Once XYZ Corp. has fully virtualized its computing workload, the server layout would look much like that shown in Figure 1-3. The physical server footprint has been reduced to two physical servers, with the five previously physical workloads now running as VMs. These workloads continue to function as though they are still physical boxes, which is the core function of our hypervisor—Hyper-V.

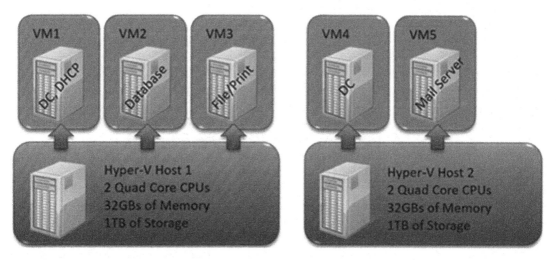

Figure 1-3. *XYZ Corp.'s now virtualized computing workload. The virtualization host's specifications are higher than the calculations from Table 1-2 would indicate, to allow for future growth of the environment.*

A question that probably will arise during a virtualization project is whether all the company's workloads are compatible with virtualization. While there may be workloads that shouldn't be virtualized, such as some specialized manufacturing software, they are becoming fewer and farther between. Software vendors are noting the mass adoption of virtualization, and they are working to make sure that their products can be virtualized. If you are unsure, check with each individual software vendor on a case-by-case basis.

Now that you have a view of what a virtualized environment looks like, it's time to review the Hyper-V architecture in more detail.

Hyper-V Architecture

Figure 1-4 shows the Hyper-V architecture. Let's review what each component does in turn.

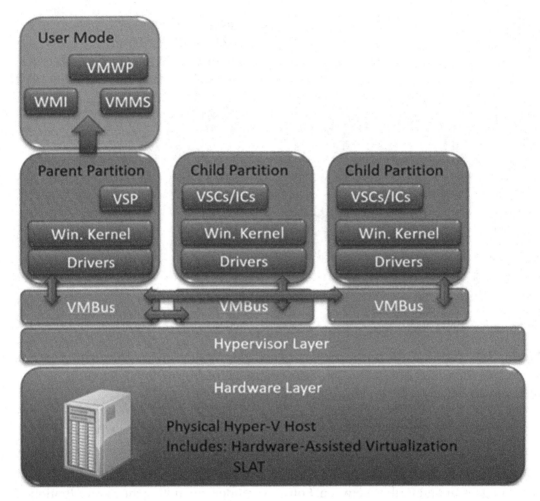

Figure 1-4. *High-level Hyper-V architecture*

Hardware Layer

The hardware layer is the physical hardware on which Hyper-V is installed. There are some requirements that must be met:

- Hyper-V expects that the machine will have hardware-assisted virtualization, such as Intel-VT or AMD-V.

- SLAT (second-level address translation) is also a requirement.

These are computing technologies that are contained within the CPU on your Hyper-V host. Hardware-assisted virtualization and SLAT both provide enhanced computational capabilities when dealing with virtualized workloads. Most new hardware supports these requirements, but some options may still have to be enabled in the systems BIOS. Check your system's documentation for details.

Hypervisor Layer

The hypervisor controls access to CPU and memory and allocates them as resources to various partitions (or VMs) running on top of them. When the Hyper-V role is installed, the OS of the physical server is made virtual during the process and becomes the parent partition shown in Figure 1-4.

VMBus

This is a virtual bus that enables communication between the host system and the VMs running on the host. If a virtual machine has the Hyper-V integration services installed, it will be able to utilize this bus for information exchanges with the host.

Parent Partition

This partition (or VM) is a "hidden" VM that acts as the management OS and controls the hypervisor. After you install the Hyper-V role on a Windows server, the hypervisor layer is placed between the hardware and the OS. The installed OS effectively becomes a VM running on Hyper-V, which is used to provide device drivers, power management services, storage, and networking functionality to the VMs running on the host.

Virtualization Service Provider (VSP)

VSP is only in the parent partition. It provides support for virtualized devices with full driver capabilities contained within the child VMs over the VMBus, that is, it provides optimized access to hardware resources to child VMs.

Virtual Machine Worker Process (VMWP)

The VM worker process (one separate process for each running VM on the Hyper-V host) provides management functionality and access from the parent partition to each of the child partitions. These processes run in user mode.

Virtual Machine Management Service (VMMS)

The VMMS is responsible for managing the state of all virtual machines (or child partitions) running on the Hyper-V host. The VMMS runs in user mode, within the parent partition.

Child Partition

Child partitions are the VMs hosted on your Hyper-V installation that are given access to CPU and memory by the hypervisor. Access to storage and networking resources is granted through the parent partition's VSP. There are two different types of child partitions: enlightened and unenlightened. An enlightened VM will have the integration tools installed, have full synthetic device support, and utilize the VMBus for enhanced support and features. An unenlightened VM will not have the integration tools and will have emulated virtual devices instead of synthetic. Emulated devices do not perform as well as synthetic devices. We'll be talking about enlightened and unenlightened VMs later on in this book.

Virtualization Service Client (VSC)

The VSC in each child VM utilizes the hardware resources that are provided by the parent partition. Communication is via the VMBus.

Integration Components (ICs)

These components, also known as integration tools, allow the child partition to communicate with the hypervisor and provides a number of other functions and benefits. We'll be discussing integration components in a few chapters.

Note   The use of the term *partitions* can be confusing at times. In the case of Hyper-V, the word *partition* can be used interchangeably with the term *virtual machine*, and you can expect to see this terminology throughout the text.

As you can see, there are a lot of components in this technology. You may not grasp the Hyper-V architecture right away, but don't fret! As you read the book, understanding the underlying architecture, and having an idea of how things are laid out, will help you comprehend why some functions and features in Hyper-V are set up and used the way they are.

We mentioned, at the top of the chapter, that we're concentrating on Windows Server 2019 and Windows Server 2016 in this book. Microsoft has complicated the picture regarding Windows server versions, as we'll explain next.

Windows Server Versions

Hyper-V was introduced with Windows Server 2008. At that time, Microsoft's strategy with the server product was to introduce a major version approximately every four years. An interim version, referred to as the R2 version, was introduced between major versions. This means that the following versions of Windows Server are currently supported by Microsoft for installing Hyper-V:

- Windows Server 2008

- Windows Server 2008 R2

- Windows Server 2012

- Windows Server 2012 R2

- Windows Server 2016

Microsoft has a ten-year support policy (though the support period is often extended), so support for Windows Server 2008 and 2008 R2 ends at the start of 2020. Windows Server 2012 and 2012 R2 will no longer be supported after October 2023.

This model changed with Windows Server 2016. Microsoft has moved to a continuous support policy similar to that introduced for Windows 10. There are now two release channels for Windows Server customers.

The first channel is the Long-Term Servicing Channel (LTSC). This is effectively the historical model used by Microsoft with new major versions of Windows Server released every two to four years. These releases have the same ten-year support life cycle that Microsoft has used for previous versions of Windows Server. The current LTSC version (as of this writing) is Windows Server 2016, with Windows Server 2019 expected toward the end of 2018. Releases from this channel are suited to scenarios requiring functional stability, for instance, exchange servers or large database servers. LTSC releases can receive updates (security and other) but won't get new features or functionality during their lifetime. LTSC releases are available as Server Core (though installation calls it Server, and it is the default option!) and Server with Desktop Experience (GUI).

The new channel is the Semi-Annual Channel (SAC). Releases in this channel occur every six months (March and September) and are designated as Windows Server, version YYMM, in which YY is the two-digit year and MM is the two-digit month. The first release in this channel was Windows Server, version 1709 (September 2017) followed by Windows Server, version 1803 (March 2018).

SAC releases have a supported lifetime of 18 months, as opposed to the 10 years for the LTSC releases. New functionality and features are introduced through SAC releases for customers who wish to innovate on a quicker cadence than the LTSC release. New features and functionality introduced through SAC releases should be rolled into the next LTSC release. SAC releases are currently only available as Server Core to Software Assurance and cloud customers.

The advantage of using SAC releases is that you get new functionality much quicker. The disadvantage is that your servers have a maximum life cycle of 18 months. SAC releases are currently recommended for containerized applications, container hosts, and applications requiring fast innovation.

We'll give a brief summary of the changes in the Windows Server versions, concentrating on features that may affect your Hyper-V environment.

The first SAC release (1709) introduced a number of new features, mainly for container support.

- Nano Server is now *only* for container images and is 80% smaller.

- Server Core container image is 60% smaller.

- Linux containers are now supported.

- VM start order can be controlled.

- Virtualized persistent memory

Windows Server version 1803 introduced the following features:

- Server Core base container image reduced by 30% over version 1709

- Curl, tar, and SSH support

- Windows Subsystem for Linux

- Container networking enhancements and increased Kubernetes functionality

Windows 2019 will include the new features of the 1709 and 1803 releases, plus

- Shielded VMs can now be Windows or Linux installs

- Network encryption

- Extending Windows Defender into the OS kernel

- Further shrinkage of the Server Core container image

- Increased support for Kubernetes

- Hyper-converged infrastructure

Windows Server, version 1809, will be the SAC release that corresponds to the feature set of Windows Server 2019.

Nano Server

Nano Server is a very small footprint installation option introduced with Windows Server 2016. It was a headless server that has to be managed remotely. Nano Server supports a limited number of OS features, including container host, Hyper-V, IIS, file server, and clustering.

In Windows Server, version 1709, Nano Server was reduced to a container image OS only. You can't create a Nano Server VM or install it on a physical machine.

We recommend that you use Nano server only as a container image, owing to this change.

Hyper-V Server

There is also the option of running Microsoft Hyper-V server. This is a low-footprint version of the server OS that is optimized for use as a Hyper-V host. It contains the Windows hypervisor, the driver model, and virtualization components. You can't install other server features, such as file server or IIS.

Hyper-V server machines don't provide a GUI and have to be managed remotely. They are an ideal virtualization platform, as minimum resources are consumed by the host, which maximizes what is available to the VM workloads.

Windows 10

Hyper-V has been available in the Windows client since Windows 8 and continues in Windows 10. Hyper-V on a Windows client machine has a subset of the features present in the server version. Using a client machine as a virtualization platform is good for development or demonstration purposes but can't be used in production.

You've likely had enough of the theoretical discussions by now, so we've provided some lab questions as a refresher. In the next chapter, you'll discover the Hyper-V management utilities that you'll be working with, as you get deeper into the Microsoft virtualization stack.

Lab Work

Please complete the following questions. Keep the answers handy, as you may find them useful as you read the rest of the book.

1. What is a hypervisor?

2. What are the key benefits of the virtualized computing model?

3. What is the parent partition, and how is it created?

4. What are the key differences between a parent partition and a child partition?

5. What is the primary purpose of the VMBus?

6. What is the primary purpose of the integration components?

CHAPTER 2

Configuring Hyper-V Host Settings

We've been digging through introductions and theory for some time, so it's now time to put that to practical application. We'll start by configuring the host settings of a stand-alone Hyper-V host. Hyper-V Manager will be used to complete these tasks, as it provides all of the needed functionality to connect to hosts, create virtual machines (VMs), and manage them.

Note A Hyper-V host may be referred to as a host or parent, while a VM may be referred to as a VM, guest, or child. The terms are interchangeable, and all will be seen throughout this book.

In This Chapter

This chapter will prepare you for future chapters, in which you'll create, and modify, VMs. Please be aware that some sections of Hyper-V Manager will simply be seen or mentioned in this chapter and may not be explained in full. Certain items within the interface warrant further discussion, requiring a deeper understanding of the basics, before we venture beyond the default settings. This includes topics such as VM configuration options and the setup and configuration of Hyper-V Replica.

We'll start this chapter by discussing Hyper-V Manager. Additionally, we'll be talking about configuring Hyper-V host settings—items that affect the way that the host functions and have an impact on the production workloads running on the host. Finally, you'll learn how to connect to a VM, which you'll be doing a lot, once you start working with Hyper-V. Let's get started. You may not have a VM to connect to yet, but understanding the process ahead of time will help ensure that you don't feel lost once we get to the next chapter and walk through creating a VM.

17

© Andy Syrewicze, Richard Siddaway 2018
A. Syrewicze and R. Siddaway, *Pro Microsoft Hyper-V 2019*, https://doi.org/10.1007/978-1-4842-4116-5_2

What Is Hyper-V Manager?

Hyper-V Manager is a Microsoft Management Console (MMC) snap-in that provides basic administrative capabilities for managing one or more stand-alone instances of Hyper-V. One of the most common things that new Hyper-V admins struggle with is the management ecosystem. It's not because it's a bad ecosystem, but that it's different from competing platforms, such as VMware, in the sense that there are potentially five different management interfaces available, depending on the size of the environment being managed. We'll briefly discuss each one and show you when each management utility comes into play.

Hyper-V Manager

This is primarily designed to manage stand-alone hosts or multiple hosts that are not clustered. It's the entry-level Hyper-V management tool with which all beginners should start. We'll be using Hyper-V Manager for the next several chapters. This utility can be launched from Administrative Tools in the Windows Control Panel.

Failover Cluster Manager

Failover Cluster Manager is similar in feel to Hyper-V Manager (as it's also an MMC) but offers more capabilities. It's designed to manage small clustered Hyper-V environments. If you have a clustered environment, this should be your default management tool for Hyper-V. This often confuses people, but instead of reinventing the wheel, Microsoft was able to leverage some of the already existing clustering technologies provided by this Windows Server role. This utility can be launched from Administrative Tools in the Windows Control Panel.

System Center Virtual Machine Manager

We'll cover this topic toward the end of the book. System Center Virtual Machine Manager (or SCVMM, for short) could easily have its own book. SCVMM is designed to manage the largest of Hyper-V deployments. It's probable that only large enterprise environments will see this in use, but it provides some of the more amazing Hyper-V feature sets, such as Network Virtualization and Service Templates. SCVMM requires a separate installation and appears in the Start Menu under SCVMM.

PowerShell

PowerShell isn't specifically a Hyper-V utility. It's Microsoft's automation engine and scripting language that is available on all Windows editions. PowerShell can be utilized, for instance, when you have to perform a task many times. You can deploy a script across several machines at once. Throughout this book, keep an eye out for useful PowerShell cmdlets and code snippets to experiment with as you learn. PowerShell can be launched from the Start Menu.

Windows PowerShell v5.1 is installed on Windows Server 2019 and Windows Server 2016. PowerShell v6.x is the cross-platform, open source version of PowerShell and is where future development will occur. The Hyper-V module is designed for Windows PowerShell v5.1 but appears to run in PowerShell v6.x. Other modules, such as Active Directory, won't run in PowerShell v6.x at this time. We recommend that you use PowerShell v5.1 to provide access to the maximum functionality. If you need to access Linux VMs, then PowerShell v6.x will have to be used.

Windows Server 2016 introduced PowerShell Direct. This is a method of providing remote access to VMs from the Hyper-V host. PowerShell Direct isn't dependent on networking connectivity to access the VM, because it uses the VMBus. There are a number of requirements for PowerShell Direct, including the following:

- PowerShell v5.1 or later versions

- Hyper-V host is Windows 10 or Windows Server 2016 or later

- Virtual Machine is Windows 10 or Windows Server 2016 or later

You create a PowerShell remoting session using the `-VMname` parameter, rather than `-ComputerName`; otherwise, accessing the VM through PowerShell Direct is the same as a standard PowerShell remoting session. The folder containing the PowerShell executable must be included in the PATH environment variable of the VM, for PowerShell Direct to work.

Windows Admin Center

Windows Admin Center (WAC, previously known as Project Honolulu) is the new kid on the block when it comes to management tools for Hyper-V. WAC is a web-based tool that is designed to manage hyperconverged infrastructure (HCI) in the emerging cloud era. It's designed to manage hosts, VMs, storage, and more. Microsoft has even made WAC extensible, so that third-party vendors can write add-ons for it. You may be wondering, if it's so great, why isn't it the main tool we'll be using. In short, it's still early days for WAC. It will be developed independently from the long-running MMC tool set. We bring it up here, so you'll be aware of it, as you may see mention of it later in this book.

WAC uses PowerShell remoting and WMI to manage the remote servers. The latest iterations of WAC can show the PowerShell code that is being used to perform the management tasks. This can be useful if you're trying to learn how to manage Hyper-V, VMs, and Windows servers in general, through PowerShell.

Connecting to Hyper-V Hosts

Before you can manage your Hyper-V environment, you must first connect to the system with the Hyper-V role installed. On the client machine, you must have the Remote Server Administration Toolkit (RSAT) tools of the same or newer version installed, in order to connect to the intended Hyper-V Host.

Note   Each version of the RSAT tools is a separate download. An Internet search is the quickest way to locate them. The RSAT tools are only available in a limited number of languages, and the culture of your client machine must match the language of the RSAT tools you're trying to use.

For example, connecting to a Windows Server 2012 R2 Hyper-V host with the Windows 7 era RSAT tools wouldn't work, but connecting to a Windows Server 2012 R2 Hyper-V host with Windows 10 era RSAT tools would be viable. Let's connect to a host now.

1. Launch Hyper-V Manager from Administrative Tools on the host itself or a management workstation.

2. Right-click the root of the tree in the left-hand pane and select Connect to server.

3. Fill out the select computer form, as seen in Figure 2-1, and click OK.

4. Verify that the target host now shows in the left-hand pane under the root and is selectable.

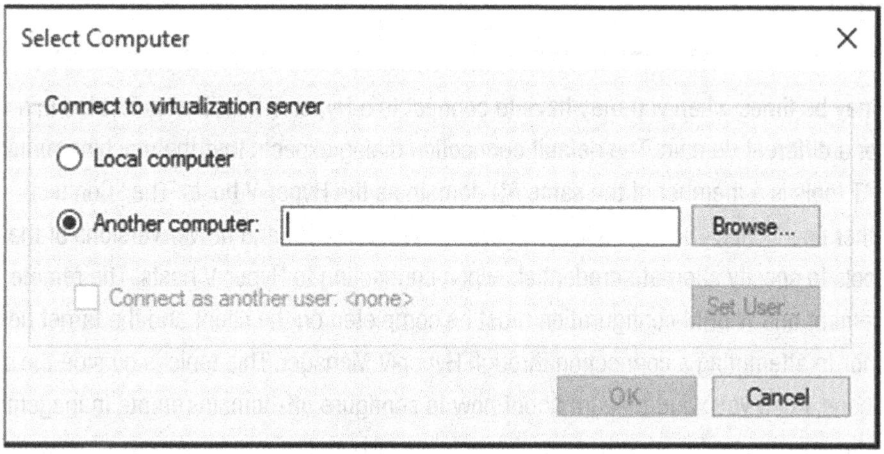

Figure 2-1. *Hyper-V Host connection dialog*

TRY IT YOURSELF

Following the instructions in this section, connect to your Hyper-V host from your client machine.

Adding hosts into the management utility is quite simple. Hyper-V Manager is a typical MMC snap-in, so you can add multiple targets into the left-hand tree as well. So, if you have multiple independent, stand-alone Hyper-V hosts in your environment, you can manage them all centrally from one instance of Hyper-V Manager. There is no need to connect to each host one at a time, which is an excellent time-saver.

Note   You'll need the correct security permissions to connect to any Hyper-V host. Any member of the domain administrators group will have the needed rights to connect to the target machine. Also, any user in the local Hyper-V administrators group on the target machine will have the correct rights to connect to that machine. You should make users members of the relevant Hyper-V administrators group on each host, rather than adding them to the domain administrators group. Create a group for Hyper-V administrators in your AD domain and add that group to the Hyper-V administrators group on each host, rather than managing each host individually.

MORE TO LEARN

There may be times when you may have to connect to a Hyper-V host that is located in a work group or a different domain. The default connection dialog expects that the machine running the RSAT tools is a member of the same AD domain as the Hyper-V hosts. The "Connect as another user" check box will allow Windows 8, Windows 10, and newer versions of the RSAT tools to specify alternate credentials when connecting to Hyper-V hosts. The remote management and WinRM configuration must be completed on the client and the target host also, prior to attempting a connection through Hyper-V Manager. This topic is outside the scope of this book, but if you want to learn about how to configure off-domain remote management, a great how-to can be found at `https://technet.microsoft.com/en-us/library/jj647785(v=ws.11).aspx`.

Navigating the Hyper-V Manager UI

Now that you've successfully connected to a Hyper-V host, basic management tasks can be completed. If the host you've connected to has some existing VMs, it may look like that in Figure 2-2. If it doesn't, don't worry, you'll be learning how to create a new VM in the next chapter.

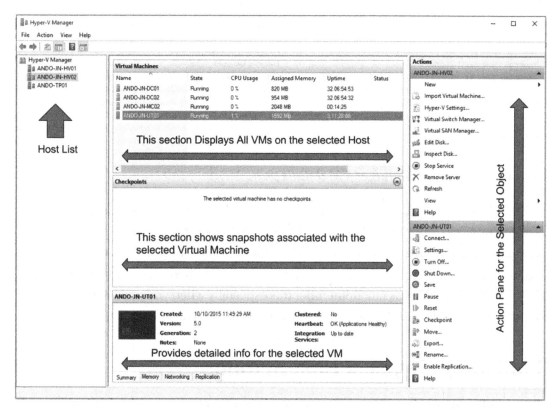

Figure 2-2. *Hyper-V Manager*

In Hyper-V Manager, as shown in Figure 2-2, hosts are listed on the left. VMs, their status, and any associated checkpoints (which we'll get into later) are listed in the center column, and actions associated with the selected object are listed in the right-hand column.

The Hyper-V host in Figure 2-2 contains a number of running VMs. If you select one of them and review the details section near the bottom, you can see basic information and monitoring data for the VM. For example, in Figure 2-2, the VM ANDO-JN-UT01 is highlighted, and the summary tab has been selected. This tab gives us basic information about the VM, such as generation, version, and clustering status. The other tabs provide information about memory, networking, and replication settings, such as in Figure 2-3, which displays the memory summary for the VM ANDO-UB01.

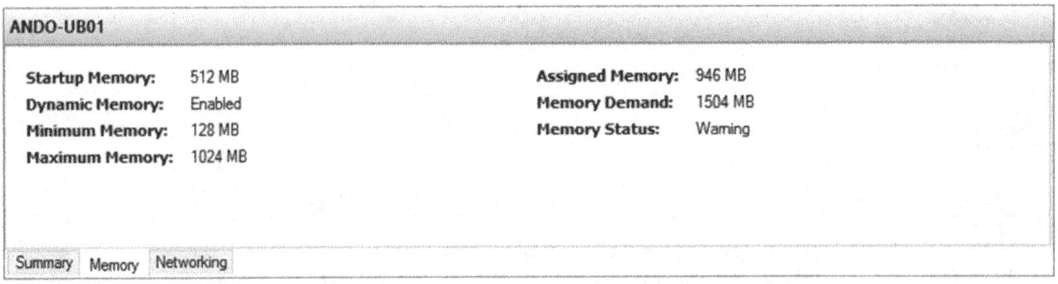

```
ANDO-UB01

  Startup Memory:    512 MB              Assigned Memory:   946 MB
  Dynamic Memory:    Enabled             Memory Demand:     1504 MB
  Minimum Memory:    128 MB              Memory Status:     Warning
  Maximum Memory:    1024 MB



  Summary   Memory   Networking
```

Figure 2-3. *Hyper-V Manager VM details pane Memory tab*

This all adds up to be a very important single-pane-of-glass view of your virtual infrastructure. It's important to know how this utility looks and feels, because when you start managing Hyper-V, this is ground zero for troubleshooting and optimization. Hyper-V Manager will give you the most clear-cut and simplified access to running VMs in the event all other methods fail. Remember this especially when you need to troubleshoot connectivity issues for a VM. Let's move on to configuring Hyper-V host settings.

Configuring Hyper-V Host Settings

When you first set up a new Hyper-V host, there are a number of items that should be configured before you start building VMs. It may also be necessary to modify some of these host settings in the future, if changes occur within your infrastructure. As an example, let's examine some of the basic settings.

1. Open Hyper-V Manager. Select the Hyper-V host in the left pane and click Hyper-V settings in the action pane. You'll see the dialog shown in Figure 2-4.

2. Make sure the Virtual Hard Disks section is selected on the left pane and select a location to store your virtual hard disks. You can pick a location or leave it as it is.

3. Select Virtual Machines in the left-hand pane and a location to store other VM related files. You can pick a location or leave it as it is.

4. Select the Live migration section and make sure that the maximum configured live migrations is 1. (For the purposes of a lab, no more is needed at this time.)

5. Click OK to close the window.

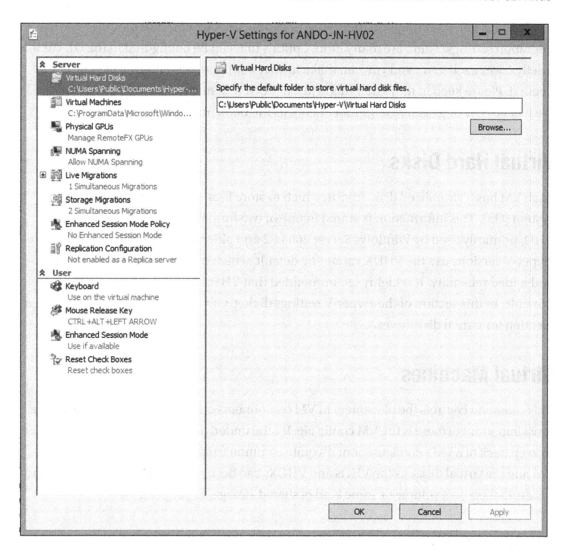

Figure 2-4. *Hyper-V settings dialog*

TRY IT YOURSELF

Connect to a Hyper-V host using Hyper-V Manager and examine host configuration. Make any changes that are required and detailed in this section.

Thus far, you've configured the storage location for your VMs and modified the live migration settings. There are many more options that can be configured in the UI. We'll briefly cover each item, and you can make further configuration changes in your lab, as needed. Please keep in mind that this is just a preview of most of the features mentioned. We will be covering each item in more detail as the book progresses.

Virtual Hard Disks

Each VM has a virtualized disk drive in which to store files and the VM's operating system (OS). This information is stored in one of two formats. The older file format is VHD, primarily used by Windows Server 2008 R2 and older instances of Hyper-V. Newer Hyper-V versions use the VHDX variant by default, which provides enhanced features and added reliability. It is highly recommended that VHDX files be utilized whenever possible. In this section of the Hyper-V settings dialog, you can define the default storage location for virtual disk drives.

Virtual Machines

This submenu controls the placement of VM components other than the virtual disks. The most important of these is the VM config file. It's the underlying file that Hyper-V references to keep track of a VM's configuration. It's quite common to see different locations for the VM and the virtual disks, as the VHDs and VHDXs can become quite large and may have to reside on their own volume or some kind of shared storage, as you'll see later.

Physical GPUs

This section is mainly intended for use in virtual desktop infrastructure (VDI) scenarios. There are times when increased graphical performance provided by in-host graphics processing units (GPUs) and the Microsoft RemoteFX display protocol is required. This is where you configure this feature.

NUMA Spanning

Non-uniform memory access (NUMA) provides VMs more efficient access to the physical memory of the host system. This gives better performance in *most* cases. There are a few configurations for which it is not needed, and it's desirable to disable this setting on the host. It's best to leave NUMA enabled at the host level and then enable or disable it on each individual VM. NUMA can be useful for workloads such as SharePoint or Exchange that actively support NUMA. If you are unsure if a particular workload is NUMA-capable, check with the software vendor.

Live Migrations

Live migration is a technology that enables you to move a VM from one physical Hyper-V host to another, without any downtime. In this section, the administrator can configure default behavior for live VM migrations to and from this specific host. This includes specifying a particular IP and associated network interface for migrations. Additional enhanced features control the type of authentication used between migration source and destination, as well as the transmission behavior.

Storage Migrations

This setting allows the administrator to define the number of simultaneous storage migrations that can occur. This setting is usually best left at the default of two, unless you *know* your infrastructure can handle more. Most small environments will leave this at the default.

Enhanced Session Mode Policy

This setting controls the administrator's experience with the console when managing VMs. Enhanced Session Mode is disabled by default. When enabled, it provides features such as clipboard functionality from host to guest and local drive redirection, which can make it easier to move files to new VMs in high-security environments. This must be enabled at the individual VM level as well.

Replication Configuration

Hyper-V has disaster recovery and replication built right into the product. Hyper-V replica enables replication of VMs between two or more host systems. We will be covering this in future chapters.

The sections listed under User (see Figure 2-4) are the controls for working within the console window of a particular VM, including how the keyboard functions and which key combination will release the mouse from a VM console window. Most of the defaults should be sufficient for most users.

Configuring Hyper-V Host Settings with PowerShell

It is also possible to configure host settings using Windows PowerShell, which is most useful when you have to automate a large number of changes to multiple hosts.

Let's take a look at how this can be done.

1. On your Hyper-V host, right-click the PowerShell icon and click Run as Administrator.

2. Run the command `Update-Help` and wait for the command to complete. This only has to be done once, after the OS has been installed. You can run it periodically, if desired, to download any changes to the help information.

3. Run the command `Get-Help Set-VMHost -online` and review the online documentation. Viewing the help online is the preferred option, as the online help is updated more frequently than the downloadable help files.

4. Run the command `Set-VMHost -MaximumVirtualMachine Migrations 3 -MaximumStorageMigrations 1`.

5. Open Hyper-V Manager and select the same Hyper-V host you used for steps 1–4.

6. In the right-hand action pane, click Hyper-V Settings.

7. On the Live Migration and Storage Migration tabs, verify that each value is set as specified previously.

8. Change simultaneous live migrations back to 2 and set simultaneous storage migrations to 1.

9. Click OK to exit Hyper-V Settings.

```
┌────────────────────────────────────────────────────────────────────┐
│                          TRY IT YOURSELF                           │
└────────────────────────────────────────────────────────────────────┘
```

Use PowerShell to view and modify the settings of your Hyper-V host.

Now that you understand the basics of connecting to a Hyper-V host and managing host settings, you're ready to move on to the next chapter and begin creating VMs. Prior to doing that, complete the following hands-on lab.

Lab Work

Complete any outstanding Try It Yourself sections and then

1. Using Hyper-V Manager, determine the memory demand for a running VM.

2. Using Hyper-V Manager, take note of the existing virtual hard disks storage path in Hyper-V Settings. Modify the path to point to a different location.

3. Using only `Get-Help` and the `Set-VMHost` cmdlets in PowerShell, determine the correct syntax to change the path for virtual hard-disk storage back to the original location.

4. Once completed, verify that the path is correct in Hyper-V Settings.

CHAPTER 3

Creating Your First Hyper-V Virtual Machine

You've had introductions to Hyper-V's architecture, and you've learned how to configure the core Hyper-V host settings. In this chapter, you'll be setting up a new virtual machine (VM), which will contain an operating system (OS) and its own virtual hardware. Remember that a VM is its own isolated entity that functions much the same as a physical server. As you complete the exercises in this chapter, you'll find that working with a VM is no different than interacting with a remote physical server.

In This Chapter

You'll first learn the components that make up a VM, then you'll run through the process of configuring a new VM, as follows:

- Specifying name, generation, and location of the VM

- Configuring basic hardware settings for memory and networking

- Configuring and connecting storage to the VM

- Defining how the guest OS will be installed inside the VM

By the end of this chapter, you'll have a working VM whose settings you'll modify further in the next chapter. Building new VMs is a task that you'll be doing often when working with Hyper-V. Workloads change frequently, and new servers must be provisioned all the time. Learning how to properly establish a new VM will prepare you for this new, fast-changing IT landscape.

© Andy Syrewicze, Richard Siddaway 2018
A. Syrewicze and R. Siddaway, *Pro Microsoft Hyper-V 2019*, https://doi.org/10.1007/978-1-4842-4116-5_3

What Components Make a Virtual Machine?

Before you create a new VM, it's best to understand all of the components that enable a VM to work. A virtualized OS functions in much the same manner as a physical server. It must have the same components that modern OSs depend on, just in an intangible state. This includes device drivers, BIOS, and core system devices. As there is no actual physical hardware in your VMs, virtual devices are created. The hypervisor layer provides the VM access to CPU and memory, while the parent partition provides access to networking and storage.

Static items, such as the VM configuration, and file-storage related items must reside on a file system. There are several file types that exist at the VM configuration path configured in the Hyper-V host settings, as discussed in Chapter 2.

Virtual Machine Config File

As you'll see shortly, it's quite easy to use the UI to set up and make changes to a new or existing VM. The configuration for a given VM is tracked and stored in a VM config file. In Windows Server 2012 and 2012 R2, this config file is stored in XML format and is saved with the file name in globally unique identifier (GUID) format, in the VM path you defined in Chapter 2. This can be seen in Figure 3-1.

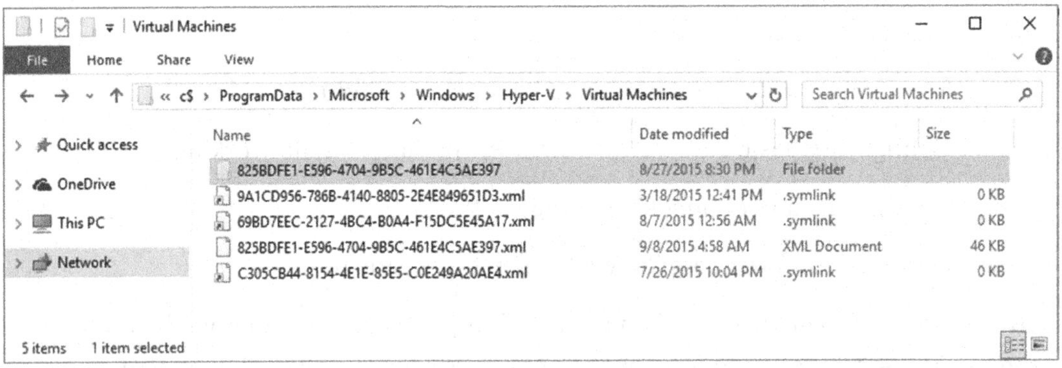

Figure 3-1. *Directory containing VM config files*

The files shown in Figure 3-1 are the config files for the VM. You'll also see that there are subfolders in this location as well. These folders contain the supporting files required for a VM.

FINDING THE GUID FOR 2012 R2 AND OLDER HOSTED VMS

It can be difficult to associate a hostname with a GUID. In the case where you may be looking for the config file for a specific VM, you can find the associated GUID using

```
Get-VM –Name "<VM NAME HERE>" | select Name, Id
```

Looking at the XML file for a VM will provide more information about the VM than you likely ever wanted to know, including a list of any checkpoint files associated with the VM. Think of a checkpoint as a picture in time that can be used to revert to how the VM was when the checkpoint was taken. We'll be talking about checkpoints in a later chapter in this book.

Virtual Machine Config Files in Windows Server 2016 and 2019

The storage and use of VM config files is different in Windows Server 2016 and later versions. Microsoft replaced the XML format with a new binary file type with a VMCX extension. Windows 10 also uses this type of configuration file. There are a number of reasons behind this change.

- Increased performance at scale

- Protection from the end user making a bad change in the config file

- More resilient and reliable storage of the VM configuration

Parsing XML files in environments with a large number of VMs (some large enterprises will have many thousands of VMs, and Microsoft Azure even more) can be very CPU-intensive. At larger scales, keeping track of the VM configurations takes resources away from hosting the VMs. This is not a good thing!

Additionally, a number of administrators have found themselves in bad situations after making incorrect or unintentional changes to a VM config file. This is a prime reason to leave this file alone, unless you're in the direst of circumstances, as you can quickly break your VM, if this file is edited incorrectly.

This new file type has the added benefit of not allowing administrators to manually edit the config file and potentially shoot themselves in the foot. Plus, the new file format is more resilient to environmental factors, such as storage outages or power failures. The file type has protections baked in, to help prevent any type of corruption to the config file.

MORE TO LEARN

As Windows Server 2016 has matured, it is now possible to modify a .VMCX VM config file, *if you REALLY need to.* For more information on doing this, please see this link:

https://blogs.msdn.microsoft.com/virtual_pc_guy/2017/04/18/editing-a-vmcx-file/

This really does fall into just-because-you-can-doesn't-mean-you-should territory. Directly editing the .VMCX file should be your ultimate last resort. You have been warned!

Virtual Machine BIN and VSV Files in 2012 and 2012 R2

Now, going back to the folder containing the VM config files, remember the subfolder that is named after the GUID of the VM? There are a couple of relevant files stored in this folder, and the BIN file is one of them. You'll find that this particular file can get quite large, because it will always be the same size as the memory assigned to the associated VM. If you assign 4GB of memory to a VM, it's BIN file will also be 4GB in size.

The BIN file is used to store a copy of the VM's memory to disk, in the event that the VM receives a stop command from the hypervisor. The default action is to "save" the VM state and is most common in sudden and unexpected host reboot situations. Hyper-V will save the contents of the VM's memory to disk, in the BIN file, and will retrieve it when the VM comes out of the stop state. At this point, the VM will be in the same state it was in before the host reboot.

This function is not always needed, so in the event you need to save some disk space, you can change the behavior of a VM to "Shut Down" on host reboot, instead of "Save." When a VM is configured in this manner, you will no longer see the BIN file. This setting can be modified in the properties section of a VM. We'll look at it in Chapter 4.

The VSV file is responsible for keeping track of all the device information associated with the VM.

Note   In Windows Server 2016 and 2019 Hyper-V, the BIN and VSV files have been replaced by the .VMRS file type for storage of the VM's runtime state data.

VHD and VHDX Files

The storage devices attached to the VM, such as a hard drive, are virtualized also. This information is stored on physical disk via VHD or VHDX files. These files are stored at the path you defined for virtual hard disk storage in Chapter 2.

Note   VHD is the older format introduced in Hyper-V 2008. It has a size limitation of 2TB. The VHDX format was introduced in Windows Server 2012, increasing the maximum size to 64TB and adding protection against storage connectivity issues and power outages. VHDX is the default format for every version of Hyper-V since 2012 R2.

Virtualized hard disks are stored at the location defined when a VM is created and are attached to the VM, to be presented as a block device, such as the C: volume. There are options as to how these files consume the assigned space. The default is "dynamically expanding," meaning the disk will only consume physical storage as it's used within the VM.

The other option is referred to as a "fixed disk." If you create a 500GB fixed disk and attach it to the VM, that 500GB is immediately consumed in the physical storage. This is useful in situations in which you want to make sure you don't over-provision your storage. Generally speaking, if you have very little oversight on your storage and/or you don't have a dedicated storage administrator, stick to fixed disks to prevent over-provisioning.

AVHD Files

AVHD files are very similar to VHD and VHDX files, in that they store the data contained within the VM. By default, there will be no AVHD files associated with a VM. When a checkpoint is taken, an AHVD file is created, and the VM config file is modified to redirect all incoming disk writes to it. We'll be covering checkpoints in more detail in Chapter 7.

Creating a New Virtual Machine

Now that you understand the underlying architecture and the files associated with a VM, you are ready to create one.

Let's launch the New Virtual Machine Wizard and create a VM.

1. With Hyper-V Manager open, select the target host that will run the new VM.

2. In the right-hand action pane, click New, then select Virtual Machine, as shown in Figure 3-2.

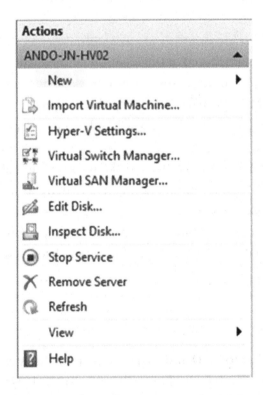

Figure 3-2. *Click New ➤ Virtual Machine to start the VM creation wizard*

VM CREATION WIZARD

The New Virtual Machine Wizard guides you step by step through the process of assigning resources to a VM. You can set the resources that you want the VM to have and how the hypervisor should treat this specific VM.

The first page of the wizard contains a Next button and a Finish button. Both are clickable. This can be confusing. How can we finish the wizard before we've even configured anything? Clicking the Finish button, in this situation, will create a VM with a default configuration that contains incorrect memory for most workloads and a 127GB dynamically expanding disk.

Over the years, we've found that being able to configure each option through the wizard is far more helpful than having to go back and change it later. *Most* items configured with the wizard can be modified at a later time, if required. Flexibility is one of the primary benefits of virtualization, and it wouldn't be helpful to lock you into the choices made through the wizard.

3. Click the check box "Do not show this page again," to prevent the starting page from displaying again.

4. Click Next.

5. On the "specify name and location" section of the wizard, you first must define a name. This will be the VM name, as displayed inside of the Hyper-V management tools. Additionally, you can define a different location in which to store the VM. By default, this field will be populated with the paths that we defined in the Hyper-V host settings in Chapter 2.

6. Click Next.

Note   The VM name is *not* the hostname of the running VM. Remember, you're creating the shell of the VM, and later on you'll install an OS within that shell.

7. You'll now be on the Specify Generation screen, shown in Figure 3-3.

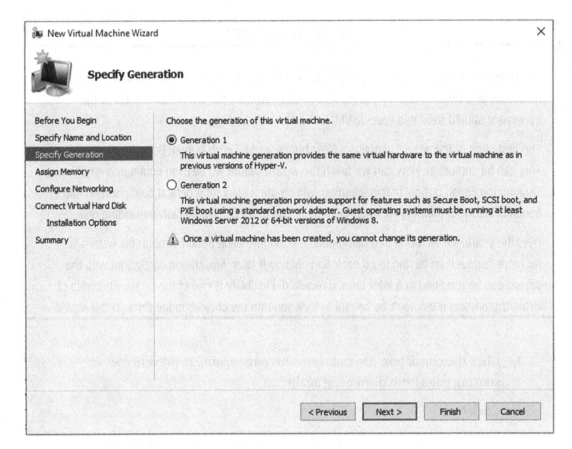

Figure 3-3. *Selecting the generation of the VM*

MORE TO LEARN

Windows Server 2012 Hyper-V introduced the concept of VM generation. As new advances in virtualization technology were introduced, some older features would have to be phased out in favor of those advancements. However, this had to be done in a way that would not alienate or hinder those organizations that were still running older technologies. Thus, the concept of a VM generation was created.

The VMs hosted on Hyper-V hosts prior to Server 2012 were given the designation "Generation 1" VMs. All new VMs with modern OSs running within them would be created as "Generation 2" VMs, although users still would have the option of building a VM with the older Generation 1 type, for environments that might still have some of the older Windows Server 2008/2008 R2 Hyper-V hosts in production.

A Generation 2 VM has a number of useful benefits, such as secure boot and UEFI firmware support. All new enhancements moving forward will be provided for this generation type. At the time of this writing, the following Windows OSs are supported Generation 2 OSs:

- Windows Server 2019

- Windows Server, version 1803

- Windows Server, version 1709

- Windows Server 2016

- Windows Server 2012 R2

- Windows Server 2012

- 64-bit versions of Windows 10

- 64-bit versions of Windows 8.1

- 64-bit versions of Windows 8

We would expect future SAC releases of Windows Server to be Generation 2, until a Generation 3 is created at some future time.

For a list of supported Linux distributions that are able to run as Generation 2 VMs, refer to `https://docs.microsoft.com/en-us/windows-server/virtualization/hyper-v/Supported-Linux-and-FreeBSD-virtual-machines-for-Hyper-V-on-Windows`.

8. Select Generation 2.

9. Click Next.

Caution   Be very careful and sure of your decision when selecting the VM generation, because once it's configured, it remains for the life of the VM. This is one of the very few items that cannot be modified once the machine is created!

The next screen of the wizard is the memory configuration screen, as seen in Figure 3-4. This section of the wizard dictates how much memory the VM will start with and whether Dynamic Memory is enabled. Dynamic Memory is a technology in which the Hyper-V host and the guest VM work together to determine the amount of memory the VM should be assigned for optimal performance. If Dynamic Memory is left in a disabled state, the amount of memory defined in the "startup memory" field will be the static amount of memory that the VM will run with at all times.

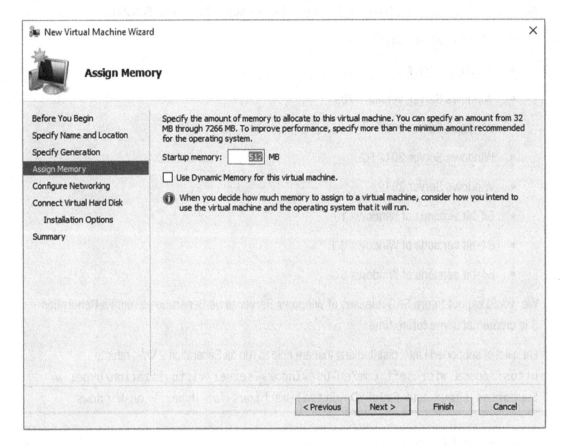

Figure 3-4. *Defining the startup memory and Dynamic Memory feature state*

10. Define the needed amount of memory; the default is 512MB. A minimum of 1024MB is required to install Windows Server.

11. Leave Dynamic Memory disabled at this time.

12. Click Next.

At this point, you'll be asked to configure the networking for the VM. A prerequisite for this section of the wizard is to have defined a virtual switch that can be used for communication (see Chapter 8). The VM we create in this chapter will not be able to talk with the physical network, but we'll configure that when we discuss networking.

13. Leave the Connection drop-down set to "Not Connected."

14. Click Next.

15. The many storage options are shown in Figure 3-5.

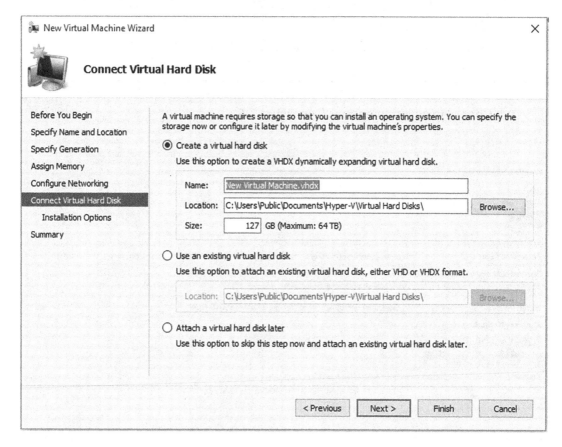

Figure 3-5. *Connect Virtual Hard Disk*

The default option here is to create a new virtual hard disk that lets you select the size of the virtual disk and also whether you want to store it in the default virtual hard disk path. You also have the option to use a preexisting VHD or VHDX file or attach a virtual hard disk at a later time. The latter is particularly useful when you simply want to run a live OS from an ISO, such as a live Linux distribution.

16. Keep the default location for the VHDX file.

17. Define the size of the virtual disk you want to create (make sure you have enough space!).

18. Click Next.

MORE TO LEARN

It is possible to pre-create a virtual hard disk with some of the advanced preferences mentioned earlier, such as fixed disks or specifying the older VHD file type. This can be done by launching the New Virtual Hard Disk wizard, by clicking New ➤ Hard Disk in the action pane in Hyper-V Manager. Once the new virtual disk is created, you simply select the "Use existing virtual hard disk" option in Figure 3-5 and navigate to the path where the file is stored.

---

19. Choose installation options (see Figure 3-6).

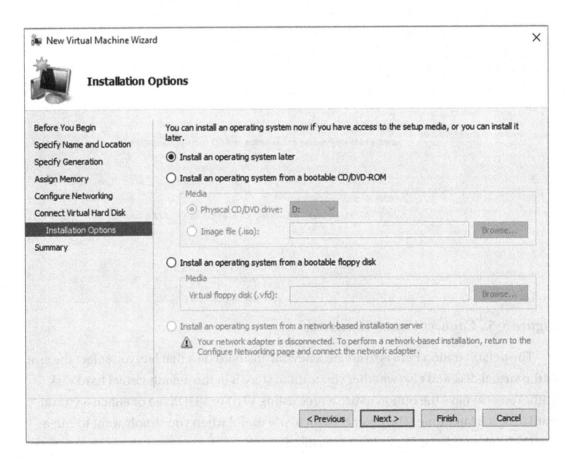

Figure 3-6. *Installation Options*

The default option is to install an OS at a later time, but if you're creating a new VM, you can't do much with it without an OS! The second option allows the VM to use the physical DVD drive of the host as an installation source. Finally, you can also use an ISO file. The hypervisor will attach the ISO to the virtual DVD drive of the new VM. You can also use a floppy disk or network source for installation of the OS, but these approaches are used less commonly.

20.   Select Install an OS from a bootable CD/DVD-ROM.

21.   Select Image file (.iso) and navigate to your Windows Server 2016 or 2019 ISO location.

22.   Click OK. Click Next.

Note   Attaching this ISO doesn't allow Hyper-V Manager to install the OS on your behalf. You still must boot the VM and run through the installation procedure for the intended OS.

---

23.   On the last screen of the wizard, review and confirm your settings, then click Finish.

Hyper-V Manager will create the VM with the settings you defined in the New Virtual Machine Wizard. Congrats! You've just created your first VM on Hyper-V!

TRY IT YOURSELF—CREATE A VIRTUAL MACHINE

Use the instructions in this section to create a new VM, if you have not already done so.

Connecting to Virtual Machines

The entire point of a Hyper-V host is to serve up virtualized workloads. How do we connect to and work with these virtualized workloads? If the VM has a Windows OS and is available and reachable on the network, you could use the Remote Desktop Protocol (RDP), if the protocol is enabled. In addition, you could connect to a Linux VM, if SSH is installed and enabled.

What happens in those situations where you're working with a new VM or you're troubleshooting network connectivity for a particular workload? How do you gain access to the machine? This can be done by opening the VM console for the target VM. Let's do so now.

1. In Hyper-V Manager, click the target host in the left-hand pane.

2. Select the VM you just created from the center pane.

3. Click "Connect" in the action pane located on the right.

4. You should see a window that looks similar that shown in Figure 3-7.

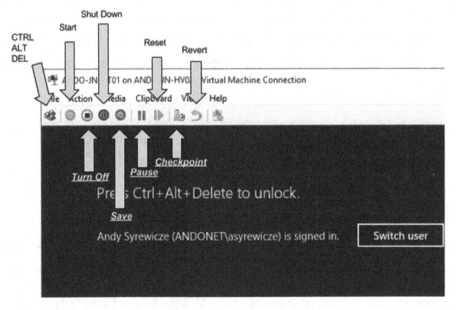

Figure 3-7. *VM console window*

The view in Figure 3-7 is the same as you would see from a physical monitor attached to a physical server. When all attempts fail to connect to a VM hosted on Hyper-V remotely, this view is your next stop. Hyper-V Manager connects to the VM via the VMBus, so network connectivity is not a requirement. You can now work normally with your virtualized OS. Using the console is a common approach for the initial configuration of the guest OS, until the remote access protocols are configured.

Note   If you connect to the console of a VM to find nothing but a black screen, remember that the VM console is the same as a physical monitor. The screen saver rules of the guest OS still apply, so click in the console window and shake the mouse, to wake the screen. Also, should your mouse ever appear to be stuck in the console window, holding Ctrl+Alt while pressing the left arrow will free the mouse, assuming the default keyboard controls were not changed during the configuration of the host.

TRY IT YOURSELF—CONNECTING TO A VM CONSOLE WINDOW

Connect to a VM in your environment using the console. Set the screen saver on the machine and leave the console for a while. Use the mouse to stop the screen saver.

Windows Server 2012 R2 and later versions have an enhanced session mode. This must be enabled in the Hyper-V host settings and selected for the individual VM console (View ➤ Enhanced Session). You'll gain access to a number of local resources, including audio, clipboard, printers, and USB devices. With Windows Server 2016 and later versions, you can resize the VM console, by dragging the corners (as with any other Windows application), once you've logged on to the VM.

Managing the Virtual Machine Console

Now that you have the console window open, you'll have noticed that there are additional controls along the top of the console window, such as Ctrl+Alt+Del and power state controls.

Note   Turn Off and Shut Down are two separate buttons. When clicked, the Shut Down button will perform a graceful OS shutdown. Clicking the Turn Off button is the same as pressing the power button on a physical server. Down it goes, with no graceful closure of any of the running processes. Be mindful of this when working with the power state of your guest VMs.

You'll also notice, along the top of the console window, buttons for saving and pausing the virtualized workload. Both of these options achieve the goal of temporarily stopping the virtualized workload.

- Pause will save the workload's state and keep a hold on its assigned memory, while stopping its use of host CPU.

- Save will save the VM's state to disk and release all uses of both CPU and memory.

Coming out of a paused state will be quicker than coming out of a saved state, as no disk operations will be required to determine the last known state of the VM.

The option to reset a VM is the same as a hard reboot. The checkpoint controls will be covered in Chapter 7. The drop-down menus provide some additional functionality.

- Media allows the administrator to attach media, such as an ISO file or floppy disk image.

- Clipboard provides clipboard functionality from the machine running Hyper-V Manager into the VM; however, copy and paste for files isn't available.

- View modifies the view of the console, including the ability to go to full screen and enter enhanced session mode.

TRY IT YOURSELF—CONTROLLING THE POWER STATE OF A VM

1. Click the Shut Down button at the top of the console screen. What happens?

2. Click the Start button. Observe the boot process. How is it different from a physical server?

3. Click the Pause button on the control panel and review the VM's status in Hyper-V Manager.

4. Click Resume. Can you now access the machine?

Installing the Guest OS

Now that the VM has been created, you must install a guest OS, such as Windows Server 2016 or 2019. Let's do so now.

1. In Hyper-V Manager, select the target host on which you created the new VM.

2. Right-click the newly created VM in the center pane and then click Connect.

3. In the VM console window, click the Start button, to boot the VM.

4. Click into the console window and press any key to start the Windows installation.

5. Walk through the OS installation process.

Note   Before the installation process is complete and the integration components are running inside the VM after the OS installation, the mouse curser may be unable to move in and out of the VM freely. To release the console's hold over the input controls, press Ctrl+Alt+left arrow.

Once the OS is installed, you'll have a fully virtualized workload running on Hyper-V, though it will be unable to talk to the physical network at present (see Chapter 8).

Navigate around the VM to get a feel for its behavior. It functions no differently than a physical server. Keep this VM aside, as we will continue to use it throughout the course of the book. You can either shut it down from within the OS, or you can use the shutdown option on the VM console control panel.

TRY IT YOURSELF—INSTALLING A GUEST OPERATING SYSTEM INSIDE A VM

Install an OS in your new VM, if you have not done so already.

Creating a New VM with PowerShell

It's also possible to create a new VM with PowerShell. This is especially useful when you must automate your VM creation. Let's do so now.

1. Open PowerShell directly on the Hyper-V host by right-clicking the PowerShell icon and clicking Run as Administrator.

2. Execute the following command:

   ```
   New-VM –Name TESTMACHINE –MemoryStartupBytes
   1GB –NewVHDSizeBytes 25GB `
   –NewVHDPath C:\TESTMACHINE.VHDX
   ```

3. Wait for the command to complete. Open Hyper-V Manager. You'll see the new VM.

4. In the right-hand pane, click Inspect Disk. Select the VHDX that was just created.

5. Verify that the maximum size is set to 25GB.

6. Right-click the new VM and click Delete.

7. Click Delete again on the confirmation screen.

8. Open File Explorer. Navigate to the root of the C: drive. Select the TESTMACHINE.VHDX file and delete it.

Creating a VM using PowerShell is quite simple. First, name the machine with the –Name parameter, then define the startup memory with the –MemoryStartupBytes parameter. Finally, define the VHD size and path with the –NewVHDPath and –NewVHDSizeBytes parameters. When you create a new VM in Hyper-V Manager, the GUI is simply calling this command and a collection of parameters under the hood.

When deleting a VM, Hyper-V Manager will not delete its VHD/VHDX files. This is a safety measure. You must perform a manual deletion.

Note   For more Hyper-V-related PowerShell cmdlets, run `Get-Command -Module Hyper-V`, to get a complete list of available cmdlets. You can then use the `Get-Help` cmdlet to get more information on any of them.

TRY IT YOURSELF—CREATING A NEW VM WITH POWERSHELL

Use the New-VM cmdlet to create a VM. Can you delete a VM with PowerShell?

Let's wrap up this chapter with a lab, to tie everything together.

Lab Work

Complete all of the Try It Yourself exercises. If you have not already done so, then

1. Create a new VM with the following requirements:

   - Generation 2 VM type

   - 1024MB of memory

   - Dynamic Memory disabled

   - Disk size of 20GB

   - Installed OS of your choice

2. Delete the VM and any associated virtual disks.

3. Repeat the process, using PowerShell. If you need assistance with the syntax, don't forget to use the Get-Help command!

4. Delete the VM and any associated virtual disks.

CHAPTER 4

Configuring Basic Virtual Machine Resources and Settings

In Chapter 3, you learned how to create a virtual machine (VM) from scratch, and configure resources attached to the VM. However, what was accomplished in Chapter 3 isn't a complete view of the settings and configuration of a VM. Nor are you stuck with the configuration defined in Chapter 3, which would be counterproductive and break one of the primary benefits of virtualization: flexibility! No, there is far more that can be done with a VM, once it is established. The goal of this chapter is to review the options and settings that aren't available through the New Virtual Machine Wizard.

In This Chapter and Beyond

In this chapter, we'll build on Chapter 3. We'll take one of the VMs we created, and we'll modify and change its configuration to better suit our needs. This will include modifying settings for

- CPU resources

- Memory resources

- Storage resources

This is important material, because you'll be modifying existing VMs quite often as the needs of your business change. Without this knowledge, your IT operations lose flexibility.

© Andy Syrewicze, Richard Siddaway 2018
A. Syrewicze and R. Siddaway, *Pro Microsoft Hyper-V 2019*, https://doi.org/10.1007/978-1-4842-4116-5_4

At the end of this chapter, you'll know how to modify a VM's resources. Additionally, you'll become familiar with the core underlying functionality provided by Hyper-V, on a VM-by-VM basis. You'll once again notice that virtual networking is missing from this chapter. Virtualized networking is complicated, so it receives an entire chapter later in the book.

Note   In this chapter, we'll cover the most commonly used settings. Some of the items will be covered in more detail later in the book. When we do refer to a later section of the book, we'll specifically call it out.

Configuring Virtual Machine CPU Resources

If you were paying close attention to Chapter 3, you may have noticed one very critical resource missing from the wizard used to provision the VM, namely CPU! By default, the New Virtual Machine Wizard will assign a single Virtual CPU (vCPU) to the target VM. If you require any additional vCPUs, you do so after the VM has been created.

Note   The changes we are about to make require that the target VM be in a powered off state. Anytime you make fundamental changes to the CPU settings of a VM, it is recommended (and a requirement for some settings) to power down the VM. For the purposes of the following exercise, it is recommended that you use one of the VMs created in the previous chapter. If they are still powered on, you must power them off.

Adding a vCPU is quite straightforward and can be completed using Hyper-V Manager. Let's get started.

1. In Hyper-V Manager, select the target host that hosts the VM.

2. If the target VM is still powered on, shut it down, by selecting the VM in the VM list in the center pane and then clicking Shut Down in the action pane on the right.

3. Select the VM in the VM list in the center pane and click Settings,
    in the action pane on the right. You will be greeted with the VM
    settings page for the selected VM, as shown in Figure 4-1.

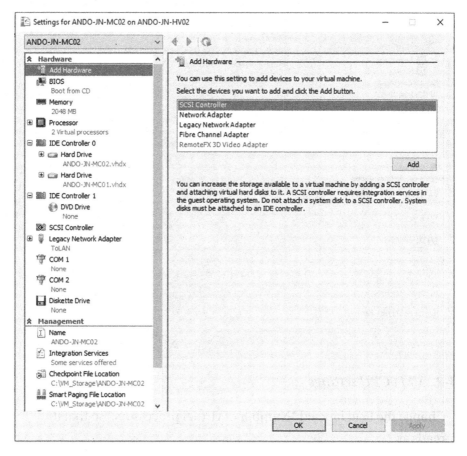

Figure 4-1. *VM settings dialog*

4. Wait for the VM to enter a powered down mode, which will be
    indicated by a state of Off in the VM list in the center pane.

5. In the left-hand pane of the VM settings utility, expand the
    Processor section and then click the root of the Processor section
    (see Figure 4-2).

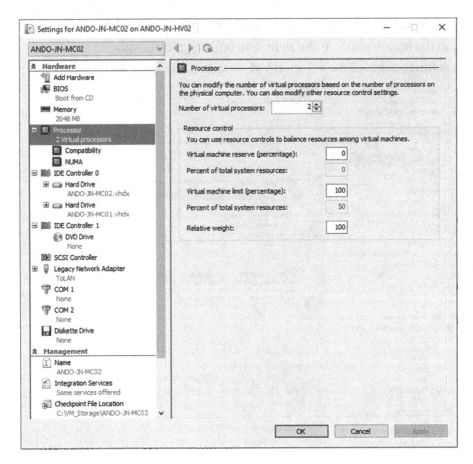

Figure 4-2. *VM vCPU settings*

6. Change the field labeled "Number of virtual processors," so that it reads as 2.

7. Click OK.

POWERSHELL CMDLET

PowerShell can also be used to modify the VM's CPUs. In this example, the Set-VM cmdlet changes the CPU count to 2 for ANDO-JN-MC02.

```
Set-VM -Name ANDO-JN-MC02 -ProcessorCount 2
```

The preceding exercise increased the number of virtual CPUs the VM has assigned to it. The Hyper-V was told to assign more CPU resources to this particular workload, and it will adjust things accordingly under the hood.

TRY IT YOURSELF—INCREASE CPU RESOURCES ASSIGNED TO A VIRTUAL MACHINE

Use Hyper-V Manager to increase the number of virtual CPUs on your VM. Repeat using PowerShell. Is there a number beyond which you can't increase the number of vCPUs for a VM?

The inevitable question at this point is, how do virtual processors (or vCPUs) correlate to physical CPUs? Remember that Hyper-V manages all available resources and delegates them to the guest OSs, as needed. This is no different for processing threads. The hypervisor doesn't take a physical core and forever tie it to a VM, as most processing threads spend the majority of their time idle.

You should think of CPU in Hyper-V as a pool of CPU resources. This metric gives a particular VM more of the available processing time with the physical host CPU, which removes computing resources from the pool. This is the primary function of the CPU scheduler. The CPU scheduler determines that process A from VM B will use physical CPU core 3. Once a computation is completed or paused, the core is freed, so the hypervisor can assign another process to it for the same or perhaps a different VM.

ABOVE AND BEYOND

Hyper-V process scheduling is a complex topic. For most purposes, you only have to know that increasing the vCPU count increases the amount of processing time the VM gets at the hypervisor level. If you'd like to learn more about how this process works, Eric Siron has an excellent article on this topic, available at `www.altaro.com/hyper-v/hyper-v-virtual-cpus-explained/`.

Another item you'll see in Figure 4-2 is resource control. These options control how the CPU scheduler treats CPU allocation for this VM and determine how that VM should consume CPU resources. We've found over the years that it's often best to just let the CPU scheduler do its job and handle all CPU allocation. There are certain situations in which you may require finer grain control over virtual CPU behavior, for example, in the case of resource contention. If a host system is ever starved for resources, you could ensure that one VM gets more access to CPU resources than another. This is very useful when you have a mission-critical workload that you want to make sure never gets starved for resources. Let's look at each potential setting and review how each affects CPU utilization.

Virtual Machine Reserve (Percentage)

This allows you to reserve a percentage of the assigned vCPUs to a VM. For example, a physical host that has two quad core CPUs have eight logical processors, meaning they have eight available threads for computations to be completed. If you assign two vCPUs to a VM, you're giving that VM access to two CPU threads. Changing this setting to 100% would then ensure that those two threads are dedicated to that VM. In that same situation, if the setting was 50%, the hypervisor would ensure that one of those threads is always available for the VM. This isn't something you want to do with ordinary VMs, as the more you use this, the less VMs you'll be able to place on a particular host, owing to increased CPU demand. However, it is useful for high CPU workloads.

Percent of Total System Resources

This field is associated with both the reserve and limit fields. This field updates automatically to reflect the total amount of host CPU resources this VM has in reserve or in limitation.

Virtual Machine Limit (Percentage)

This field limits the amount of CPUs a VM can consume, based on the allocated number of CPUs. As an example, if a physical host has two quad core CPUs adding up to eight logical processors, setting the limit to 50% will only allow the VM to access one of the processing threads. This is rarely used. The only time that this particular setting is of use is when you have a virtualized workload that can periodically consume all of its assigned resources and raise the resource usage on the host above acceptable levels. Another way around this issue is to simply reduce the number of assigned CPUs, thus removing CPU contention on the host.

We'd like to reinforce the idea that you should only use these items when you *absolutely* have to. It's best that the CPU scheduler take care of everything itself, but these controls are here if needed.

Virtual Machine CPU Compatibility

In the VM CPU settings, you'll notice a subtree item under Processor labeled "Compatibility" that contains only some text and a single check box. This is used mainly in situations in which you have different CPU families across your Hyper-V hosts.

When a VM is booted, it is presented with the host system's underlying instruction sets. Think of an instruction set as an advanced function or feature of the CPU. The guest OS will take advantage of these instruction sets when available. However, if you attempt to live migrate the VM to another host with a different processor type, you'll get an error message stating that the VM is not compatible with the processor that is present in the destination host machine.

In this situation, the VM is utilizing the available instruction sets of the new CPU presented by the current host. The destination host's CPU may be missing some of the newer instruction sets. If it is older, the OS of the guest VM can't simply stop using those instruction sets. The VM will have to be powered off to be moved to the older host.

Powering off VMs to enable migration to a different physical host isn't the preferred method of doing things. Enabling the Processor Compatibility check box disables the extra CPU instruction sets for that particular VM, ensuring that live migration between hosts with different processor generations occurs without issues.

SET CPU COMPATABILITY WITH POWERSHELL

CPU compatibility mode can also be configured on a VM that is shut down using PowerShell. In this example, we're setting the compatibility flag for the VM ANDO-JN-MC02.

```
Set-VMProcessor ANDO-JN-MC02 –CompatibilityForMigrationEnabled $true
```

What About NUMA?

Another item that you'll see mentioned throughout this chapter is non-uniform memory access (NUMA). The topic of NUMA could consume many pages. For the purposes of this book, it's only required to know that it provides NUMA-aware applications, such as SQL Server or SharePoint, more efficient access to memory. If you're interested in learning more about NUMA, the TechNet article available at https://technet. microsoft.com/en-us/library/dn282282.aspx will provide all the information and background that you could want.

Configuring Virtual Machine Memory Resources

Next on our list of configurable items are VM memory resources. Memory is one of those resources that has to be modified while workloads are live. Hyper-V 2012 R2 (and later versions) enables this with advanced features, such as Dynamic Memory, but first, let's see what increasing memory looks like without having Dynamic Memory enabled.

During our exercises in Chapter 3, we set the Startup RAM for our VMs. Let's modify that value.

1. In Hyper-V Manager, select the target host that hosts the VMs you created in Chapter 3.

2. If the target VM is still powered on, shut it down by selecting the VM in the VM list in the center pane, then click Shut Down in the action pane on the right.

3. Select the target VM in the center pane. Click the settings link in the action pane.

4. In the Virtual Machine Settings UI, select the memory section in the left-hand pane. You'll see a screen such as that shown in Figure 4-3.

5. Click in the Startup RAM field and add another 512MB of memory to the selected VM.

6. Click Apply and then click OK, to apply the changes.

7. Select the VM in the center pane of Hyper-V Manager and then click Start in the action pane on the right, to boot the guest OS back up.

8. Wait for the VM to boot and then click Connect in the action pane. Log in to the system and verify that the additional memory has been added.

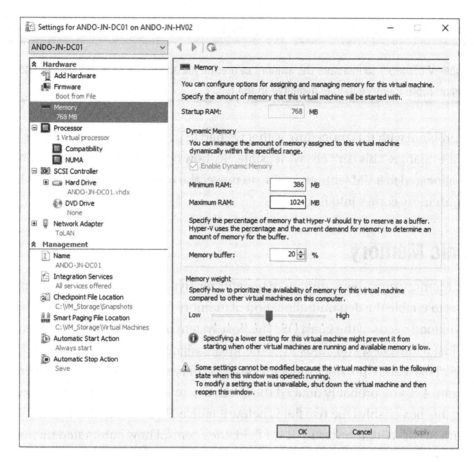

Figure 4-3. *VM memory settings. Note that Startup RAM is grayed out because VM is running.*

You've now successfully increased the amount of memory allocated to this VM. The host system will now provide more RAM to this particular VM for future needs. Additionally, if you want to, you can configure the Memory weight, which controls the priority that this VM has in relation to physical memory, in the event the host runs into issues with memory contention.

TRY IT YOURSELF—INCREASE MEMORY RESOURCES ASSIGNED TO A VIRTUAL MACHINE

Use Hyper-V Manager to increase the amount of memory assigned to a VM. What happens if you assign more memory than is available to the host?

One problem with this procedure is that we had to power the VM off, in order to conduct the change. This isn't always feasible. So, how do we increase the amount of memory allocated to a VM without having to power the machine down? This is where Dynamic Memory comes into its own.

Dynamic Memory

Dynamic Memory provides a number of benefits for Hyper-V administrators. Its primary function is to enable the dynamic allocation of memory from the host system, based on the workload needs of the guest OS. The host system monitors the current memory demand inside the guest and adjusts the memory assigned to the VM, based on the VM's properties. This feature provides more efficient memory use across the host system.

In Figure 4-3, you probably noticed the check box to Enable Dynamic Memory. Checking this box enables the two fields below it labeled "Minimum RAM" and "Maximum RAM." With the Startup RAM field, they control how automated memory resourcing occurs.

Startup RAM

This is the amount of memory that the VM starts with. It doesn't change when Dynamic Memory has been enabled. The VM starts with the configured amount of memory, and the amount of memory used by the VM will be adjusted up or down from there.

Minimum RAM

This is smallest amount of memory that you want this VM to consume. If the workload inside the VM doesn't have a demand higher than this value, the VM will consume only this amount of memory.

Maximum RAM

This is the VM's memory ceiling. Dynamic Memory will incrementally increase the amount of memory a VM has assigned to it, until it hits this amount and no further.

Memory Buffer

When a VM receives a request to increase the memory during a Dynamic Memory operation, it will do so in increments defined by this value. By default, this is 20%, meaning that when a VM configured with 1024GB of startup memory starts to exceed that amount, Hyper-V will add additional memory to the VM, first starting with an amount of 204MB. A 20% increment is acceptable for nearly all use cases.

Note   Dynamic Memory is not compatible with NUMA. It's one or the other, which can be defined on a per-VM basis. The questions you must ask yourself, though, when determining NUMA vs. Dynamic Memory for a VM are: Am I running a NUMA-aware workload inside this VM? and Will the VM consume more resources, processors, or memory than are available on a single NUMA node? The first question can be answered by the software vendor. As for the second question, you can determine the size of a NUMA node on a host via the processor section in the Virtual Machine Settings UI we reviewed earlier in the chapter.

So, how do you configure a VM to use Dynamic Memory? You can use Hyper-V Manager like this:

1. In Hyper-V manager, select the target host.

2. If the target VM is still powered on, shut it down, by selecting the VM in the VM list in the center pane and then clicking Shut Down in the action pane on the right.

3. Select the target VM in the center pane and then click the settings link in the action pane.

4. Set the Startup Memory field to 1024MB.

5. Click Enable Dynamic Memory check box.

6. Set the Minimum Memory to 512MB and set the Maximum Memory to 2048MB.

7. Click Apply, then click OK to apply the changes.

8. Select the VM in the center pane of Hyper-V Manager and click Start in the action pane on the right, to boot the guest OS backup.

9. Wait for the VM to boot and then click Connect in the action pane. Log in to the system and verify and start some applications.

10. In Hyper-V Manager, select the VM that was modified and monitor the assigned memory in the Memory tab, as you launch and close applications inside of the VM.

CONFIGURE DYNAMIC MEMORY WITH POWERSHELL

It is also possible to configure Dynamic Memory using PowerShell. In the example, ANDO-JN-MC02 is configured to use Dynamic Memory with a minimum of 512MB of RAM and 4GB at maximum.

```
Set-VM –Name ANDO-JN-MC02 –DynamicMemory –MinimumMemoryBytes 512MB –
MaximumMemoryBytes 4GB
```

TRY IT YOURSELF—ENABLING DYNAMIC MEMORY FOR A VIRTUAL MACHINE

Use Hyper-V Manager or PowerShell to configure Dynamic Memory for a VM.

Configuring Additional Virtual Machine Storage Resources

In Chapter 3, we created a basic virtual hard disk for our VMs using the New Virtual Machine Wizard. How do we go about adding more virtual hard disks to a VM? Let's go ahead and create a new virtual hard disk and attach it to one of our VMs, to get a feel for the procedure.

1. In Hyper-V Manager, select the target host.

2. Select the target VM in the center pane and then click Settings in the action pane to open the Virtual Machine Settings UI.

3. Depending on the generation level of the VM, select either an IDE controller or an SCSI controller in the left-hand list.

4. Select type Hard Drive in the right-hand list and click Add, to open the add Hard Drive dialog, as seen in Figure 4-4.

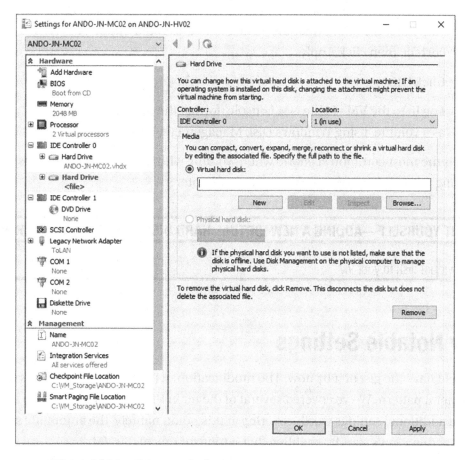

Figure 4-4. *VM Add Hard Drive dialog*

5. Click New, to open the New Virtual Hard Disk Wizard.

6. Click Next, select the VHDX type disk format, and click Next again.

7. Select the Fixed size disk type and click Next.

8. Store the disk in a location that has 10GB of free space. Note the defined path.

9. Make sure that the "Create a new blank virtual hard disk" radio button is selected and then modify the Size to 10GB. Click Next.

10. Verify that the settings are correct on the summary screen and click Finish.

11. Back on the Virtual Machine Settings UI Add Hard Drive Dialog, verify that the path under the virtual hard disk radio button is correct, then click Apply.

12. Click OK.

13. Log in to the VM via the NM console, format the disk, and attach it as a volume, using Windows Disk Management.

This is the most common scenario when working with a VM's storage settings. We'll be covering more VM storage-related topics in Chapter 9.

TRY IT YOURSELF—ADDING A NEW VIRTUAL HARD DISK TO A VIRTUAL MACHINE

Add a virtual disk to your VM.

Other Notable Settings

You should have the gist of it by now. The modification of the VM settings follows the same general pattern. We've covered several of the main VM components. There are a couple of additional settings worth covering at this point, namely, the automatic start and stop actions. Let's start by enabling this setting for one of our VMs.

1. In Hyper-V Manager, select the target host.

2. Select the target VM in the center pane and then click Settings in the action pane, to open the Virtual Machine Settings UI.

3. In the left-hand pane, click on Automatic Start Action near the bottom of the list, to open the Automatic Start Action dialog, as seen in Figure 4-5.

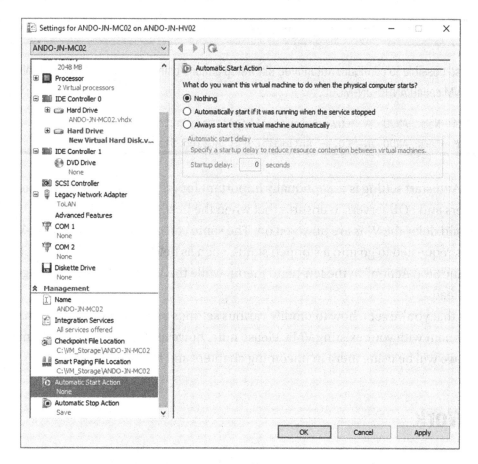

Figure 4-5. *Automatic Start Action dialog*

4. Click the "Always start this virtual machine automatically" radio button.

5. Set the Startup Delay field to 300 seconds.

6. Click Apply and then click OK, to exit the Virtual Machine Settings UI.

TRY IT YOURSELF—ENABLING VIRTUAL MACHINE AUTOSTART

Enable autostart for your VM.

CONFIGURE AUTOSTART WITH POWERSHELL

It is also possible to configure automated start/stop actions using PowerShell. The examples use a VM called ANDO-JN-MC02.

```
Set-VM –Name ANDO-JN-MC02 –AutomaticStopAction Shutdown
Set-VM –Name ANDO-JN-MC02 – AutomaticStartAction Start
```

The Autostart setting is exceptionally important for critical VMs, such as domain controllers and SQL servers. It ensures that when the host system boots, there's a 300-second delay the VMs are powered on. The same can occur when the Hyper-V service is requested to go into a stopped status, such as before a reboot. You select "Automatic Stop Action" in the left-hand menu, while the Virtual Machine Settings UI is open instead.

Now that you've seen how to modify various settings of a VM, feel free to continue to experiment with your existing VMs. Please note, however, do not to delete them yet, because we will be using them in upcoming chapters and for the following lab.

Lab Work

1. Complete the Try It Yourself sections, if you have not already done so.

2. Choose one of your two VMs as the target and perform the following modifications:

   - If the VM is powered on, use the UI to shut it down.

   - Open the Virtual Machine Settings UI.

   - Increase the CPU count for the selected VM by 1 vCPU.

   - Enable Dynamic Memory on the machine and set the startup memory to 1024MB, the maximum to 2048MB, and the minimum to 512MB.

   - Add an additional virtual hard disk to the VM.

- Log in to the VM console.

- Verify that the additional CPU is showing in taskmgr.

- With Task Manager open, launch a number of applications and watch the amount of reported memory closely.

- Using Disk Manager, format and assign a drive letter to the new vDisk.

3. Can you repeat these actions using PowerShell?

CHAPTER 5

Managing and Maintaining Hyper-V Integration Services

Over the last several chapters, you've learned about creating and working with virtual machines (VMs). You've also learned that in order to facilitate some of the advanced functionality that Hyper-V provides, the guest operating system (inside a VM) must pass information to the hypervisor. Owing to the separation that virtualization provides, how does this process occur?

This function is performed by a component called Guest Integration Services. These services conduct a number of tasks, ranging from time synchronization and performance metric sharing to providing the ability to copy files from host to guest over the VMBus, without requiring a network connection between the two. Let's review these services in more detail.

In This Chapter and Beyond

We're going to switch gears a bit in this chapter. In Chapters 3 and 4, you learned how to create new VMs and how to modify the virtual hardware settings. Both of these topics are very important common tasks that are performed regularly, so it's important that you're proficient in them.

This chapter, however, will cover integration services and their functions. Then you'll learn how to manage them, using the UI and PowerShell, and how to go about keeping them up to date, which ensures that your VMs get the latest functionality and bug fixes. Keep in mind that on most newer Windows versions, the integration services will be

© Andy Syrewicze, Richard Siddaway 2018
A. Syrewicze and R. Siddaway, *Pro Microsoft Hyper-V 2019*, https://doi.org/10.1007/978-1-4842-4116-5_5

preinstalled, but there will be certain situations, such as working with older Windows versions, in which the services may have to be installed or enabled/disabled.

The information covered in this chapter helps round out the knowledge you've gained in the last couple of chapters regarding VMs, their components, and how to manage and maintain them. Let's start by defining the different integration services and their functions.

What Are Integration Services?

There's a symbiotic relationship between the guest OS running in a VM and the virtualization host running that VM. Some form of information exchange has to occur, so that the host OS can be aware of conditions inside the VM. That relationship is managed and facilitated by the Hyper-V Integration Services.

The Hyper-V Integration Services are the unsung heroes of the Hyper-V world. They can very easily be taken for granted, as most virtualization administrators just come to expect them to be running and available. It is certainly noticed when they aren't running. There are a number of different integration services that make up the entire suite, and they are presented within the guest OS as running services.

You can view the current state of the integration services for a VM using Hyper-V Manager:

1. With Hyper-V Manager open, select the Hyper-V host containing one of the VMs you created in Chapter 3.

2. In the center pane, select a VM and click Settings in the action pane on the bottom right.

3. In the left-hand pane of the VM Settings dialog, scroll down and click Integration Services. You should see a list of the integration services similar to that shown in Figure 5-1.

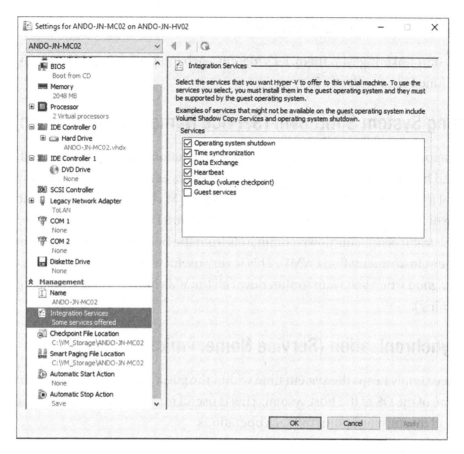

Figure 5-1. *Hyper-V Integration Services*

4. Click the check box to enable Guest services.

5. Click Apply, then click OK, to exit the Settings screen.

TRY IT YOURSELF—ENABLING HYPER-V INTEGRATION SERVICES WITH THE GUI

Follow the preceding instructions, to enable the Guest Services on a VM in your environment.

If you did this with one of the newly created VMs from Chapter 3, you'll notice that all services are enabled, with the exception of the guest services. If we wanted to disable all integration services, we could do so by un-checking the box next to each service, but once you know the function each of these services performs, you'll understand that there are ramifications for doing so.

Integration Services Defined

Before we start tinkering with them, let's identify each integration service and talk a bit about the function of each one in turn.

Operating System Shutdown (Service Name: vmicshutdown)

This may appear to be one of the less important integration services, but it's greatly appreciated by most administrators. This service allows administrator to shut down the guest OS of a VM, without having to interact with the VM via the VM console window or some type of remote access, such as the Remote Desktop Protocol (RDP). In this case, the administrator sends shutdown commands from the host system using Windows Management Instrumentation (WMI). This is very useful when working with lots of VMs (especially good when you want to shut down all the VMs in your lab at the end of a night's writing).

Time Synchronization (Service Name: vmictimesync)

This service simply keeps the system time within the guest OS synchronized with the system time of the OS of the host system. This is useful for keeping time in sync between systems and during checkpoint rollback operations.

Note   Even though the time synchronization service is enabled by default, it is recommended that it be disabled in the case of virtualized domain controllers. It is still recommended that domain controllers update their system time from a certified external source and not be synchronized with the system time of the hypervisor.

Data Exchange (Service Name: vmickvpexchange)

The data exchange service gathers information from within the guest OS of the running VM and provides that information to the host. This includes information used for monitoring and reporting, and for use by third-party utilities. Examples of the information gathered include

- Major and minor version numbers of the installed guest OS

- Build number of the guest OS

- Reported processor architecture
- Fully qualified DNS name of the guest OS

Heartbeat (Service Name: vmicheartbeat)

This service provides a means for the host system to monitor the status of the OS contained within the guest VM. The host will send periodic heartbeat requests that essentially say "Everything OK?" to which the guest OS should respond saying "Yes, I'm fine."

If the guest OS stops responding, the host will log the event until it is able to reestablish contact with the guest OS. This service allows administrators to act on such events with scripted actions and third-party utilities, as needed. You could create scripts to react to events by performing tasks such as automatically power cycling the VM, attempting a graceful reboot, or running a script.

Backup (Volume Checkpoint) (Service Name: vmicvss)

Assuming the OS running within the guest VM has support for Volume Shadow Service (VSS), this service allows the Hyper-V host system to make VSS requests of the guest VM, to aid in backup operations. This enables software from third-party vendors to back up these workloads at the hypervisor layer, instead of having to install backup agents into the VM.

Guest Services (Service Name: vmicguestinterface)

This service is relatively new. It was added as a post-release patch in Windows Server 2012 R2 Hyper-V. Despite its name, it is this service that creates a secure method for file transfers to occur between the host and guest. This is particularly useful in high-security environments in which you must get a file to a newly created VM, but you do not want to send it over the network. This service allows the host to utilize the VMBus to get the needed file from the host to the guest OS. We'll be covering this process shortly.

Supported Windows Server Guest Operating Systems

An official list of the OSs supported by integration services is hosted at `https://docs.microsoft.com/en-us/windows-server/virtualization/hyper-v/supported-windows-guest-operating-systems-for-hyper-v-on-windows`. At the time of writing, the supported list of OSs are those shown in Tables 5-1 and 5-2.

Table 5-1. *Windows Server Operating Systems Supported by Hyper-V Integration Services*

Operating System	Installation Notes
Windows Server 2019	Built-in
Windows Server 2016, including the SAC releases Server 1709 and Server 1803	Built-in
Windows Server 2012 R2	Built-in
Windows Server 2012	Built-in
Windows Server 2008 R2 with Service Pack 1	Install the integration services after you've set up the OS inside the VM.
Windows Server 2008 with Service Pack 2	Install the integration services after you've set up the OS inside the VM.
Windows Home Server 2011	Install the integration services after you've set up the OS inside the VM.
Windows Small Business Server 2011	Install the integration services after you've set up the OS inside the VM.
Windows Server 2003 R2 with Service Pack 2	Install the integration services after you've setup the OS inside the VM.
Windows Server 2003 with Service Pack 2	Install the integration services after you've set up the OS inside the VM.
CentOS 5.x, RHEL 5.x, SLES 11, OpenSUSE 12.1, Ubuntu 12.04 OSs and later	Built-in, via the Linux Integration Services package contained in the newer versions of the Linux Kernel.

Table 5-2. *Windows Client Operating Systems Supported by Hyper-V Integration Services*

Operating System	Installation Notes
Windows 10	Built-in
Windows 8.1	Built-in
Windows 8	Install the integration services after you've set up the OS inside the VM.
Windows 7 with Service Pack 1	Install the integration services after you've set up the OS inside the VM.
Windows 7 *Home Editions not supported	Install the integration services after you've set up the OS inside the VM.
Windows Vista with Service Pack 2 *Home Editions not supported	Install the integration services after you've set up the OS inside the VM.
Windows XP with Service Pack 3 *Pro Edition Only	Install the integration services after you've set up the OS inside the VM.
Windows XP x64 Edition with Service Pack 3 *Pro Edition Only	Install the integration services after you've set up the OS inside the VM.

We've deliberately included Windows XP and the Windows Server 2003 families in the table, even though these products are regarded as end-of-life and are no longer supported by Microsoft. In our experience, many organizations retain systems, usually because of a "special application that can't be upgraded," well past their official end of life.

Note   OSs that have the integration services built in receive updates to the integration services through Windows Update, so you don't have to do anything beyond patching to keep those machines up to date.

Now that you have an appreciation for the tasks that Hyper-V Integration Services provides, it's time to see how these services are managed.

Managing Hyper-V Integration Services

In this section, you'll learn to perform the four most common tasks associated with Hyper-V integration services:

- Installing integration services

- Enabling and disabling integration services

- Transferring files with integration services

- Updating integration services

First up is installation.

Installing Integration Services

Most modern OSs automatically install the integration service components, as shown in Tables 5-1 and 5-2. So, how do we get these services installed into the older OSs?

ABOVE AND BEYOND—INTEGRATION SERVICES ISO FILE

In this section, we're discussing installing the integration services. Remember: This is only necessary for *older* OSs that don't have the services built in.

If your Hyper-V host is Windows Server 2016 (or a later version) or Windows 10 (and later versions), you won't find the option to install the integration services via the Action menu. You also won't find the required ISO file on these platforms. This is because Microsoft has assumed that you won't be running the older OSs that require you to install integration services on these platforms.

If you have to run an older OS on a modern Hyper-V host, you'll have to acquire a copy of the integration services ISO file. If you have a Windows Server 2012 R2 or earlier version, Hyper-V host, you can find the integration services ISO—VMGUEST.ISO—in the C:\Windows\System32 folder.

Otherwise, it is easiest to download a copy of Hyper-V Server 2012 R2 from the Microsoft evaluation center at www.microsoft.com/en-us/download/details.aspx?id=3512. Mount the downloaded ISO file. Open the \sources\install.wim file (use 7-Zip or another utility that can read WIM files) and extract VMGUEST.ISO from the Windows\System32 folder.

Put the VMGUEST.ISO somewhere safe on your Hyper-V host and use the Media option on the menu bar to open vmguest.iso in the VM's DVD drive, if the option to load the integration services disk isn't available on the Action item of the menu bar.

You can use the VM console window for the VM to perform the installation, or you can use PowerShell. Let's start with the GUI approach.

To install integration services using Hyper-V manager, do the following:

1. With Hyper-V Manager open, select the Hyper-V host containing the VM you created in Chapter 3.

2. Start a VM, if necessary. Right-click one of the running VMs in the center pane and click Connect.

3. Once the VM console window is open, click the Action menu in the Action bar, and click "Insert Integration Services Setup Disk."

4. Inside the VM, you will notice that an ISO image has been mounted to the virtual DVD-ROM drive. If the setup file does not start automatically, you can run it by executing the `setup.exe` file located at `D:\support\x86\setup.exe`.

5. Run through the installation wizard and reboot once complete.

6. Verify that the services mentioned earlier in this chapter exist, by using the services MMC snap-in on the target virtual machine.

TRY IT YOURSELF—INSTALLING HYPER-V INTEGRATION SERVICES

If you have a suitable VM, install the integration services. If not, create a VM, using a suitable system, and install the integration services.

Installing integration services is performed on a machine-by-machine basis, but if you have to enable or disable some, or all, of the integration services, you want to be able to automate the task.

Enabling and Disabling Integration Services

So far, you've seen how we can use the Hyper-V Manager UI to enable and disable the various integration services for a VM. This is fine when you're only working with one or two VMs at a time, but as you know, things in IT have a way of scaling much larger than we originally planned, and there may be times when we need to work with ten, twenty, or even a hundred different VMs simultaneously.

How do we enable and disable integration services at a large scale? If you've been working in the Microsoft ecosystem in recent years, the answer is quite simple: PowerShell.

As you've seen so far in this book, PowerShell can be very useful when working with Hyper-V. The Hyper-V PowerShell module includes cmdlets for working with integration services. Let's discover the active integration services on a given VM using PowerShell, and then take it a step further and deactivate the guest services service you enabled earlier using the GUI. First, to discover the active integration services using PowerShell,

1. Open PowerShell directly from your Hyper-V host. If this is a Windows Server Core box, from the command line, simply type "PowerShell" (without the quotes) and press Enter. Make sure that you run PowerShell with elevated privileges (Run as Administrator option). Server Core systems will automatically run PowerShell with elevated privileges.

2. Type

    ```
    Get-Command –Module Hyper-V –Name *Integration*
    ```

    to get a list of available commands with ties to Hyper-V Integration Services.

3. Type

    ```
    Get-VM
    ```

    to get a list of VMs and their running state.

4. Type

    ```
    Get-VMIntegrationService –VMName <VM Names in comma
    separated list>
    ```

You'll receive output like that shown in Figure 5-2.

```
[ANDO-JN-HV02]: PS C:\Users\asyrewicze\Documents> Get-VMIntegrationService -VMName ANDO-JN-DC01,ANDO-JN-DC02

VMName         Name                        Enabled PrimaryStatusDescription SecondaryStatusDescription
------         ----                        ------- ------------------------ --------------------------
ANDO-JN-DC01 Time Synchronization         True    OK
ANDO-JN-DC01 Heartbeat                     True    OK                       OK
ANDO-JN-DC01 Key-Value Pair Exchange       True    OK
ANDO-JN-DC01 Shutdown                      True    OK
ANDO-JN-DC01 VSS                           True    OK
ANDO-JN-DC01 Guest Service Interface       False   OK
ANDO-JN-DC02 Time Synchronization         True    OK
ANDO-JN-DC02 Heartbeat                     True    OK                       OK
ANDO-JN-DC02 Key-Value Pair Exchange       True    OK
ANDO-JN-DC02 Shutdown                      True    OK
ANDO-JN-DC02 VSS                           True    OK
ANDO-JN-DC02 Guest Service Interface       False   OK
```

Figure 5-2. *Output of the* `Get-VMIntegrationService` *cmdlet*

5. To enable the Guest Services integration service on a VM, run the following:

    ```
    Enable-VMIntegrationService -Name 'Guest Service
    Interface' `
    -VMName <VM names in comma separated list>
    ```

6. Type

    ```
    Get-VMIntegrationService -VMName <VM names in comma
    separated list>
    ```

    to verify that the Guest Service integration service now has an enabled state of true.

TRY IT YOURSELF—ENABLING/DISABLING HYPER-V INTEGRATION SERVICES WITH POWERSHELL

Use the PowerShell cmdlets to enable and disable integration services for a VM.

Managing the enabled/disabled state of the various integration service components is quite easy with PowerShell. If you want to quickly view the status of the integration services on all the VMs on your host, you can use

```
Get-VM | Get-VMIntegrationService | sort Name
```

ABOVE AND BEYOND

There may be times when you run into a VM that returns a PrimaryStatusDescription of "No Contact" even though the service is enabled. This is most likely owing to the service within the VM being in a hung or stopped state.

Simply start the service, and you'll be good to go again. Additionally, in Linux VMs, not all capabilities are available, depending on the distribution of Linux contained within the NM. So, you may always have some services returning this status when Linux VMs are in play.

There are times when you'll need to copy files to a VM. Integration services provide one way of performing this task.

Transferring Files with Integration Services

There are certain high-security environments in which you don't want to risk moving sensitive information over the network via file transfers and potentially risk someone grabbing it in transit. Another potential use case for file transfer using integration services would be during the initial setup phase of a VM.

You may have to install a software package inside the VM, but guest networking may not be set up yet. This is especially true if your IT department is siloed, with different teams being responsible for parts of the environment, like many are today in corporate environments. It could be your network team is unavailable at the time. Using integration services gives you a way to move forward on your own.

Other potential use cases include perimeter networks and isolated security zones in which you may not have direct access to the VM. Nothing is more frustrating when attempting to get an application installed than when you have to fight tooth and nail just to get the setup file where you need it.

Hyper-V Integration Services, as of Server 2012 R2 (and later versions), allows administrators the option of pushing files from the Hyper-V host to guest VMs via PowerShell. The transfer occurs over the VMBus, rather than the network. Remember that the VMBus allows the host and guest VM to pass information to each other directly.

This function is provided by the Guest Services integration service that we enabled on both VMs earlier in this chapter. As long as the service is enabled and running on the target VM, we can now push a file from the host system directly to the VM. Let's assume we have a file that must be copied to multiple VMs. This capability is currently exclusive to PowerShell, and, as such, we can target multiple servers at once with PowerShell. Let's do so now, with a dummy text file.

1. Using Notepad, create a blank text document and save to a location on your Hyper-V host, naming it IntegrationServicesTest.txt.

2. Open PowerShell directly from your Hyper-V host. If this is a Windows Server Core box, from the command line, simply type "PowerShell" (without the quotes) and press Enter. PowerShell must be running with elevated privileges.

3. Create a variable called $targetvms by running

    ```
    $targetvms = Get-VM –Name <VM Names in comma separated
    list>
    ```

4. Verify that the Guest Services integration service is in an enabled state on the target VMs, by running

    ```
    $targetvms | Get-VMIntegrationService
    ```

5. If enabled, proceed with the file copy by running

    ```
    $targetvms | Copy-VMFile –SourcePath <path to
    IntegrationServicesTest.txt> –DestinationPath <Target Path
    on target VMs> -CreateFullPath –FileSource Host
    ```

6. Navigate to the targeted destination path on each VM and verify that the file exists.

TRY IT YOURSELF—MOVING FILES BETWEEN HOST AND GUEST WITH INTEGRATION SERVICES

Use PowerShell to copy a file to one or more VMs, using integration services.

Congratulations! You've successfully moved a file from one machine to another without requiring the use of a network in any way! This is just one additional way that Hyper-V can add flexibility to your IT operations and facilitate more secure solutions for your business.

Note   It's not currently possible to pull files from the guest VM to the host. Many VMs are hosted in third-party datacenters, and businesses want to be sure that the hosting company isn't able to pull files out of the running VMs.

ABOVE AND BEYOND—COPYING FILES WITH POWERSHELL

You can create a PowerShell remoting session to your VM and copy files to, and from, the VM across the remoting session. You can use a standard WSMAN-based remoting session or PowerShell Direct.

PowerShell Direct is available on Windows Server 2016 and Windows 10 (or later versions) Hyper-V hosts with PowerShell v5.1. You can create a PowerShell remoting session from the Hyper-V host to the VM over the VMBus, rather than using a network.

If anything is guaranteed in IT, it's that you'll need to keep things up to date to get the maximum from your environment.

Updating Integration Services

This may seem obvious, but it's immensely important that the integration services package be kept up to date at all times. This ensures that the latest bug fixes and feature sets are available and also verifies that these critical services stay in a running state.

The only time you may want to keep the integration services version down-level is if you temporarily move a VM to a Hyper-V host with a newer host OS and then move it back shortly thereafter. For example, if you moved a VM host on a Windows Server 2008 R2 Hyper-V host to a Windows Server 2012 R2 Hyper-V host, things would continue to run. If you intended to keep that VM in that location, you would want to upgrade the integration services. However, if you ever intend to move the VM back to the 2008 R2 Hyper-V host, you may want to retain the old version. The newer installed integration services package will dumb itself down to the 2008 R2 level, but this may not be clean enough for all administrators. It will depend on your environment and your situation.

As far as applying updates goes, Microsoft has made that quite simple for us. They already have a great update mechanism in place in the Windows Update service and WSUS. Integration services updates will be pushed as part of that process for all VMs running the Windows OS. For those of us running Linux OSs, you'll have to review the update procedure with your individual distribution's documentation. Additionally, another option for pushing upgrades is by using System Center Virtual Machine Manager (SCVMM).

ABOVE AND BEYOND

In the event you are curious about using SCVMM to conduct these updates, there is a great article by Ben Armstrong, of the Hyper-V product group, on how to do this. It is available here: `http://blogs.msdn.com/b/virtual_pc_guy/archive/2014/01/21/updating-integration-services-with-scvmm.aspx`.

Managing integration services may seem like a trivial task, but they are important for the proper functioning of your virtual environment.

Let's finish this chapter with some lab work that reinforces what you've just learned.

Lab Work

You should complete the following exercises, to gain practical experience in the techniques presented in this chapter:

1. Complete the Try It Yourself sections.

2. Choose a VM to act as the target for rest of the exercises.

3. Using Hyper-V Manager, disable all the integration services for that VM.

4. Using PowerShell, start all of them once again and verify that they are in a running state.

5. Using the services MMC snap-in inside the target VM, stop one of the integration services.

6. Use the Get-VMIntegrationService cmdlet to review the status. Take note of how the stopped services change the status of the output of this cmdlet.

7. Restart the service and test it, using Get-VMIntegrationService.

8. Using the Copy-VMFile cmdlet, move a large file, such as a movie file or an ISO image, from the host to the guest OS, using the VMBus.

CHAPTER 6

Managing and Modifying Virtual Machine Files

In previous chapters, you've learned to use Hyper-V Manager and PowerShell to create and modify virtual machines (VMs). VMs can be considered to be a collection of files, at their most basic level. There are some management and operational tasks around the VM files that you need to be aware of and consider when managing Hyper-V environments. These tasks include locating and managing the underlying VM files, determining their default locations, and extending virtual hard disks. This is what you'll learn in this chapter.

In This Chapter and Beyond

You have a strong foundation now in creating and managing VMs. In this chapter, we'll cover moving VM files manually and how to modify a virtual hard disk. While not common, these actions usually have to be done in a time-sensitive-manner, as projects are often dependent on these types of changes.

The task of extending the size of a virtual hard disk is a very common one that you'll be expected to perform if you are responsible for managing a Hyper-V solution. Additionally, you can't modify these underlying VM files if you don't know where to locate them. We'll start this chapter by locating the VM files in their folder structure, and then we'll make some modifications to them. Overall, this will round out your administration skills when it comes to working with VMs.

By the end of this chapter, you'll have a firm understanding of how to work with VM objects in a Hyper-V environment, including the setup of new VMs and the modification of existing VMs and their components. Subsequent chapters will look at Hyper-V checkpoints and then focus on the configuration of resources and settings on the host.

© Andy Syrewicze, Richard Siddaway 2018
A. Syrewicze and R. Siddaway, *Pro Microsoft Hyper-V 2019*, https://doi.org/10.1007/978-1-4842-4116-5_6

File Types and Their Default Locations

We've briefly covered the file types that make up a VM and their functions, but we didn't discuss their locations. It's important to know the function and location of each file type. There may be situations in which you must traverse the VM folder structure to troubleshoot an issue, and you need to be aware of what is considered to be normal behavior for these files types. Without knowing that, you may deem something that is completely normal to be an issue to be fixed, thus making your troubleshooting much more difficult. Without understanding the structure of the VM, you may make things worse! We won't spend much time discussing each component, because we've already covered this, but Table 6-1 supplies a quick refresher, along with the default location of each file.

Table 6-1. *List of Hyper-V Default File Locations*

File Type	Purpose	Default Location
VM Config File (XML) VMCX in 2016 and later versions	Holds the master configuration for a VM	`C:\ProgramData\Microsoft\Windows\ Hyper-V\Virtual Machines`
BIN File	Save State location for Virtual Machine Memory	`C:\ProgramData\Microsoft\Windows\ Hyper-V\Virtual Machines\{UUID}\`
VSV File	Save State Device Information Storage	`C:\ProgramData\Microsoft\Windows\ Hyper-V\Virtual Machines\{UUID}\`
VHD/VHDX	Primary Storage for a VM	`C:\Users\Public\Documents\ Hyper-V\Virtual Hard Disks`
AVHD/AVHDX	Checkpoint File	Same Location as Parent VHD/VHDX files

Table 6-1 lists the default locations. If you're looking at an already established environment, other locations may have been used. So, how do we verify whether the files in your environment are stored at the default paths or not? Well, that is going to be next on the agenda.

It's important to know how to discover VM file locations, especially when troubleshooting. Many of the common problems in configuring and operating a Hyper-V environment are related to folder paths and permissions issues. Symptoms of this could be a VM that doesn't start or a VM that can't see the secondary hard drive you've configured. Troubleshooting that type of issue requires you to know how to locate the files.

The two best tools to verify VM file locations are Hyper-V Manager and PowerShell. In Hyper-V Manager, you can leverage the VM settings and host settings sections. Keep in mind that this is the default location. Someone could have saved an individual VM in a different location during creation or moved the relevant files at a later time. You'll have to look at the relevant paths inside each individual VM's configuration for confirmation. PowerShell is a bit quicker, but you must know the syntax going in. Let's try using both methods, first starting with Hyper-V Manager.

Locating Virtual Machine Files Using Hyper-V Manager

To locate a VM's files,

1. With Hyper-V Manager open, select the Hyper-V host containing the two VMs you created in Chapter 3.

2. In the right-hand pane, click Hyper-V Settings.

3. You'll be greeted with the Hyper-V Settings UI, and the information we're looking for is readily available right away, as seen in Figure 6-1.

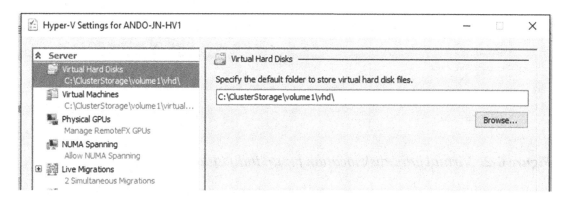

Figure 6-1. *Default VHD/VHDX storage path located in Hyper-V Manager*

4. Take note of the default folder location for virtual hard disks.

5. In the Hyper-V Settings UI, click Virtual Machines in the left-hand pane.

6. Take note of the default location for Virtual Machines.

7. Close the Hyper-V Settings UI.

8. Open the Virtual Machines Settings UI for one of the two VMs that we've created thus far.

9. Select the virtual hard disk associated with the target VM in the left-hand pane. It will look very similar to Figure 6-2.

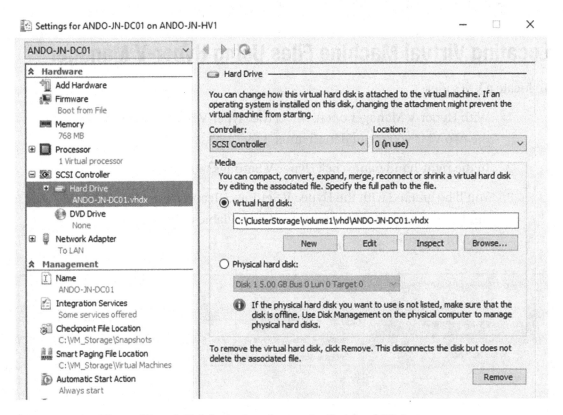

Figure 6-2. *Virtual hard disk location for an individual VM*

10. Take note of the virtual hard disk location shown in the right-hand pane. Is it located in the same path as the default location recorded earlier?

11. Click Checkpoint File Location in the left-hand pane.

12. Take note of the defined location for checkpoints.

13. Do the same for the Smart Paging File Location, also located in the left-hand pane.

14. Close the Virtual Machine Settings UI.

TRY IT YOURSELF—VIEW VM FILE LOCATIONS

Confirm the locations of the VMs in your test lab using Hyper-V Manager.

When using the Hyper-V Manager UI for this task, there are several areas that you must view, to verify you're looking in the correct location. You start with the host-level defaults for the whole system, but because the paths are changeable at the time of VM creation, you have to verify the paths on a per-VM basis as well. There is a quicker way to gather this information, using PowerShell, which we'll get to in a second, but first, we must discuss the Smart Paging File.

Smart Paging File

If you've been paying attention, you likely saw the Smart Paging File section and said, "Hey, we haven't discussed this yet." You're correct. We haven't, and the main reason is that if all is going well, you shouldn't have reason to even think of the Smart Paging File. Its sole purpose is in situations in which a host is having resource contention issues. Imagine a scenario in which you have Dynamic Memory enabled on a VM. For example, the VM has a startup memory value of 2048MB and a minimum memory value of 512MB. Then, let's assume that the VM is operating at about the minimum value of 512MB of memory. If a reboot of the VM is needed, 2048MB of memory will be required to start the VM. What happens if the host doesn't have that much to spare?

This is where the Smart Paging File comes into play. The Hyper-V host will use the Smart Paging File as a temporary location for memory storage. This will allow the VM to boot. Then, over a short period of time, usually not lasting longer than five or ten minutes, the memory usage of the VM should drop back down to the lower amount, as the startup processes finish, and the Smart Paging File will be removed and purged.

Really, you shouldn't be running that tight on memory. You always want to leave, at a minimum, 20% to 30% for spare resources, as it takes time to order and install hardware, if you need to scale up the host. Also, in the event you have to use the Smart Paging File, Microsoft has provided the ability to manually define its location. This allows you to choose a storage location that is seeing little or no traffic for increased performance. Again, the best course of action is to avoid the need for the feature, but you should know it's there, if needed.

Locating Virtual Machine Files Using PowerShell

We mentioned earlier that there's a quicker way of gathering all of this path information, using PowerShell.

1. Open PowerShell as an administrator on your Hyper-V host. If this is Windows Server Core box, simply type PowerShell and press Enter.

2. Type

   ```
   Get-VMHost | Select VirtualHardDiskPath,VirtualMachinePath
   ```

   and press Enter to return the default storage paths for the selected host.

Note   If you're working interactively, you can use PowerShell's ability to understand wildcards to use `Get-VMHost | select *path`, instead of typing full property names. If you're using a script, you should always use the full property names, for ease of understanding and maintenance.

---

3. Type `Get-VM` and press Enter to return a list of VMs being hosted by the Hyper-V host.

4. Run `Get-VM |`

    `Select Name, ConfigurationLocation,SnapshotFileLocation,`
    `SmartPagingFilePath`

5. Press Enter to return the location of VM configurations and
    Snapshot and Smart Paging File paths.

Note   If the output from the previous command is too wide for your console, you could change the code to `Get-VM | select Name, ConfigurationLocation, SnapshotFileLocation,SmartPagingFilePath | Format-List`, which will present the output in a list format rather than a table.

---

6. On the same Hyper-V host, type

    `Get-VM | Get-VMHardDiskDrive | Select VMName,Path`

7. Press Enter to return the location of any virtual hard disks
    associated with the VM.

8. Take note of the existing paths, as you'll be using this information
    shortly.

PowerShell enables you to find the information much quicker than looking through multiple locations in the UI. When troubleshooting an issue with paths or permissions, if you're not sure where a VM is stored, this will be one of the first steps you take in troubleshooting the issue. Remember: The most likely scenarios will be a VM that can't boot, or one that is complaining about not being able to read all of its virtual hard disks. The preceding method will allow you to verify this information quickly, so you can start the troubleshooting process.

TRY IT YOURSELF—VIEW VM FILE LOCATIONS

Confirm the locations of the VMs in your test lab, using PowerShell.

Simply gathering this information isn't the only thing we can do here. We can also change the default locations for these files at the host level, as discussed in Chapter 2. The main reason you would change this from the default is that you have storage set aside specifically for VMs. This could be a secondary volume on the host or network storage. Changing the VM default storage path can be performed with either the Hyper-V Settings UI or the Set-VM Host cmdlet in PowerShell.

Moving Virtual Machine Files

Now that you know how to locate the various files associated with a VM, what types of things can we do with them? Well, generally, you're going to be leaving them alone. One of the rare cases where you may actually have to do something with these files is when you must move them.

Some of these files can be moved manually, but it's best not to move things manually, as breakage can occur, unless you know exactly what you're doing. VM config, BIN, VSV, and Smart Paging Files should not be moved manually, and in most cases, you will not be allowed to move them, owing to the files being in use. It's best to let the management utilities do the moving for you, as it is much less error-prone. We'll be talking more about VM migration between locations and between Hyper-V hosts in a later chapter. Moving VM files other than the VHDs will be covered in that chapter.

Moving the virtual hard disks associated with a VM is possible to do manually. There are storage migration functions built into Hyper-V, but if you want to copy a VM's virtual hard disk somewhere else, you would create a new blank VM, and instead of configuring a new virtual hard disk during provisioning, you would attach an existing disk and point it at the newly copied VHD/VHDX file. This is useful in many situations, for example, you could make a copy of a VHD for testing purposes, or you could attach a problematic OS disk to another VM, for troubleshooting.

Virtual Machine Configuration File

We would say a VM's VHD and VHDX files rank number one in importance, with the VM config file being a close second. The virtual hard disks are responsible for holding data, while the configuration file tells Hyper-V how a VM is pieced together, for example, how much memory it's supposed to have, how many vCPUs should be assigned, and the locations of virtual hard disks.

Caution   Anytime you are making changes, or even viewing a VM configuration file, you should proceed with the utmost caution.

Many an administrator has found VMs unstartable, after making some unintended modification to the configuration of a VM. In some cases, the fix may be relatively easy to identify; other times, an entirely new blank VM will have to be created, with the older virtual disk attached. So, again, caution is heavily advised when working with VM config files.

The VM configuration file is an XML file, so any text editor supporting XML can be used to view and modify it (with caution!). You may have to make a copy of the configuration file to another location, owing to the file being in use by the hypervisor. Just keep this in mind moving forward.

Note   In Windows Server 2016 and later versions, the VM configuration file will no longer be in XML format. The new file format will be a binary format that will require you to use PowerShell to perform modifications.

So, we've figured out where this file is stored, let's actually take a look at it.

1. Take the VM you selected earlier and review the path information.

2. Using File Explorer, navigate to the VM path.

3. Once in that directory, copy the XML file that is named with the corresponding GUID of the target virtual machine.

Note   Just a reminder from Chapter 3. You can find the GUID of the target VM by running Get-VM "<VM NAME HERE>" | select Name, Id.

4. Paste the XML file on a machine with an XML-friendly text editor, such as WordPad, and open it.

5. Review the file and take note of the XML attributes and elements. You will notice that many of these correspond with the settings contained within the Virtual Machine Settings UI in Hyper-V Manager.

6. Close the file and save it in a safe location for now.

TRY IT YOURSELF—VIEW VM CONFIG FILE

View the contents of the configuration files for the VMs on your system.

In Windows Server 2016 and later versions, you must use PowerShell to retrieve the configuration information.

Note   As a best practice, PowerShell scripts should output objects. We know that the following script breaks that rule. It's a deliberate decision, as the script is meant as a demonstration of the various cmdlets and as a report on the configuration of a VM. We cite `Get-ComputerInfo in PowerShell v5.1` and later versions as an example. If it's good enough for the PowerShell team, it's good enough for us.

A sample script that demonstrates the use of the various cmdlets you can use, and the information you'll find, follows:

```
function get-vminfo {
  [CmdletBinding()]

  param (

    [string] $vmname

  )

  $vm = Get-VM -Name $vmname

  "Settings for $($vm.Name)"

  ""

  "Memory"
  $vm | Get-VMMemory |
  select VMName, DynamicMemoryEnabled,
  @{N='Minimum(MB)'; E={$_.Minimum / 1MB}},
  @{N='Startup(MB)'; E={$_.Startup / 1MB}},
  @{N='Maximum(MB)'; E={$_.Maximum / 1MB}} |
  Format-List
```

```
"Processors"
$vm | Get-VMProcessor |
select VMname, Count |
Format-List

"SCSI controllers"
$vm | Get-VMScsiController |
select VMname, ControllerNumber |
Format-List

"Drives"
$vm | Get-VMScsiController |
select -ExpandProperty Drives |
select Name, Path |
Format-List

"Network adapters"
$vm | Get-VMNetworkAdapter |
select  VMName, Name,  IsManagementOs,
SwitchName, MacAddress,
Status, IPAddresses |
Format-List

"Integration services"
$vm | Get-VMIntegrationService |
select VMname, Name, Enabled |
Format-List

"Other management information"
$vm | select Name,
ConfigurationLocation,
CheckpointType, CheckpointFileLocation,
SmartPagingFilePath,
AutomaticStartAction, AutomaticStopAction |
Format-List
}
```

The function in the script should be used as:

```
PS> get-vminfo -vmname <VM name>
```

The script works through the settings you'll see in the Hyper-V Manager settings dialog for a VM and displays the relevant information. You could use a script such as this to find all of the required information or use just the individual cmdlets, to get specific information for one or all cmdlets.

TRY IT YOURSELF—VIEW VM CONFIGURATION WITH POWERSHELL

View the configuration of a VM using the PowerShell cmdlets.

The virtual disks you have attached to the VM are probably its most important components.

Virtual Hard Disks—VHDs and VHDXs

The last file types that we're going to discuss are the virtual hard disk file formats. Pre-Windows Server 2012, we had the VHD file format, which had a number of limitations, such as a 2TB maximum file size and slow operational times when provisioning fixed type VHDs.

In Windows Server 2012, Microsoft introduced the VHDX file format, which enables a maximum file size of 64TB. It also provides advanced functionality, such as data corruption prevention and better alignment of block storage on large sector disks. This file format is the default virtual hard disk format on Windows Server 2012 R2 hosts and later versions. You can select the older VHD type during virtual hard disk creation. When in doubt, use VHDX.

Note   The only time you should be using the older VHD file format is in situations in which you have a Windows Server 2008 R2 host that might have to host the VM, or if you ever intend on moving the VM into Microsoft's pre-ARM (Azure Resource Manager) Azure public cloud service, as the older Azure portal does not utilize the new VHDX file format.

Converting Virtual Hard Disks

In most cases, you'll build your virtual hard disk, defined as either VHD or VHDX, attach it, and you'll be done. You'll likely never give it a second thought, unless you're extending the disk. However, there may be times when you have to modify the disk files. For example, you may have a VHD file that requires the benefits that the VHDX file format provides. Then, on the other hand, you may have a VHDX file that must be attached to a VM running on an older Windows Server 2008 R2 Hyper-V host during a migration or cutover. Is it possible to change the type after creation? The answer is yes, and it's what we'll be doing in our next Try It Yourself.

Note   In the following exercise, we'll walk you through the creation of two small 2GB virtual hard disks. These virtual hard disks are not connected to any virtual machine. They are simply there for you to practice on.

To create a new virtual disk,

1. Open PowerShell as an administrator on your Hyper-V host.

2. Type: `New-VHD -Path C:\Test\ConversionTest.vhdx - SizeBytes 2GB` and press Enter, to create a 2GB virtual hard disk at the root of `C:\`.

3. Type `dir C:\Test` and press Enter to verify the file's existence and file extension.

4. Type `Convert-VHD -Path C:\Test\ConversionTest. vhdx -DestinationPath C: \Test\ConversionTest.vhd - DeleteSource` and press Enter, to create a new VHD file. Copy the contents of the VHDX and delete the source file, once completed.

5. Open Hyper-V Manager and select the same Hyper-V host in the left-hand pane and click Edit Disk in the right-hand pane.

6. Click Next at the opening screen of the wizard and then browse to the `ConversionTest.vhd`, located at the root of `C:\Test` on the host, and click Next.

7. Select the "Convert" radio button and then click Next.

97

8. Select disk format VHDX and click Next.

9. On the disk type screen, keep the default of Dynamically Expanding and click Next.

10. Select `C:\Test\ConversionTest.vhdx` as the destination path and click Next and then Finish.

11. Verify the existence of the file and then run `Get-ChildItem C:\Test\Conversion* | Remove-Item`.

TRY IT YOURSELF

Create a new virtual hard disk in VHDX format and convert it to VHD and back to VHDX.

Converting the file after creation is quite simple in both Hyper-V Manager and PowerShell. If you don't specify the `-DeleteSource` parameter, the old file will still be present. Microsoft will always err on the side of caution to make sure the source file is still there, if needed. However, you need twice the amount of space to convert a virtual disk. For example, if you have a 200GB VHD file and you want to convert it to a VHDX, you need 400GB of hard disk space available—200GB for the source file, and 200GB for the new virtual hard disk.

Virtual Hard Disk Types

VHD and VHDX are the file formats associated with virtual hard disks. There are a number of types of virtual hard disks, with different functions and use cases. Each type consumes physical hard disk space differently, and without knowing how the virtual disk is meant to work, you could wind up running out of storage.

In Windows Server 2012 R2 and later versions, the default is dynamically expanding disks, which is perfect for the vast majority of use cases, but let's review the other options briefly.

Fixed Disk

A fixed disk is the easiest to understand, because it has a 1:1 ratio of physical to virtual storage. If you provision a 200GB fixed VHDX, 200GB of disk space will instantly be consumed on the physical storage. This is the safest way to provision virtual storage, because all space is accounted for, and it's impossible to provision more storage than is available. However, you'll have a lot of wasted space, as most VMs do not consume all of the disk space available to them. This is where dynamically expanding disks come into play.

Dynamically Expanding Disks

Dynamically expanding VHDs and VHDX files are very similar to fixed disks but consume physical disk space differently. A fixed disk will consume the full amount immediately, but dynamically expanding disks will only consume physical disk space as required, providing a more efficient use of physical disk space.

Note   Dynamically expanding disks are also referred to as thin-provisioned disks. If you're using a SAN for your underlying storage, you may find that the disk space is also thin-provisioned. A scenario with thin-provisioned storage supporting thin-provisioned virtual disks means that you must monitor your storage very carefully, to ensure you don't run out of disk space.

Using dynamically expanding disks, you could provision more disk space than you actually have. For example, let's say your Hyper-V host has a maximum of 100GB for VM storage. If you provision two VMs with a 100GB VHD each, and the guest OSs inside those VMs grows to 50GB each, your VMs will stop functioning. Even though the guest OSs inside the VMs think they have 100GB of total space, once the host is out of disk space, there is no way for the guest VMs to consume any more.

When using dynamically expanding disks, you must keep track of total storage consumption, so you don't run into this situation. Additionally, there is a slight disk performance overhead for running in this mode, as additional disk writes have to be performed to increase the VHD/VHDX size before the data payload can be committed to disk.

Note   When creating a new VM using Hyper-V Manager, the default virtual disk type is dynamically expanding. If you want to create a fixed or differencing disk, you will have to create the disk manually first and then attach it to the target VM.

Differencing Disks

You won't run into this type of disk very often, as it is primarily utilized for virtual desktop infrastructure (VDI) workloads or testing and experimental environments. Picture the following situation. You have ten Windows 10 virtual machines. Each virtual machine has a portion of disk space that is identical between all ten, so you are storing ten copies of the same OS information. This is very wasteful on disk space.

Differencing disks allow you to define a master VHD file that contains the vast majority of the static (common) data (the Windows 10 OS, in this case). A differencing disk is created for each VM that keeps track of the data that is different between instances. This reduces the amount of disk space required in VDI deployments significantly. Like the dynamically expanding disk type, there is a disk performance overhead associated with running differencing disks.

Extending and Shrinking Virtual Hard Disks

Another common operation when working with VHDs and VHDXs is the need to extend them as workload sizes increase. Conversely, you may have to shrink a virtual hard disk, if you're running out of disk space elsewhere in your environment. Growing virtual hard disks is quite straightforward. Shrinking them is another matter, as there are some limitations.

Note   Remember this when you're sizing out a virtual machine. It's *very* easy to scale up. It's more difficult to scale down.

As a best practice, always size your VMs as small as you think they can be and still give you the needed performance, then scale up from there. Let's scale up a virtual disk now, and then we'll shrink it.

1. Open PowerShell as an administrator on your Hyper-V host.

2. Type New-VHD -Path C:\Test\GrowShrinkTest01.vhdx
    -SizeBytes 2GB and press Enter, to create a 2GB virtual hard disk.

3. Type New-VHD -Path C:\Test\GrowShrinkTest02.vhdx
    -SizeBytes 2GB and press Enter, to create a 2GB virtual hard disk.

4. Type dir C:\Test and press Enter, to verify that both files exist.

5. Type Get-VHD -Path C:\Test\GrowShrinkTest01.vhdx |
    select size and press Enter. Take note of this value.

6. Type Resize-VHD -Path C:\Test\GrowShrinkTest01.vhdx -
    SizeBytes 10GB and press Enter, to increase the maximum size of
    the VHDX to 10GB.

7. Type: Get-VHD -Path C:\Test\GrowShrinkTest01.vhdx |
    select size and press Enter. The value has changed, indicating
    that you've grown this virtual disk.

TRY IT YOURSELF

Create a test virtual hard disk and then increase its size.

Extending a disk with PowerShell is very simple. You've turned a 2GB hard drive into a 10GB hard drive, as far as the VM is concerned. If this were a production environment, your next step would be to log in to the disk management utility inside the guest OS and modify the file system to consume the new space.

Hyper-V Manager can be used to change virtual disks, using the Edit Disk Wizard.

1. Open Hyper-V Manager. Select the Hyper-V host for the VMs you
    created in Chapter 3.

2. Click Inspect Disk in the right-hand pane.

3. Browse to C:\Test\GrowShrinkTest02.vhdx and click Open.

4. Take note of the Maximum Disk Size Value, as shown in Figure 6-3.

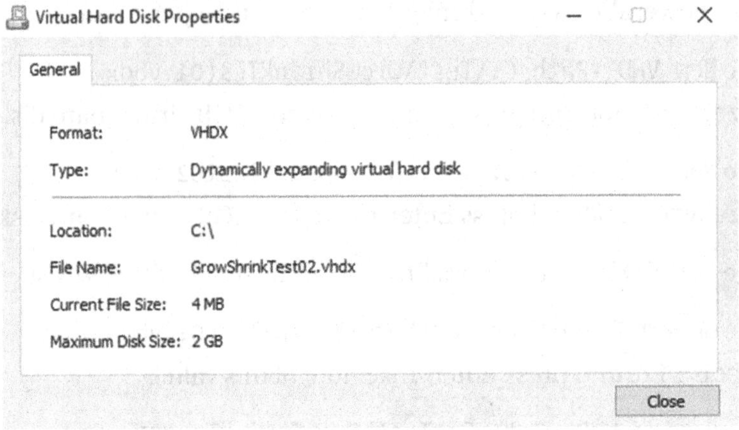

Figure 6-3. *Virtual Hard Disk Properties view*

5. Click Close and then Edit Disk, in the right-hand pane of Hyper-V Manager.

6. Click Next and then Browse.

7. Browse to `C:\Test\GrowShrinkTest02.vhdx` and click Open. Then click Next.

8. Select the Expand radio button and then click Next.

9. Place a 10 in the New Size field, to grow the disk to 10GB, then click Next.

10. Verify the settings and then click Finish.

11. Using the Inspect Disk Wizard, verify that the virtual hard disk has a 10GB maximum size.

TRY IT YOURSELF

Use Hyper-V Manager to increase the size of a virtual hard disk connected to a running VM.

In a production situation, you would log in to your guest OS and tell the filesystem to consume the additional disk space. Over time, new data would get written to the additional sections of the VHD/VHDX file.

Now let's say that after a while, you found that you provisioned too much space. The file didn't need to be 10GB, but 5GB. Is it possible to go back? The answer is, it depends, the reason being that the NTFS filesystem has to be shrunk first, and the amount of that shrinkage depends on the data layout on disk.

If data was written fairly deep into the newly allocated disk space, you may only be able to shrink the NTFS filesystem to 8GB, and so only shrink the size of the VHD or VHDX to 8GB as well.

ABOVE AND BEYOND

As this book focuses on Hyper-V related items, we won't be covering the intricacies of shrinking an NTFS filesystem. But a good how-to can be found on TechNethere:

`https://technet.microsoft.com/en-us/library/cc772210.aspx.`

It's much easier to scale up disks than scale down, so it's certainly worth asking yourself when growing a virtual hard disk, "Do I *really* need to add this much additional space?"

Note   Our recommendation is to scale up small increments, 5GB or 10GB at a time, to reduce the chances of you having to shrink a volume.

Let's now assume that you've shrunk the NTFS filesystem within the guest OS on one of these two virtual hard disks you've created. How do we shrink the size of the VHD to reclaim physical hard disk space on the host?

This task can be performed via Hyper-V Manager or PowerShell. Let's shrink both of our test files. First, you'll have to write a filesystem to the virtual disk; otherwise, the shrink commands will error out, as they won't be able to determine the minimum safe file size contained within the filesystem on the virtual disk.

Use the following process to shrink virtual hard disks:

1. Open PowerShell as an administrator on your Hyper-V host.

2. Type `Mount-VHD -Path C:\Test\GrowShrinkTest01.vhdx` and press Enter, to mount the VHD as a disk on the host OS.

3. Use either Disk Management or DiskPart to create a small 4GB partition on the disk. Don't assign a drive letter. You'll have a 4GB partition and 6GB of unallocated space.

Caution   Make sure you're working with the 10GB disk when working with either of these tools! Making changes to the wrong disk could damage your running host, so proceed with caution.

---

4. Complete the previous steps for the `C:\Test\GrowShrinkTest02.vhdx` file.

5. In Hyper-V Manager, select your Hyper-V host.

6. Click Edit Disk in the right-hand pane.

7. Browse to and select `C:\Test\GrowShrinkTest01.vhdx` and click Open, then click Next.

8. Select the Compact radio button and then click Next.

9. Click Finish, to compact the file to its smallest possible size.

10. Using Inspect Disk Wizard, browse to and select `C:\GrowShrinkTest01.vhdx` and take note of the new size.

11. Back in PowerShell, type `Resize-VHD -Path C:\Test\GrowShrinkTest02.vhdx -ToMinimumSize` and press Enter, to shrink the virtual disk.

12. Type: `Get-VHD -Path C:\Test\GrowShrinkTest02.vhdx | Select Size`, press Enter, and take note of the new size. Notice how it knew there was only a 4GB partition?

13. Type `Dismount-VHD -Path C:\GrowShrinkTest01.vhdx` and press Enter, to dismount the virtual disk from the system.

14. Repeat the command with the `C:\GrowShrinkTest01.vhdx` virtual disk.

Shrinking a disk is more complicated than expanding it. The shrinking process looked at the filesystem in the VHDX and determined that there was only a 4GB partition out of 10GB of raw space on the virtual disk. Thus, the shrink operation was able to shrink the virtual disk by 6GB. The amount you can shrink a virtual disk depends on how small you can make the NTFS filesystem.

COMPACTING VIRTUAL DISKS

The virtual disks attached to your VM, especially the system disk, will grow in time. When you first create the VM, the virtual disk may only occupy 5GB of physical disk space. As you add and remove features or software, copy files to and from the VM, and perform patching, the size can increase significantly.

In many cases, you can reclaim the unused disk space by compacting the virtual disk. The easiest method is to shut down the VM and use the following PowerShell code:

```
Mount-VHD -Path <path to the virtual disk> -ReadOnly
Optimize-VHD -Path <path to the virtual disk>  -Mode Full
DisMount-VHD -Path <path to the virtual disk>
```

You could even create a script to loop through your VMs and compact the disks on all VMs.

Alternatively, you can compact the disk through the Hyper-V Manager, as described previously.

You should now have a firm understanding of how to locate all the various pieces of a VM in the host's storage. This should be one of the first steps in troubleshooting anything at the VM layer. Additionally, we discussed changing the virtual hard disks. Remember: This is a very common operation, and you will be doing it a lot as data sizes change inside of your organization. In the next chapter, we will spend a little more time working with VM objects. Specifically, we will be working with Hyper-V checkpoints, and then we'll be moving onto host-specific resources.

Lab Work

To get the most from the chapter, complete the Try It Yourself sections and then, using your second NM (not used in this chapter), complete the following:

1. Using PowerShell, determine the location of the VM's config file, VHD, BIN, and VSV files.

2. Review the VM configuration file and take note of any configuration items that may coincide with settings from within the Virtual Machines Settings dialog.

3. Using PowerShell, grow the virtual disk by 10GB; create a new 2GB partition; and then shrink the virtual disk down to its minimum size.

4. Repeat the exercise using Hyper-V Manager.

CHAPTER 7

Utilizing Hyper-V Checkpoints for Software Upgrades

If you've been in IT world for any length of time, you know that software upgrades are a part of life. Every month, you get a list of patches from Microsoft that must be applied to both the operating system (OS) and all of the Windows Server roles and features inside your environment. Eventually, something breaks as a result of applying a patch. If only there were a way to quickly roll back a failed patch. Or maybe you have a testing routine in place in your organization that would be made easier if you could simply click a go-back button. Well, we're going to talk about one such technology throughout this chapter: Hyper-V Checkpoints.

In This Chapter and Beyond

We've spent the last several chapters talking about how virtual machines (VMs) are built and how they work. In this chapter, we're going to build on top of that knowledge, with Hyper-V Checkpoints. This chapter is the last part of the text focusing on the creation and use of VMs. After this chapter, we'll concentrate more on host concepts and configuration.

© Andy Syrewicze, Richard Siddaway 2018
A. Syrewicze and R. Siddaway, *Pro Microsoft Hyper-V 2019*, https://doi.org/10.1007/978-1-4842-4116-5_7

It's important to know how to use checkpoints, because you'll be using them on a regular basis. Checkpoints are normally used prior to such things as software upgrades and patch testing, but they are really useful anytime you're making a fundamental change within the guest OS of the VM, such as a file relocation or a large settings change within an application.

Note   Richard regularly uses checkpoints to roll back changes when testing demonstrations for presentations at conferences.

You should train yourself to think about a checkpoint anytime you get ready to do some sort of software change within a VM.

Note   Simply taking a checkpoint could save you a ton of time, and possibly your job, by allowing you to undo a change relatively quickly.

This technology is able to save you huge amounts of time, and effort, *if utilized properly*. The ability to hit an undo button on everything that's occurred to a VM since the last checkpoint is immensely powerful. However, there are pitfalls. Checkpoints can be dangerous, if used improperly. We'll be covering the proper use cases and how *not* to use them as well, so you can use this technology without potentially causing data loss within your organization. Yes, you read correctly. Misuse of checkpoints can, and does, cause data loss. So, let's start working through the chapter, to help you utilize this technology properly.

What Are Hyper-V Checkpoints

The simplest explanation is to think of a checkpoint as a snapshot in time for a VM. You're taking a copy of a VM at a point in time and then setting it aside for later use. The checkpoint can be taken while the machine is live. The guest OS inside the VM doesn't even know that is being done. If you decide a day or two later that you want to revert the VM configuration to when the checkpoint was created, you apply the checkpoint, and the VM reverts to the state it was in when you originally took the checkpoint. This is one of those things that is easier to understand by seeing it in action, so let's do so now.

Using Hyper-V Checkpoints via Hyper-V Manager

Checkpoints can be managed with Hyper-V Manager or PowerShell. In this section, we'll show you how to use checkpoints in Hyper-V Manager. To create a checkpoint, take the following steps:

1. In Hyper-V Manager, select your Hyper-V host.

2. Choose one of the VMs and open the machine's console window.

3. Log in to the VM with an account that has administrator privileges. Using Notepad, create a new text file and save it as PRE-CHECKPOINTSTATE.txt onto the desktop of the guest OS.

4. At the top of the VM console window, click the Action drop-down, then click Checkpoint.

5. On the Checkpoint Name dialog screen, type "Pre-Software Installation" and click Yes.

6. Monitor the checkpoint status using the Status column next to the target VM in Hyper-V Manager and wait for completion.

7. To verify that the checkpoint was taken successfully, review the Checkpoint section in Hyper-V Manager, with the target VM selected. It should look like Figure 7-1.

Figure 7-1. *Hyper-V Manager Checkpoints view*

8. Delete the CHECKPOINTSTATE.txt file that we placed on the desktop earlier.

9. Open a PowerShell console with elevated privileges within the VM.

10. Type `Install-WindowsFeature –Name 'WDS'`

   and press Enter, to install the Windows Deployment Services Role.

11. Type `Get-WindowsFeature –Name 'WDS' | Select InstallState` and verify that the `InstallState` is "Installed."

12. In the VM console window, click the Action drop-down and then click Revert.

13. Monitor the state of the VM with Hyper-V Manager while the machine turns off and the checkpoint that was taken earlier is restored.

14. Once the checkpoint is restored, verify that the PRE-CHECKPOINTSTATE.txt file exists on the desktop.

15. Open a PowerShell prompt with an account that has administrative privileges.

16. Type: `Get-WindowsFeature –Name 'WDS' | Select InstallState` and note that the `InstallState` now shows as "Available," meaning that the role is no longer installed.

17. Leave the checkpoint in place. We will be using it later in the chapter.

TRY IT YOURSELF

Take a checkpoint using Hyper-V Manager.

Revert the checkpoint.

Is there any difference between the original configuration and after reverting the checkpoint?

We took the checkpoint, made file changes, installed additional software, and then we told Hyper-V to forget those changes and take us back to where we started.

How many times have you, or a colleague, installed a piece of software or a patch that caused some kind of failure and you had to spend hours fixing it? In this case, that breakage would be fixed in minutes, instead of hours. This is the power of Hyper-V Checkpoints.

Managing Multiple Checkpoints with Hyper-V Manager

Earlier, you performed a single snapshot procedure and revert operation, but the checkpoints view in Hyper-V Manager displays the checkpoints in tree format. This is because Hyper-V is capable of tracking multiple checkpoints for a VM at any given time. This is extremely useful for operations, such as software revision testing, for which you may be testing different software versions and different software combinations on the same server. Checkpoints allows you to move between the different configurations with ease. Let's try this now to get a feel for it.

1. In Hyper-V Manager, select your Hyper-V host.

2. Select the VM that was used in the previous exercise and that contains the Pre-Software Installation checkpoint.

3. Using PowerShell within the guest VM, install the WDS role once again.

4. Rename the PRE-CHECKPOINTSTATE.txt file on the desktop to CONTAINSWDS.txt.

5. In the Checkpoints section for the VM in Hyper-V Manager, right-click the Pre-Software Installation Checkpoint and then click Apply.

6. The Apply Checkpoint dialog appears, as shown in Figure 7-2. Click Create Checkpoint and Apply.

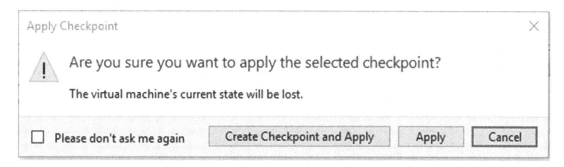

Figure 7-2. *Apply Checkpoint dialog*

7. Monitor the creation of the new Checkpoint in Hyper-V Manager.

8. Note the new checkpoint in the checkpoints tree for the VM. The default format of "VMNAME – Date" will have been used for the new checkpoint.

9. Right-click the new checkpoint and click Rename. Rename the checkpoint "Contains Windows Deployment Services."

10. Verify that the VM is back to its original state and then open PowerShell with a user with administrative privileges.

11. Type `Install-WindowsFeature –Name 'DHCP'` and press Enter to install the Windows DHCP service inside the VM.

12. Type: `Get-WindowsFeature –Name 'DHCP' | Select InstallState` and verify the `InstallState` is "Installed."

13. Rename the PRE-CHECKPOINTSTATE.txt file on the desktop to CONTAINSDHCP.txt.

14. Using Hyper-V Manager, apply the "Pre-Software Installation" checkpoint. Select Create Checkpoint and Apply on the Apply Checkpoint dialog UI.

15. Monitor the creation of the new checkpoint in Hyper-V Manager.

16. Rename the checkpoint to "Contains DHCP Service."

17. Note that your snapshot tree should now look very similar to the one found in Figure 7-3.

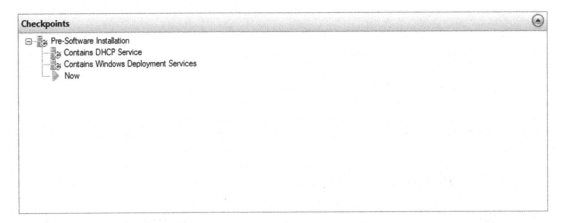

Figure 7-3. *More complex checkpoint tree in Hyper-V Manager*

18. Right-click the Contains Windows Deployment Services checkpoint and click Apply.

19. Click Apply on the Apply Checkpoint Dialog UI. There is no need to create another new Pre-Software Installation Checkpoint at this time.

20. Verify that the file on the desktop is named "CONTAINSWDS.txt" and that the WDS role is showing installed, using the `Get-WindowsFeature` PowerShell cmdlet.

21. Using Hyper-V Manager, apply the Contains DHCP Service checkpoint and repeat the previous step, to verify that the DHCP checkpoint is now in use.

22. Note how the checkpoint tree in Hyper-V Manager changes with each modification.

23. Apply the Pre-Software Installation checkpoint again, without creating an additional checkpoint in the Apply Checkpoint dialog UI.

24. Leave the checkpoints in place. We will be using them later in the chapter.

TRY IT YOURSELF

Follow the instructions in this section to create and use multiple checkpoints.

Managing and utilizing Hyper-V Checkpoints in this manner allows for very agile software testing and verification. Gone are the days of having to maintain multiple servers to be able to effectively test software procedures. Checkpoints make this process easy and safe.

Deleting and Merging Checkpoints with Hyper-V Manager

It's best practice to remove checkpoints as soon as you're done with them. If you leave them in place, all new incoming writes get written to the checkpoint and will eventually fill your storage. So, what happens to the changes contained inside the checkpoint? Well, there are two possibilities. The first option is to retain all the changes in a checkpoint and roll them into the next upstream object in the tree, regardless of whether that is the base

113

virtual disk or another checkpoint. Option 2 is to delete the changes outright, without retaining them. This is performed by using the delete action.

If you delete the currently active snapshot, Hyper-V will conduct a merge operation and roll all of the changes contained in the checkpoint into the next upstream object. If you delete a checkpoint that is not currently active, the changes within that checkpoint will be purged and lost forever.

Note   Remember: If you want to retain the changes you've made, you'll want to merge the checkpoint. If you don't want them saved, you'll simply delete it.

Again, this is one of those situations in which it's best to see by doing. Let's say we need to retain the DHCP service permanently for this particular VM, and we've determined that Windows Deployment Service isn't needed. Let's clean up our checkpoints from earlier, for practice.

1. In Hyper-V Manager, select your Hyper-V host.

2. Select the VM that was used in the previous exercise with the Pre-Software Installation, Contains DHCP Service, and Contains Windows Deployment Services checkpoints.

3. Verify that the Pre-Software Installation checkpoint is currently active. Your checkpoint tree should look like the one in Figure 7-3.

4. In the Checkpoints tree view for the selected VM, right-click the Contains Windows Deployment Services checkpoint and click Delete Checkpoint.

5. Click Delete when the Delete Checkpoint Verification UI shows up.

6. Monitor the deletion progress in the VM status column in Hyper-V Manager and wait for completion. Notice the merge process occurring?

7. Apply the Contains DHCP Service checkpoint. Do *not* create another checkpoint during the application process.

8. Right-click the Contains DHCP Service checkpoint and click Delete Checkpoint.

9. Click Delete when the Delete Checkpoint Verification UI shows up.

10. Monitor the deletion progress in the VM status column in Hyper-V Manager and wait for completion. Also, note that an extra merge process executes as well.

11. Right-click the Pre-Software Installation checkpoint and click Delete Checkpoint.

12. Click Delete when the Delete Checkpoint Verification UI shows up.

13. Monitor the deletion progress in the VM status column in Hyper-V Manager and wait for completion. Also, note that another merge operation occurs.

14. Verify that no further checkpoints are displayed in the Checkpoints tree for the selected VM. All changes have now been merged back into the VM's virtual disk.

TRY IT YOURSELF

Delete the checkpoints you created in the section "Using Hyper-V Checkpoints via Hyper-V Manager," by following the procedure in this section.

You've decided the intended changes are safe, and you've merged them back into the base virtual disk that will continue running the production workload. Clicking delete on a checkpoint may seem counterintuitive if you want to keep it, but that is how the merge process is called when the checkpoint is being deleted.

Alternatively, you could have used the Delete Checkpoint Subtree option to delete more than one checkpoint at a time. If you simply wanted to omit any of the changes, you would apply the previous checkpoint and then delete the checkpoint containing the changes you no longer want.

You've just walked through the entire checkpoint testing process. Using this method when testing and applying software updates again can save you a lot of time and heartache, and it can be a very powerful tool in your toolbox.

IMPORTANT WARNING

It is very important that upon successful testing and verification of the changes contained within a checkpoint, it's deleted and merged back into the base virtual disk as soon as possible.

When a checkpoint is created, an AVHDX file is created and associated with the VM's virtual hard disk. While the checkpoint and its associated AVHDX file exist, all incoming disk writes are occurring within the AVHDX file and *not* the virtual hard disk. So, if you write 200GB of data when a checkpoint is present on a 300GB large virtual machine, you're potentially consuming 500GB of storage, depending on how the VM's virtual hard disk has been provisioned.

With this in mind, it's best to remove checkpoints as soon as you're done with them. Otherwise, you risk consuming all the storage in your Hyper-V environment, if the checkpoint is left for an extended period of time.

Using Hyper-V Checkpoints with PowerShell

So far, you've seen how to manage checkpoints with Hyper-V Manager. PowerShell cmdlets for managing checkpoints are present in Hyper-V PowerShell Module in Windows Server 2012 R2 and later versions. Managing this process with PowerShell opens up a long list of potential automation opportunities, such as automating a checkpoint procedure prior to a scripted application installation. There also may be situations in which you don't have the GUI available to you, and PowerShell may be your only option. Not to worry! Managing checkpoints with PowerShell is as simple as doing it with Hyper-V Manager. As you now have a firm grasp of how the checkpoint process works, we'll be condensing the procedure into one exercise instead of several.

To manage checkpoints with PowerShell, do the following:

1. Open PowerShell as an administrator on your Hyper-V host.

2. Type `Get-Command -Module Hyper-V -Name *checkpoint*` and press Enter, to return a list of checkpoint cmdlets.

3. Type `Get-Command –Module Hyper-V –Name *snapshot*` and press Enter, to return a list of additional checkpoint cmdlets.

4. Type `Get-VM` and press Enter. Choose one of the VMs you created in Chapter 3, to act as the target of this exercise.

5. Type `Checkpoint-VM -Name <VM Name> -SnapshotName 'Pre-Software Installation'` and press Enter, to take a checkpoint of the VM.

6. Monitor the checkpoint's progress in the PowerShell window or Hyper-V Manager until completed.

7. Type `Get-VMSnapshot -VMName <VM Name>`

    and press Enter to return a list of checkpoints for the VM.

8. Verify the Pre-Software Installation checkpoint is displayed in the list.

9. Using Hyper-V Manager, open the console window of the target VM.

10. Open PowerShell within the guest OS with an account that has administrative privileges.

11. Type `Install-WindowsFeature -Name FS-FileServer` and press Enter, to install the Windows File Server role inside of the guest OS.

12. Using Notepad, place a text file on the desktop named POWERSHELL-CONTAINSFSROLE.txt.

13. Switch back to the PowerShell prompt on the Hyper-V host.

14. Type: `Checkpoint-VM -Name <VM Name> -SnapshotName 'Contains File Server Role'` and press Enter, to create another checkpoint.

15. Monitor the checkpoint's progress in the PowerShell window or Hyper-V Manager.

16. Type: `Get-VMSnapshot -VMName <VM Name>`

    and press Enter, to return a list of checkpoints for the VM.

17. Verify that the Contains File Server Role checkpoint is displayed in the list and take note of the ParentSnapshotName field.

18. Type: `Restore-VMSnapshot –Name 'Pre-Software Installation' –VMName <VM Name>` and press Enter, then Y, for "yes." Pressing Y confirms that you want to change the state of the VM and return it to its state prior to having file services installed.

19. Inside the guest VM, verify that the File Services role is not installed using the `Get-WindowsFeature` cmdlet, as used in previous exercises.

20. Switch back to the PowerShell prompt on the Hyper-V host.

21. Type: `Remove-VMSnapshot –Name * –VMName <VM Name>`

    and press Enter to remove all checkpoints associated with the VM. With the Pre-Software Installation checkpoint as the active checkpoint, the file-services installation will be purged and not rolled into the main virtual disk of the VM.

TRY IT YOURSELF

Use PowerShell to create, manage, and delete checkpoints.

Managing checkpoints via PowerShell is just as easy as via the GUI. Remember that there is no equivalent to the Take Checkpoint and Apply option in Hyper-V Manager. With PowerShell, you have to take each step individually to get the same effect.

ABOVE AND BEYOND

The under-the-hood details of the checkpoint process are not within the scope of this book. We're focused on learning by doing, rather than theory and processes. If you're interested in learning more about what is happening under the hood when a checkpoint is taken, refer to this TechNet article: `https://technet.microsoft.com/en-us/library/dn818483.aspx`. It will tell you all you ever wanted to know about the checkpoint process.

What *Not* to Do with Hyper-V Checkpoints

You're now a pro at handling checkpoints in Hyper-V, and you're ready to start using them in production! However, you'll remember that earlier in the chapter, we mentioned that there are some situations in which you could cause harm to your environment by using checkpoints. To be clear, it's not the checkpoint technology itself that creates these types of situations, it's checkpoints being used incorrectly that creates them. You know when to use checkpoints. Now, let's cover when *not* to use them, so that you can employ this technology safely.

Hyper-V Checkpoints Are *Not* a Replacement for a Backup

It's usually at this point in the conversation that people look at checkpoints and say "Gee, that looks an awful lot like a backup. I can replace my backup solution with this technology, can't I?" The answer is a firm "No, you can't." While, it may look like a backup, Hyper-V Checkpoints provides no retention and is still located with the NM on production storage, by default. Even if the checkpoint location is modified, only the most current writes are located in the checkpoint. The remaining data is still located in the VM's virtual hard disk. Therefore, if the virtual hard disk gets corrupted, you have no recovery method. Plan accordingly!

Hyper-V Checkpoints Are *Not* Suitable for Domain Controllers

There has been some logic added to Active Directory in Windows Server 2012 R2 and later versions that makes it more checkpoint-friendly, but it's still *not* best practice to use checkpoints with DCs. This is owing to the fact that you could inadvertently apply a checkpoint that is older than the tombstone lifetime of the DC, thus creating a major headache for yourself and your users. Your best bet is just to keep multiple DCs, and don't use checkpoints on them.

Hyper-V Checkpoints Are *Not* Suitable for Live Multitiered Applications

Many applications today rely on multiple services and servers to get their job done. For example, many web servers depend on an SQL Server back end. If you're getting ready to upgrade these workloads, and you plan on taking checkpoints prior to the upgrade, it is recommended that the VMs be powered off prior to the checkpoint. The reason is that you can't guarantee that the checkpoints will be done in an application-consistent way. Your checkpoint of the web server may not match up exactly with the checkpoint of the back-end SQL Server database, and if you have to revert, you could suffer data loss, if something in the transaction logs doesn't match up perfectly.

Do *Not* Modify Virtual Disk Layout While It Has Active Checkpoints

This is a bad one that could cause data loss. Hyper-V Manager will not let you modify a virtual hard disk that has active associated checkpoints, but it's still possible to do so with PowerShell. As all the recent writes are contained within the checkpoint and not the VM's virtual hard disk, any change to the virtual disk's size and layout will render the disk unusable. Hyper-V will no longer be able to match up the storage blocks contained in the checkpoint with the applicable blocks in the virtual hard disk. Avoid this at all cost. We've seen numerous situations in which modifying virtual disks while checkpoints exist has meant that recovery from backup was the only option available.

Following these directions and use cases is in your best interest. Remember: While checkpoints are an extremely useful technology, they can be harmful if used improperly. With that said, let's wrap up this chapter with a hands-on lab.

Lab Work

In this lab, you're going to put the power of Hyper-V Checkpoints to the test. You're going to checkpoint a VM, break an application in the OS, and then recover it.

1. Choose one of the two VMs created in Chapter 3 to act as the target VM for this exercise.

2. Take a Pre-Modification checkpoint, using your preferred method, as covered in this chapter.

3. Within the guest OS, change the file's owner to administrator, then change the NTFS permissions on the Notepad executable (`C:\Windows\System32\notepad.exe`), to give full access to the administrators group.

4. Once completed, delete the notepad.exe file.

5. Attempt to run Notepad from the run prompt of the start menu.

6. Using your preferred method, use Hyper-V Checkpoints to resolve this issue.

7. Once recovered, test Notepad's functionality once again.

CHAPTER 8

Connecting Virtual Machines to the Physical Network

So far, we've focused on the use and configuration of virtual machines (VMs). We've built a number of VMs, but they're not yet able to talk to the physical network. In this chapter, we'll configure the networking on the host, so that VMs can connect to the physical network.

In This Chapter and Beyond

We're going to focus on the Hyper-V host itself, for the next couple of chapters. You'll be learning about the basics of networking in Hyper-V in this chapter, after which, we'll go on to discuss some more advanced storage concepts in Chapter 9, because with some storage solutions, TCP/IP networking is a requirement. These topics are necessary, as they will round out your ability to manage and maintain a stand-alone host and prepare you for the later chapters. Let's get started!

Introduction to the Hyper-V Extensible Switch

You're getting a good grasp of virtualization concepts. We're taking all of these historically physical objects, such as CPU, memory, and storage, and we're abstracting them as software-defined entities. You've seen how this is done by allocating CPU time to a VM or increasing the amount of memory a VM has access to. This type of abstraction also applies to networking.

© Andy Syrewicze, Richard Siddaway 2018
A. Syrewicze and R. Siddaway, *Pro Microsoft Hyper-V 2019*, https://doi.org/10.1007/978-1-4842-4116-5_8

In earlier chapters, we've briefly mentioned virtual network interface cards (NICs). Another common name is network adapter. These virtual NICs attach to your VM's function in much the same way as a physical NIC. They use the same protocols and the same transport mechanisms. With that in mind, shouldn't they be able to talk to a physical switch as well? The answer to that question is yes, but we have to allow the traffic to get to the physical network first. This is where the Hyper-V Extensible Switch comes into play.

We're abstracting the networking layer (just like compute and storage), including the switching component. Each Hyper-V host can create one or more virtualized switching entities called a virtual switch, or vSwitch for short. You can imagine these vSwitches as similar to a VM, in that they are intangible objects that exist within the host. These entities are associated with the physical network cards in the host system.

The way we've always explained it to people is to imagine a normal switch and then pretend that the physical NICs on the host are uplink ports from that switch that connect back to the core networking infrastructure, as illustrated in Figure 8-1.

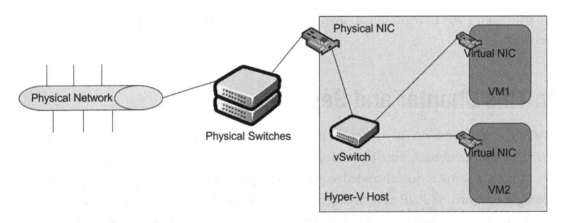

Figure 8-1. *Basic logical layout of Hyper-V networking, with connectivity to the physical network*

The virtual NICs attached to each VM are "plugged in" to a virtual switch residing on the Hyper-V host. That virtual switch in turn uses the physical NIC in the host as a type of uplink, to gain access to the rest of the switch infrastructure. In practice, it's no different than two physical switches talking to each other.

This connectivity is the most basic function of the Hyper-V Extensible Switch, and it is what we'll be focusing on throughout this chapter, because our virtualized workloads are useless if we can't talk to them over the network.

ABOVE AND BEYOND

The Hyper-V Extensible Switch has a number of integration features baked into it, so that third-part vendors can program additional functionality for it. For instance, Cisco has created the Nexus 1000x switch for Microsoft Hyper-V, which makes the Hyper-V Extensible Switch function and feel like a Cisco Nexus device. This allows your networking and support teams to support the virtualized infrastructure in much the same way that they would support the physical infrastructure. Details are available at `www.cisco.com/c/en/us/products/switches/nexus-1000v-switch-microsoft-hyper-v/index.html`. Keep this in mind as you continue to build on your Hyper-V networking knowledge throughout this book.

Virtual Switch Types in Hyper-V and Their Uses

Microsoft has provided a number of virtual switch types for use in Hyper-V environments. We have quite a bit of flexibility when it comes to controlling how vSwitches behave in Hyper-V. You have to define the switch type at the time you create it. We'll cover each type and what its primary use is.

External Virtual Switch

This is the type of vSwitch you'll be creating and using 90% of the time, usually for connecting VMs to the physical network. This virtual switch type provides communication between VMs on the host and external network connectivity. Figure 8-1 is the perfect example of an external vSwitch configuration. This is the default switch type when creating a new switch, as you'll see shortly.

Internal Virtual Switch

An internal virtual switch does not provide access to the physical network. This type of switch will allow VMs attached to it to talk to each other and to the host system. If you're running a lab in which you want to simulate entire environments and ensure that the test environment is isolated from the production network, you'd use an internal virtual switch to guarantee that isolation. Or, let's say you have a VM that requires additional network isolation because you're working in a high-security environment.

We've seen cases in which a virtualized security appliance is put on a host that has two virtual NICs, one attached to an external vSwitch and another attached to an internal vSwitch. The protected workload is then placed on that internal vSwitch and has to traverse the security appliance before it can talk with the physical network. This type of layout is shown in Figure 8-2.

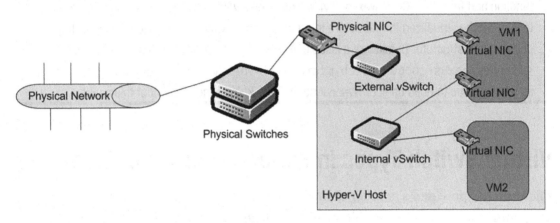

Figure 8-2. *Internal vSwitch use case example for inline security appliances*

As you can see in Figure 8-2, network traffic from VM2 has to traverse VM1 to get to the physical network. VM2 cannot talk to the network without VM1, so extra configuration needs to be performed, to ensure those two VMs stay together at all times on the same host. This idea will be covered later on when we discuss virtual machine mobility.

Private Virtual Switch

This virtual switch type is exactly the same as the internal vSwitch type, except a private virtual switch will not allow the host to talk with the VMs attached to the vSwitch. You'll still be able to connect with the console to those VMs and manage them normally, but from a networking standpoint, the host will not be able to access those workloads. You would use this vSwitch type when you don't want the host itself to be able to see the IP traffic of the VMs attached to this vSwitch. You'll see this type of switch used for internal cluster traffic when we discuss clustering.

Creating a Hyper-V Virtual Switch

Now that you've seen the three primary types of virtual switches, let's create one that will allow your VMs to talk to the physical network! We'll do this by creating an external virtual switch. To create a new switch,

1.   In Hyper-V Manager, select your Hyper-V host.

2.   In the right-hand pane, click Virtual Switch Manager. You'll be greeted by a screen similar to that shown in Figure 8-3.

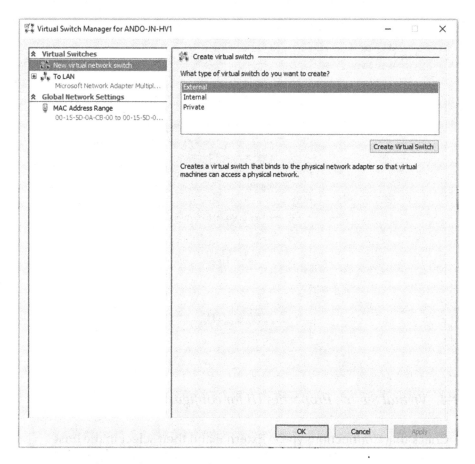

Figure 8-3. *Virtual Switch Manager UI, with which you can choose a vSwitch type*

3. Make sure virtual switch type External is highlighted, then click
    Create Virtual Switch.

4. On the next screen, as shown in Figure 8-4, give the new virtual
    switch a name and attach any notes you might want to track, such
    as subnet information.

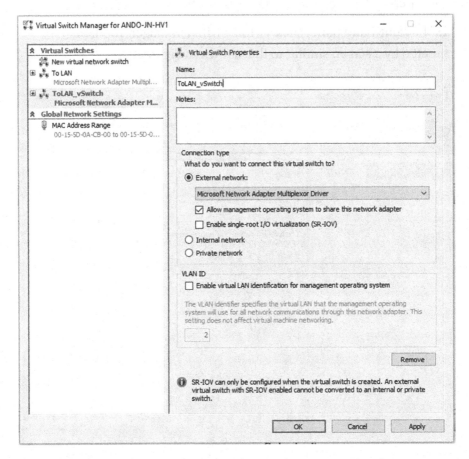

Figure 8-4. *Virtual Switch Properties UI for configuring vSwitch settings*

5. Check that Connection type is External and then select in the host
    the physical network adaptor that will be used to connect this
    vSwitch to the physical network, using the drop-down.

6. Leave the Allow management operating system to share this
    network adapter check box checked.

7. Leave Enable single-root I/O virtualization (SR-IOV), and Enable virtual LAN identification for management operating system unchecked, then click Apply.

8. When the Apply Networking Changes dialog comes up warning you that this may interrupt network connectivity, click Yes to continue.

9. Verify that the new virtual switch appears in the Virtual Switches list in the left-hand pane of the Virtual Switch Manager UI.

10. Click OK to exit the Virtual Switch Manager UI and return to the main Hyper-V Manager screen.

TRY IT YOURSELF

Create an external vSwitch on your Hyper-V host.

You should now have a functional external vSwitch on your Hyper-V host! If your organization has a separate VLAN for traffic management, you'll want to enable the option and input the VLAN ID, as requested. If you're not sure about this, you either don't require this, or you need to discuss it with your networking team.

ABOVE AND BEYOND

Another check box that you likely noticed here is that for single-root I/O virtualization. SR-IOV is a technology that allows hypervisors to gain more direct access to the networking hardware in the host, to provide better performance in high-throughput situations. This is a bit of an advanced topic, and if you're interested in learning more about it, see the MSDN overview regarding this feature here: `https://msdn.microsoft.com/en-us/library/windows/hardware/hh440148(v=vs.85).aspx`.

Attaching Virtual Machines to a vSwitch

Now that you have a working vSwitch, you need to assign a virtual NIC from a VM to the new external vSwitch, so that the VM can communicate with the physical network and your users can access the VM's workload.

The procedure to attach a VM to the vSwitch follows:

1. In Hyper-V Manager, select the Hyper-V host with the VMs you created in Chapter 3.

2. In the center pane, identify a target VM for this operation.

3. Select the target VM, then click Settings in the right-hand pane.

4. In the settings UI for the target VM, click Network Adapter, in the left-hand window, as shown in Figure 8-5.

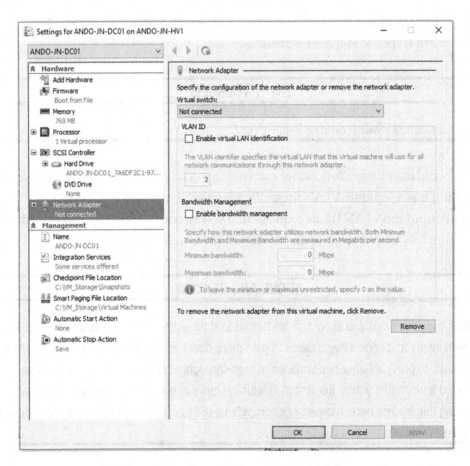

Figure 8-5. *Network Adapter Settings UI for a VM, which contains settings for the vNIC*

5. Using the Virtual switch drop-down, select the vSwitch that we created earlier.

6. Leave the two check boxes on this screen unchecked, then click Apply.

7. Close the Virtual Machine Settings UI.

8. Using Hyper-V Manager, open the console for the target VM and log in to the guest OS.

9. Open a command prompt or PowerShell window and verify that an IP was obtained by DHCP. If you don't have DHCP on this LAN segment, manually set the IP address.

10. Attempt to ping the gateway of the network. You should now have network connectivity inside of the guest OS of this VM.

TRY IT YOURSELF

Attach a VM to your external vSwitch.

The virtual switch assignment is really the only option that's needed to get the VM talking with the network, assuming you don't require the VM on a specific VLAN. If you do, you'll need to enable the VLAN ID check box and assign the appropriate VLAN ID. The other option you'll see on the VM NIC settings UI is "Enable bandwidth management." This option is especially useful, if you want to cap the amount of network bandwidth a specific VM is allowed to have, where you have one VM that likes to attempt to monopolize all of your network throughput.

Managing vSwitches with PowerShell

You can create a vSwitch and attach a VM to it, using PowerShell Cmdlets. It's a two-step process. First, create the new vSwitch.

```
New-VMSwitch -Name 'SwitchName' -NetAdapterName 'AssociatedHostNICName'
```

Next, attach a VM to the switch.

```
Connect-VMNetworkAdapter -VMname 'TargetVMName' `
-Name 'TargetVMNetworkAdapterName' -SwitchName 'NameTargetvSwitch
```

Attaching a VM to a vSwitch in PowerShell is another step in extending your automation capabilities when creating new VMs.

Management Network Considerations

There is an option in the virtual switch settings that allows the management OS to share the network adapter that was being assigned to a virtual switch. Remember that even though you're providing networking capabilities to your VM, the host system itself needs network connectivity for such things as management, patching, and monitoring. When a new virtual switch is configured, by default, Hyper-V will allow the host's OS also to use that same physical NIC for these management tasks. This is where administrators start asking whether that is a good idea, and the answer to that question is, It depends.

It depends on the type of physical network adapters you have and how many of them you have. If you're lucky enough to have a host with dual 10GB or 40GB network adapters in it, then you should be completely fine running management traffic over those NICs. However, if you have a number of 1GB NICs on the host, you may want to consider separating the management traffic.

For a single OS, 1GB of throughput is still adequate, but remember, your host may be running 5, 10, 20, or more VMs, and it's quite likely that a single 1GB NIC could quickly become saturated. If that happens, you're going to have to remote into the host, so you need sufficient network bandwidth. In that case, you may want to set aside one or more physical NICs specifically for management purposes, while the other NICs in the host are used for VMs and other tasks.

Additionally, if you want added resiliency, you can use the NIC teaming features in Windows Server, to make redundant teams of physical NICs for your management traffic and also for your VM traffic.

NIC Teaming

At some point, all physical hardware will fail, including NICs and switches. Also, physical cables frequently get bumped or pulled out, which could cause an outage. NIC teaming protects against these events, and it's doubly important when Hyper-V enters into the discussion.

When Hyper-V hosts critical production workloads, you want to ensure that the uptime is near 100%. To facilitate this, it's recommended to use NIC teaming in your

Hyper-V hosts wherever possible. Microsoft incorporates NIC teaming in Windows Server 2012 and later versions. With this technology, we can set up fault-tolerant teams of NICs for management, storage, and VM network traffic. If one NIC in a team fails, the other NIC(s) in the team will continue to send traffic through, until you can schedule downtime for the affected system to replace the NIC.

Let's set up a new NIC team on our host, and then we'll modify the virtual switch to use the new NIC team for connectivity to the physical network.

To create a NIC team:

1.   Open Server Manager on your Hyper-V host.

2.   Click All Servers in the left-hand pane and locate your Hyper-V host in the list. If your host isn't visible, add it by clicking Manage on the top control bar, and click Add Servers.

3.   Right-click the target Hyper-V host and click Configure NIC Teaming. This will open the NIC Teaming UI, as shown in Figure 8-6.

Figure 8-6. *NIC Teaming UI in Server Manager*

4. In the lower-right section of the screen, under Adapters and Interfaces, select two or more NICs, click the Tasks drop-down, and then click Add to New Team.

5. Name the New NIC Team, verify that the correct adapters are selected, and then click OK.

6. Close the NIC Team UI and then Server Manager.

7. Open Hyper-V Manager on your Hyper-V host and open the Virtual Switch Management UI once again, as shown earlier in this chapter.

8. Select the virtual switch that was created earlier in this chapter, and using the Adapters drop-down, select Microsoft Network Adapter Multiplexor Driver. (This is the name used by the NIC teaming driver.)

Note   It can sometimes be difficult to determine which NIC team to select, when you're using multiple NIC teams. In this situation, you can modify the interface description for the team, by using the following syntax: `Set-NetAdapter -Name 'AdapterName' -InterfaceDescription 'Description'`.

---

9. Click Apply and wait for the settings to take effect.

10. Verify that you can remotely ping the host system by DNS name or IP address.

11. Log in to the guest VM that was connected to the network earlier in this chapter and verify that it can still ping the gateway.

TRY IT YOURSELF

Create an NIC team on your Hyper-V host.

Now that you've configured a NIC team, if one of those two NICs fails, any virtual machines attached to that vSwitch will still have access to the network, and you'll still be able to remotely manage the host. This adds a very important layer of protection to your virtualized workloads. When specifying hardware for Hyper-V hosts, it's always helpful to have sufficient NICs to enable teaming.

You can also use PowerShell to team NICs, but you have two options:

- NetSwitchTeam for use with Hyper-V extensible switches: `https://docs.microsoft.com/en-us/windows-hardware/drivers/network/overview-of-the-hyper-v-extensible-switch`

- NetLBfo for NIC teaming

You can team the NICs in a VM, if needed. First, on the Hyper-V host, enable the VM's NICs to be teamed.

```
Get-VMNetworkAdapter -VMName <VMname> | Set-VMNetworkAdapter -AllowTeaming On
```

The team can then be formed. On the VM, use

```
New-NetLbfoTeam -Name Team1 -TeamMembers LAN01, LAN02 -Confirm:$false
```

REGARDING WINDOWS SERVER 2016

Windows Server 2016 introduced an alternative NIC teaming mode called Switch Embedded Teaming (SET) that boasts a number of improvements and enhancements when used with the new Software Defined Networking (SDN) stack. If you'd like to read up on this new feature, feel free to review the informational page located at `https://technet.microsoft.com/en-us/library/mt403349.aspx#bkmk_over`.

It's time for a lab to consolidate your learning.

Lab Work

This lab gives you a chance to practice what you've learned in the chapter.

1. Use Hyper-V Manager to create an additional vSwitch of the internal type.

2. Add a second NIC to the VM that is already connected to the physical network and attach this new NIC to the internal vSwitch you just created.

3. Attach the NIC in the second VM that you didn't use earlier to the internal vSwitch you just created.

4. Configure the virtual NICs on each VM attached to the internal vSwitch for the 10.0.50.x network with a subnet mask of 255.255.255.0 and no defined gateway or DNS.

5. Once configured, verify that the two VMs can ping each other on the 10.0.50.x network.

CHAPTER 9

Connecting Hyper-V Hosts to Storage Infrastructure

One constant in the world of IT is that data will forever continue to grow. The rate at which business organizations create new data is astounding. That data has to be safely stored and made accessible for your end users. This doesn't change in virtualization scenarios. There are a number of ways to connect a Hyper-V environment to the data, including local storage, Internet Small Computer Systems Interface (iSCSI)–based storage arrays, and SMB 3.0 file shares. Each medium has its own pros and cons, and the connectivity method and best practices are different, depending on the type of storage used. This is what we'll be talking about in this chapter.

In This Chapter and Beyond

So far, we've focused on the virtual machines (VMs) themselves, because most of the day-to-day operations are conducted at the VM level. Now that you have a good understanding of virtualized workloads, we're going to continue the exploration of host-focused topics. We covered networking in Chapter 8 and will be covering host storage in this chapter. Failover clustering and high availability will follow. These technologies provide a higher degree of resiliency and availability to your VMs.

The management of the storage attached to your Hyper-V hosts is extremely important, because that storage holds production data.

© Andy Syrewicze, Richard Siddaway 2018
A. Syrewicze and R. Siddaway, *Pro Microsoft Hyper-V 2019*, https://doi.org/10.1007/978-1-4842-4116-5_9

DATA IS IMPORTANT

We have personally followed an unspoken rule throughout our careers in that whenever we're working with data, we *must* have a firm grasp of the technology and be 300% sure of exactly what is going to happen when conducting any storage-related change or operation. Trust us, when you're working with any organization's data, you're holding a very important piece of that company in the palm of your hand, so a lot of responsibility comes with that.

In this chapter, we'll show you how to connect your Hyper-V host to different storage types. These are essential skills, because it's quite common to add or change storage devices within the lifespan of a Hyper-V deployment.

Note   We'll also be discussing storage quite extensively in Chapters 10 and 12, when we explain how to cluster Hyper-V hosts and VMs, respectively.

The other benefit of learning this is you may have workloads with different I/O needs. You may want to have your heavy I/O SQL workload on faster disks than the storage on which your backup workload resides.

We'll start by discussing local storage, as that is what we've been using up until this point in the book.

Direct-Attached Storage in Hyper-V

Direct-attached storage (DAS) is perhaps the most common storage type used for small deployments. It's the most economical and is ideal for single-host situations or a single host in your DMZ.

The most common form of DAS is the disks located inside your server chassis. Another, less common, form of DAS is a JBOD (just a bunch of disks) array directly attached to the Hyper-V host via an SAS (serial attached SCSI) connection. The SAS bus to the JBOD array can provide the same performance as internal disks. JBODs are becoming most common these days with hyper-converged workloads but are still used frequently for archival purposes.

DAS can support a limited number of VMs, usually two to ten virtual machines, depending on disk capacity in the server and assuming the VMs have a low to moderate I/O workload. A 10-disk RAID 10 array can handle the I/O needs of more VMs than a single disk, so the configuration of the local disks will affect the number of VMs you can run. It isn't an exact science, as the workloads contained within your VMs are going to play a part as well. The only way to be sure that your DAS storage will support the number of VMs you have is through monitoring and testing, which we will get into in Chapter 13.

As an example, let's say that you've inherited a stand-alone Hyper-V host with DAS, and the host is running low on storage. Shrinking the VMs isn't an option, as they need the configured storage. The only option left is to add additional storage to the host. We'll add the new storage space as a new volume, so that you can separate workloads onto separate disks for optimum performance. You may also want to separate a virtual backup appliance, so that its storage is on different physical disks to your production virtual machines.

Let's create a new storage location and move one of our VMs to it (we'll cover VM migrations in more detail in Chapter 14). We'll do this by creating and mounting a new VHDX on the host. The host will see the VHDX virtual disk as a block device. This allows us to simulate adding new storage to the host.

You need to follow these steps to add the storage:

1. Open PowerShell with elevated privileges directly from your Hyper-V host. If this is a Windows Server Core box, from the command line, simply type "PowerShell" (without the quotes) and press Enter.

2. Type `New-VHD -Path C:\Test\DASTEST.vhdx -SizeBytes 100GB` and press Enter, to create a new blank 100GB VHDX.

3. Type `Mount-VHD -Path C:\Test\DASTEST.vhdx` and press Enter, to mount the new virtual disk as usable storage.

4. Use DiskPart or Server Manager to initialize, format, and assign a drive letter to the new storage device.

5. Type `Get-Volume` and press Enter, to verify that the system sees the new storage device, and verify the correct size.

6. Open Hyper-V Manager and connect to the target Hyper-V host.

7. Select one of the VMs in the Virtual Machines pane.

8. In the Action pane, click Move.

9. Click Next on the initial screen of the Move Virtual Machine
    Wizard.

10. Select the "Move the virtual machine's storage" radio button, as
    shown in Figure 9-1, and then click Next.

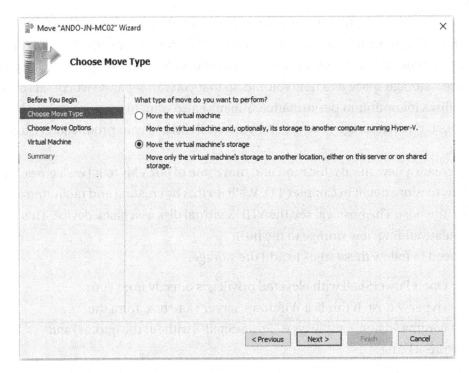

Figure 9-1. *Move Virtual Machine Storage Wizard*

11. Select the "Move all of the virtual machine's data to a single
    location" radio button and click Next.

12. Browse to the root of the new volume that was created earlier in
    this exercise and click Select Folder, to define the root of the target
    location as the desired location.

13. Take note of the VM's size and click Next.

14. On the summary page, verify the settings and then click Finish.

15. Wait for the operation to complete and review the status column in Hyper-V Manager for the selected VM for more status information, as the VM moves from one location to another.

Note   This operation can be done on a VM that is currently running, without affecting the workload inside the VM. This is done by first making a copy of the VM's storage at the new location and then copying over any disk writes that occurred while the transfer was happening, at the very end. Once completed, the hypervisor starts reading and writing from the new VHDX file and resumes normal operations.

---

16. Open PowerShell again.

17. Type `Get-Volume` and press Enter, to view the host's current storage volumes. Take note of the SizeRemaining column for the newly mounted storage volume.

18. Type `Get-VM –Name <Target VM Name Here> | select Path, ConfigurationLocation, SnapshotFileLocation, SmartPaging FilePath` and press Enter, to see the current storage paths for the selected VM, and verify that the VM now resides on the new volume.

TRY IT YOURSELF

Using the instructions in this section, add local storage to your Hyper-V host and move a VM on to the new storage location.

You've attached new local storage to the host and moved a VM to it while the VM was up and running. This provides a level of flexibility to storage changes in your environment that you may not have had before. You used to have to schedule several hours' worth of downtime for making such a change, prior to moving to a virtualization platform.

Shared Storage in Hyper-V

Thus far, we've been working strictly with local storage, but to use clustering, it's very important to understand the concepts behind shared storage. In order for two Hyper-V hosts to work together, there needs to be a common storage location that is properly formatted and in a location all the hosts can see.

You're not going to get this requirement satisfied with local disks, unless you're using a new emerging technology referred to as hyper-converged infrastructure (HCI). The idea behind HCI is that you have compute (Hyper-V) and storage in the same chassis. The hyper-converged technology then works with other nodes in a cluster, to ensure data integrity across all local disks in each cluster node.

ABOVE AND BEYOND

Windows Server 2016, and later versions contain hyper-converged capabilities in the form of Hyper-V and Storage Spaces Direct. This will be covered in Chapter 10, but if this is something that interests you, feel free to read ahead about how this architecture works, from the following link: `https://technet.microsoft.com/en-us/windows-server-docs/storage/software-defined-storage/hyper-converged-solution-using-storage-spaces-direct-in-windows-server-2016?f=255&MSPPError=-2147217396`.

In the next couple of chapters, we'll cover a number of shared storage options, but for the purposes of this chapter, we're going to deploy an open source storage appliance, which we'll then use as a storage target. Using an open source storage appliance will serve two purposes: it will give you more practice deploying visualized workloads, and it will allow you to practice connecting to a storage target using Microsoft iSCSI Initiator. We'll cover using a Windows-based iSCSI solution in Chapter 12.

iSCSI

There are many options for shared storage connection mediums, but we'll focus primarily on iSCSI in the remainder of this chapter. The main difference between iSCSI and the standard SCSI protocol is that with iSCSI, we are taking those same SCSI protocol storage commands, and we're then pushing them over the TCP/IP Protocol. This is what allows you to separate storage from compute when using iSCSI. Figure 9-2 illustrates the logical layout of the iSCSI device you'll be creating.

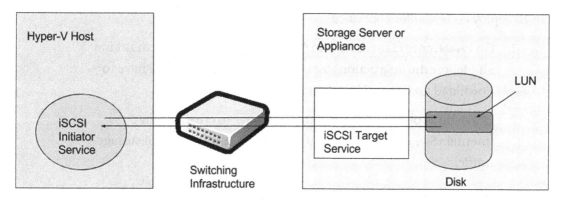

Figure 9-2. *iSCSI logical layout, showing the storage device on the right, the host on the left, and the switch infrastructure in between*

In Figure 9-2, you can see that there are a number of different components. First, you have your storage device or appliance on the right-hand side. An iSCSI target service carves off a piece of the available storage and presents it to the storage network as a logical unit number (LUN), which is a device that is addressed by the SCSI protocol. From there, an iSCSI initiator on a Hyper-V host in the environment connects to that LUN from across the network.

Deploying a Storage Appliance

We're going to deploy an open source appliance in this section. The appliance we'll be deploying for practice is called Openfiler. It's software that has been developed under the GNU General Public license and is free for use. The instructions for deploying this software are somewhat lengthy and would consume most, if not all, of this chapter. So, while this may take a little longer than other chapters, you'll get a lot of good experience out of it, and we've found that the easiest way to learn about how iSCSI works is to actually do it from end to end.

Note   You'll need at least 12GB of drive space for the VM's operating system, then you can allocate as much space as you're comfortable with for your storage LUNs. Try to allocate at least 80GB, if possible. Also, note that when configuring the LUN, you'll have to input the IP address of any host that will be connecting to the storage target. Remember: This is the storage IP, and not the IP of the appliance that is on the lab network.

To deploy an Openfiler appliance,

1. Go to www.openfiler.com/learn/how-to/graphical-installation and follow the instructions for deploying Openfiler. You'll have to download an ISO and install the OS inside of a new VM.

2. Once the appliance is deployed, you'll have to create a new internal vSwitch (see Chapter 8) that will be used for iSCSI storage traffic.

3. Once your network changes are complete, you'll have to make sure that you have two virtual NICs attached to the Openfiler VM. One of those will be on your standard LAN network, and the other should be on its own network, for example, 10.10.10.x.

4. Next, configure the second physical NIC in your lab host to be on that same storage network, and then verify that the storage IP on the Openfiler VM is pingable by the host system.

TRY IT YOURSELF

Install an Openfiler iSCSI appliance on your Hyper-V host.

The Microsoft iSCSI Initiator

We need to tell our Hyper-V host to connect to the new storage using the Microsoft iSCSI Initiator. The Microsoft iSCSI Initiator is a service that is now automatically present on all versions of Windows Server 2012 Hyper-V hosts and later versions.

To connect a Hyper-V host to the iSCSI target,

1. Open a command prompt, type "iscsicpl" (without quotes) and press Enter.

2. You'll be told that the iSCSI Initiator service is not currently in a running state, and you'll be asked if you want to start it now. Click Yes.

3. You'll be greeted with a screen like that shown in Figure 9-3.

4. Insert the storage IP that you provided to the Openfiler storage connection and then click Quick connect.

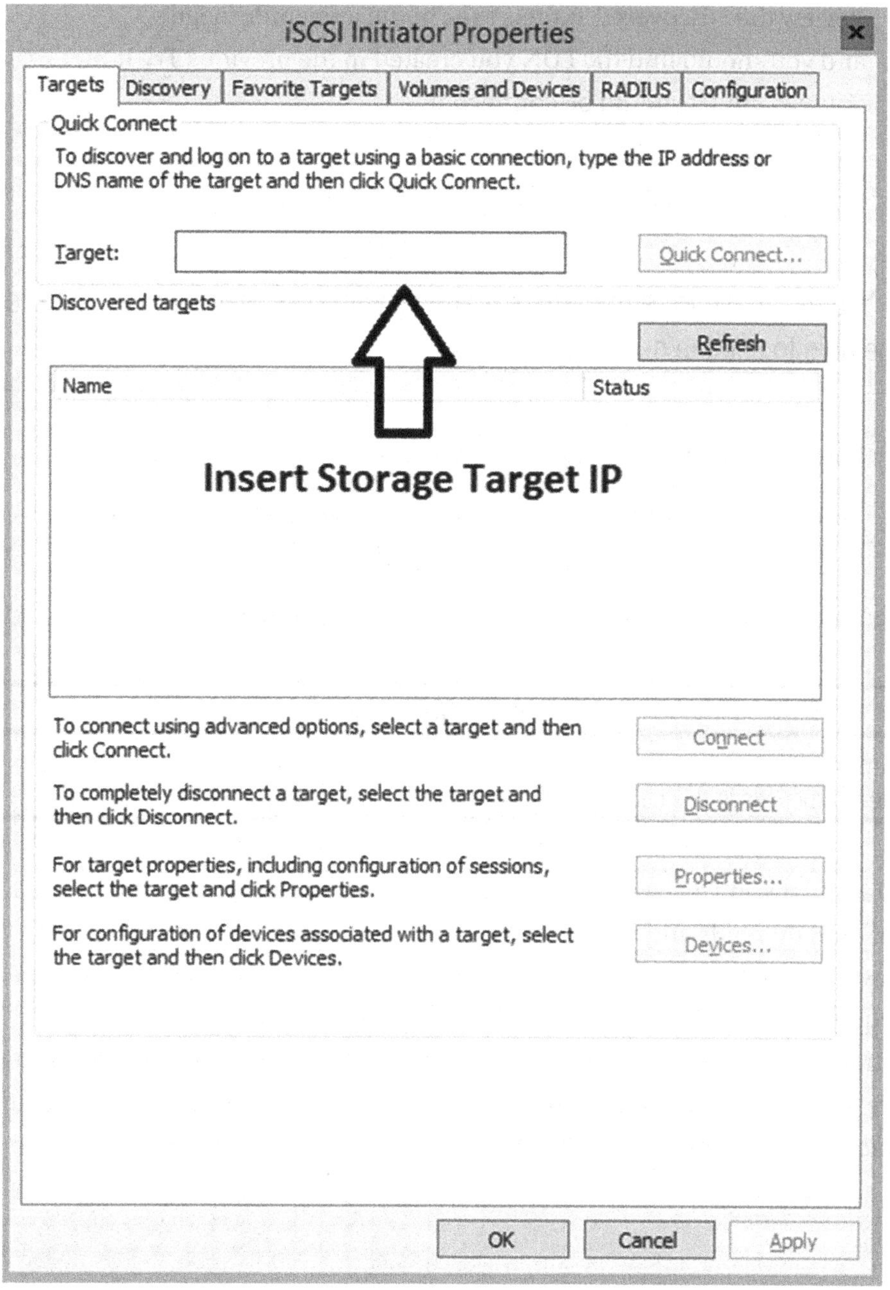

Figure 9-3. *iSCSI Initiator properties for connecting back to the storage target*

5. Review the Discovered Targets area in the area underneath,
    and you should find the LUN you created in the previous Try It
    Yourself, and it should be connected.

6. Either using Server Manager remotely, or tools on the Hyper-V
    host, log in to Disk Management and locate the new disk.

Note   You may have to refresh the storage view in Disk Management, before
you'll be able to see the new available disk.

---

7. Format the disk and create a new volume.

8. Assign a drive letter to the new volume and verify that you are able
    to navigate the file system on the new volume.

Congratulations! You've just connected the shared storage to your Hyper-V host.

TRY IT YOURSELF

Use the instructions in this section to connect your Hyper-V host to the new iSCSI Target.

The task that you've just completed is now allowing storage traffic to traverse
a network and do reads and writes on a separate piece of equipment (or a VM,
in this case). You'll find that you will be doing work with shared storage like this
quite frequently, as adding and removing storage is quite common in Hyper-V
administration. This is especially true once you start getting into clustering situations,
which we'll be doing in the following chapters. Before that, though, let's do a little
more practice with a lab.

Lab Work

These exercises will help you practice what you've learned.

1. Complete the Try It Yourself sections, if you haven't done so.

2. Using the storage migration wizard, move one of your VMs to the new shared storage volume and verify that the VM is still functional.

3. Monitor the LUNs stats in the Openfiler console to get a view of the storage infrastructure from the storage side, for a complete picture.

4. Create an additional LUN within Openfiler and use it to create another volume on your Hyper-V host.

5. Once done, move your VM back to local storage, using the move storage wizard, and then, using the iSCSI Initiator utility, disconnect the LUNs.

6. Power off the Openfiler VM, as we'll be learning about a different storage method in Chapter 10.

CHAPTER 10

Providing High Availability for Hyper-V Virtual Machines

Servers from first-tier vendors have built-in component redundancy, owing to multiple CPUs, network cards, power supplies, and so on. This means that they can last for years without failure. Your storage systems can be configured to protect your data against single or even multiple simultaneous disk failures. You can expect a server configured such as this to give reliable service for a long time, but you only have a single server. If it does fail, you've lost your data, your virtual environment, or whatever application the server is running. More important, your users have lost access to their applications, and your organization may be losing revenue. Losing a server running a single application is bad. Losing the server that hosts a number of virtual machines (VMs) could be catastrophic for your organization.

Operating system (OS) patching is an unavoidable requirement. A machine often has to be rebooted after patching. If the machine is a Hyper-V host, this means that all VMs on the host have to be restarted, leading to downtime that could be unacceptable to your organization.

The answer is to configure the systems for high availability (HA). This involves configuring two or more physical servers to work together, so that in the event of one failing, the workload is automatically migrated to another machine in the group. In this chapter, we're looking at configuring Hyper-V hosts (physical machines in your environment) to work together to provide an HA environment for your VMs.

© Andy Syrewicze, Richard Siddaway 2018
A. Syrewicze and R. Siddaway, *Pro Microsoft Hyper-V 2019*, https://doi.org/10.1007/978-1-4842-4116-5_10

DEFINING HIGH AVAILABILITY

High availability refers to a system being continuously operational, or available, for a long period of time. The required period of time is dependent on a number of factors, including business needs, operational policies, and available budget. The higher the required availability, the more it will cost!

The ideal is for 100% availability, but in reality, organizations aim for one of the following targets:

99.999% availability = 5.25 minutes of unscheduled downtime per year

99.99% availability = 52.6 minutes of unscheduled downtime per year

99.9% availability = 8.77 hours of unscheduled downtime per year
(Modern servers should achieve this.)

The Service Level Agreement (SLA) has to be taken into account, as, for instance, the organization may only be interested in the system being available during business hours and, therefore, doesn't care if the server is down for six hours overnight.

The Microsoft Failover Cluster Service (MFCS) provides high availability in a Windows environment. A group of machines, known as a cluster, is configured and managed together, using MFCS. One or more applications run on the cluster, with the ability to failover to another node, in the event of there being a problem with the applications' current node.

In the case of a cluster of Hyper-V machines, each machine in the cluster runs Hyper-V and workloads—in this case, VMs—can be moved between members (also referred to as nodes) of the cluster.

Note   There is another type of clustering available to Microsoft servers: network load balancing (NLB) clusters. These are used to load-balance network traffic between hosts, usually HTTP traffic for web servers. NLB also supplies high availability but is not suitable for providing the resiliency we need to supply HA to Hyper-V machines.

In this chapter, we'll introduce you to Microsoft failover clustering. We'll then explain the requirements for clustering Hyper-V hosts.

Note   This chapter covers creating the cluster. Chapter 11 will show you how to finalize the cluster configuration and manage the cluster. Chapter 12 will discuss creating a cluster for your VMs (guests).

As always, the chapter closes with lab work to consolidate your learning. First, let's dig into failover clustering.

Introducing Microsoft Failover Clustering

We've defined a cluster as two or more machines that work together to provide high availability to a workload. In this chapter, we'll concentrate on clustering Hyper-V hosts, although other workloads can also be clustered (see `https://technet.microsoft.com/en-us/library/hh831579(v=ws.11).aspx`), including

- Database servers

- File servers

- Business critical applications, such as financial systems

- E-mail servers

Note   Later versions of Microsoft Exchange and SQL Server use the Microsoft cluster service as an underlying support for their HA configurations, rather than being installed directly on a cluster.

ACTIVE DIRECTORY INTEGRATION FOR CLUSTERS

Microsoft failover clustering depends on Active Directory (AD). The cluster nodes must be members of an AD domain, and the user creating the cluster requires permissions to create computer objects in AD. A number of AD objects are created during cluster creation. Communication between cluster nodes requires AD authentication.

With Windows Server 2012 R2 (and later versions),it is possible to create a Hyper-V cluster outside of AD (an AD detached cluster), but this isn't recommended for Hyper-V clusters, as moving active VMs between nodes (live migration) won't work, as it requires AD authentication.

More details on failover clustering and AD are available at

https://blogs.technet.microsoft.com/supportingwindows/2014/03/24/
failover-clustering-and-active-directory-integration/.

So, what does a cluster look like? Figure 10-1 shows the major features of a Windows cluster.

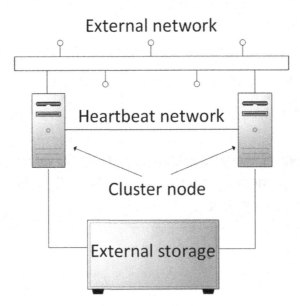

Figure 10-1. *Outline of a Windows two-node cluster. The heartbeat network is for communication between cluster nodes. The external network is for client communication to the workloads on the cluster.*

Figure 10-1 shows two machines (known as nodes) in the cluster. A Windows cluster can contain up to 64 nodes (Windows Server 2012 [R2] and Windows Server 2016). Windows Server 2019 extends effective cluster size through the use of cluster sets. A Hyper-V cluster can support up to 8000 VMs, with a maximum of 1024 on any one node.

CLUSTER SET

A cluster set enables you to scale your environment to a higher level. A cluster set is a loosely coupled grouping of failover clusters, for example, four 64-node Hyper-V clusters could be combined into a set to produce a 256-node cluster set. VMs can be migrated between clusters in a cluster set, making your environment more flexible and scalable. The nodes can be split between different physical sites, if required.

You can create fault domains and availability sets within your cluster set. An availability set is used to configure redundancy across fault domains. A fault domain determines which nodes fail together.

More information can be found at `https://docs.microsoft.com/en-us/windows-server/storage/storage-spaces/Cluster-Sets`.

Both machines are connected to the external network, which is how users access the workloads supported by the cluster. The heartbeat (or internal) network is used by the cluster members to communicate among themselves, in order to confirm that nodes are still available to the network.

The nodes in the cluster have two types of storage. First, each node has one or more disks to support the OS (not shown explicitly in Figure 10-1). Second, there is the cluster storage that is available to all nodes. This is shown as the external storage in Figure 10-1.

External storage is often used to store the cluster quorum.

Cluster Quorum

A number of cluster-based operations are based on a quorum model. This model means that a majority of the cluster members have to agree that the action can occur. Actions that are controlled by the quorum include

- Cluster startup

- Workload placement

- Workload failover between nodes

Each node in the cluster gets a single vote toward the quorum, but many clusters only contain two nodes. A witness is needed to provide an odd number of total votes, meaning that a quorum can be established. The witness can be

- *Disk*: A specific volume is designated as the witness. The witness disk must be on external storage and can be small (512MB minimum)—1GB is more than sufficient. This is most useful for clusters with non-replicated storage.

- *File share*: An SMB share (5MB minimum free space). The file server should be on a different site from the cluster nodes. The cluster information is held in a `witness.log` file, rather than a copy of the cluster database. This is most suitable for multisite clusters with storage replication.

- *Cloud*: Azure Blob (Binary Large Object) storage is used to host a read/write file that acts as the witness. Only available in Windows Server 2016 and later versions, this option is best suited to multisite clusters.

ABOVE AND BEYOND

More information on the witness and workings of the cluster quorum can be found at `https://technet.microsoft.com/en-us/library/jj612870(v=ws.11).aspx`.

The use of a cloud-based witness for Windows Server 2016–based clusters is described here: `https://docs.microsoft.com/en-us/windows-server/failover-clustering/deploy-cloud-witness`.

If you have an odd number of nodes in the cluster, you can configure the cluster to work on a node-majority basis. In this case, only the cluster nodes have a vote in the quorum, and a witness isn't required.

Cluster Storage

As stated, each node in the cluster requires dedicated storage for its OS. In addition, the nodes need access to external storage that supports the workloads hosted on the cluster. There are a number of options available for cluster storage.

- *Cluster Shared Volumes (CSV)*: These enable multiple nodes to have read/write access to volumes. This is a very common configuration for clusters of Hyper-V hosts and will be used in this chapter.

- *Fibre Channel attached storage*: Usually an SAN

- *iSCSI*: Connects to storage over network. Storage is usually a storage area network (SAN) or network-attached storage (NAS).

- *Shared virtual disk*: This is for Hyper-V guest clusters only.

- *SMB 3.0 file shares*

The option you use will be based on other storage requirements in your organization. Fibre Channel or iSCSI connections to a SAN or NAS are also a common configuration for many enterprises.

ABOVE AND BEYOND

More information on storage options for clusters can be found at `https://technet.`
`microsoft.com/en-us/library/hh831579(v=ws.11).aspx`.

Windows Server 2016 clustering enhancements are described here: `https://technet.`
`microsoft.com/en-us/windows-server-docs/compute/failover-clustering/`
`whats-new-failover-clustering-windows-server`.

Now that you understand the basics of clustering, let's look specifically at clustering Hyper-V.

Clustering Hyper-V Hosts

Many administrators view clustering as very complicated and in the "too hard" category. There are complications, but if you work through the exercises in this chapter and the next few chapters, you'll learn that it is relatively straightforward.

A Hyper-V cluster can support up to 64 nodes with a maximum 8000 VMs, although it's probable that your nodes will run out of resources before reaching that number. Each node can support a maximum of 1024 VMs. Exactly how many VMs you can get on a node will depend on the resources (CPU and memory) available to the node and how your VMs are configured.

Note   When designing a cluster, think about the workloads you'll be supporting. How many nodes do you require to support that number of VMs? Many organizations will design an extra node (called N+1 cluster) into the cluster, to ensure the cluster will function properly, even with one node offline, for example, during patching.

ABOVE AND BEYOND

The article available at `https://technet.microsoft.com/library/jj612869` discusses the hardware and storage requirements for clustering in great detail. It should be read before implementing a production cluster.

This is where we tell you that we're going to cheat in the next few chapters. We're not going to create the clusters on physical hardware, as most of us don't have a lab with sufficient machines! We're going to make use of a new feature in Windows Server 2016 and later versions—nested virtualization—that enables us to create Hyper-V hosts on our Hyper-V host. This isn't possible in earlier versions of Windows server and Hyper-V. If you can't use Windows Server 2016 or 2019 and nested virtualization, you'll need two identical physical machines for cluster nodes. You also have to use the information in Chapter 12, to use a Windows server as an iSCSI target.

Note   Use the evaluation edition of Windows Server 2016 from `www.microsoft.com/en-us/evalcenter/evaluate-windows-server-technical-preview`. You'll have to search for the Windows Server 2019 evaluation edition when it becomes available. You could use one of the SAC releases, but they're Server Core–only, which makes things more difficult. We're using the Windows Server 2019 preview, so things may change slightly after the full release. Alternatively, you'll have to use sufficient hardware to create the physical nodes for the cluster.

We will require three virtual machines, whose configurations are shown in Table 10-1.

Table 10-1. *Virtual Machines for Hyper-V Cluster*

Virtual Machine	Purpose	Virtual CPU	RAM	System Disk
W19HVC01	Hyper-V cluster node	4	4GB	125GB
W19HVC02	Hyper-V cluster node	4	4GB	125GB

Initially, each machine should have a single network adapter. A startup memory of 1024MB and having Dynamic Memory enabled can create the machines, although we'll have to modify these settings for the cluster nodes later, as nested virtualization doesn't support Dynamic Memory.

TRY IT YOURSELF

Create the VMs listed in Table 10-1, using the Windows Server Datacenter edition. Configure each machine with a static IP address and join it to your domain.

You'll be using Storage Spaces (a feature of Windows Server 2016 and later versions) and CSV to create the shared storage for the cluster. This means you must use the Datacenter edition of Windows Server.

Networking for Hyper-V Clusters

You are going to need at least three networks for your cluster nodes, as shown in Table 10-2.

Table 10-2. *Networks Used by the Cluster Nodes*

Network	Purpose
LAN	General network connectivity for users to access VMs
Heartbeat	Private communication between cluster nodes
MGMT	Management network. Used by administrators.

The management network is often not utilized, so we won't install that one for now. If you're using iSCSI for storage, you should create a separate network for that traffic (see Chapter 12).

The idea behind using different networks is to segregate network traffic. You can run all cluster traffic—public, private, and management—over a single network. It all depends on your server configuration. If you have two or more 10GB NICs in your servers, you can team them and run all traffic over the team. If have 1GB NICs in your servers, you'll have to segregate the traffic. If in doubt, segregate the cluster traffic from the workload traffic. The best practice is to separate the traffic, as shown in Table 10-2.

You should create additional VMs to facilitate the network traffic separation, if you are creating your cluster on a Hyper-V host.

Note   If you are creating the Hyper-V cluster with physical machines, you should create virtual networks (VLANs) to perform the traffic segregation. Talk to your network team.

An internal switch enables network connectivity between the host and the VMs and between virtual hosts. No traffic is sent outside of the Hyper-V host. The heartbeat traffic is purely between VMs and so could utilize a private or internal virtual switch. In this case, we'll use a private switch.

```
New-VMSwitch -Name Heartbeat -SwitchType Private
```

TRY IT YOURSELF

Create the virtual switch on your Hyper-V host, to support the cluster. You should create a switch for at least the heartbeat network. The switch for the management network can be created later, if desired.

With the switch for the heartbeat network created, you can add virtual network adapters to your nodes and configure their IP addresses. We prefer to use a separate addressing scheme for the heartbeat network; it helps to keep things organized. In this case, we'll use 192.168.40.1 for the heartbeat adapter on W19HVC01 and 192.168.40.2 on W19HVC02.

The following adds the new adapter to a machine:

```
$vm = Get-VM -Name 'W19HVC01'
$switch2 = Get-VMSwitch -Name Heartbeat | select -ExpandProperty Name
Add-VMNetworkAdapter -VM $vm -SwitchName $switch2 -Name 'Heartbeat'
```

Repeat for W19HVC02.

Configuring the IP address has to be performed on the VM itself, either by logging on to the machine or through a PowerShell remoting session. For W19HVC01, use

```
Get-NetAdapter -Name Ethernet | Rename-NetAdapter -NewName 'HeartBeat'

$index = Get-NetAdapter -Name HeartBeat |
select -ExpandProperty ifIndex

New-NetIPAddress -InterfaceIndex $index -AddressFamily IPv4 `
-IPAddress '192.168.40.1' -PrefixLength 26
```

W19HVC02 uses the same code, except the IP address is 192.168.40.2.

TRY IT YOURSELF

Create and configure the heartbeat network adapters in your cluster nodes. The heartbeat is, in effect, a ping (but a bit more sophisticated) between the nodes. Test that the heartbeat network can function, by pinging 192.169.40.2 (W19HVC02) from W19HVC01 and 192.169.40.1 (W19HVC01) from W19HVC02.

If the ping doesn't work, what could be causing the problem?

Make sure that you can ping between the nodes, using the heartbeat addresses, before proceeding.

Once you have the two VMs created, and the network configuration work done, it's time to configure the storage and create the cluster.

Creating a Hyper-V HA Cluster

Now we get to build the cluster. This is a three-stage process.

1. Create and configure the storage. There will be additional configuration steps post cluster creation.

2. Create and configure the cluster nodes.

3. Create the cluster.

Establishing an ordered process like this breaks down a complex process into manageable steps and reduces errors. It also leads to a more repeatable process, if you create many clusters. In many organizations, the storage and node configuration will be handled by different teams and may well occur simultaneously.

In the previous section, you created a number of virtual switches for use with the cluster. You should have IP addresses available for the various networks. It's a good practice to document the network addresses before you start creating the cluster, so that you know which address ranges you're using for what and don't change the wrong thing by mistake. Start with the networks, as in Table 10-3.

Table 10-3. *Network Address Ranges for Hyper-V Cluster*

Network	Address Range	Subnet Mask
LAN	10.10.54.0	255.255.255.0
Heartbeat	192.168.40.0	255.255.255.192

The heartbeat network is limited to 62 hosts, because of the subnet mask. If you must use the full 64 nodes available to your cluster, change the subnet mask to 255.255.255.128. All IP address ranges are private addresses, as defined in https://technet.microsoft.com/en-us/library/cc958825.aspx. If your organization has different addressing schemes, substitute accordingly.

The VMs are already created, so the next job is to configure the storage.

Configure Storage

We stated earlier that there were a number of options available to you for configuring storage on your cluster. In this example, we're going to show you how to use Storage Spaces Direct, which is a feature of Windows Server 2016 and later versions. If you're using iSCSI, you'll have to adapt the instructions in Chapter 12.

Storage Spaces Direct (S2D is Microsoft's acronym) enables you to build highly available storage systems that are virtually shared across your servers. The great advantage is that you use local disks to provide the physical storage, rather than an external storage system. S2D is software-defined storage. The use of Storage Spaces Direct enables you use disks types, such as SATA disks, that would have been unavailable to clusters in the past.

S2D uses disks that are exclusively connected to one node in your cluster. Storage pools are created from those disks. The "virtual disks" known as spaces that are created from the pool have their data spread across the disks in the different nodes of the cluster. This protects your data in the same way as a traditional RAID 1 (mirror) or RAID 5 (parity) storage system.

Note   Using Storage Spaces Direct on the same nodes as your running Hyper-V is an example of converged infrastructure, which is a current industry goal among major vendors.

We stated earlier that we're going to cheat. The disks we'll use in this chapter are Hyper-V virtual disks configured as shown in Table 10-4.

Table 10-4. *Disk Configuration for the Cluster*

Virtual Machine	Disk	Purpose	Size
W19HVC01	W19HVC01.vhdx	System disk	125GB
W19HVC01	HVC01data01.vhdx	Data disk	1TB
W19HVC01	HVC01data02.vhdx	Data disk	1TB
W19HVC02	W19HVC02.vhdx	System disk	125GB
W19HVC02	HVC02data01.vhdx	Data disk	1TB
W19HVC02	HVC02data02.vhdx	Data disk	1TB

Each VM has one disk as the system disk (125GB) and two data disks, each of 1TB in size.

Note   When you create the virtual disks, double-check that you've made them dynamic. We don't have enough storage in our test systems to accommodate 4TB of virtual disks and suspect that you don't either.

We also decided to put the data disks onto a separate virtual SCSI controller than the system disk. This isn't totally necessary but shows you another piece of the VM administration puzzle. In a production system, you'd want to separate the disks onto multiple controllers, to avoid the controller becoming a performance bottleneck or a single point of failure.

Note   Adding a new virtual SCSI controller to a VM requires that the VM be shut down. Virtual disks and network adapters can be hot-added but not SCSI controllers.

Shut down the two cluster nodes, then add the SCSI controllers.

```
$vms = 'W19HVCO1', 'W19HVCO2'

foreach ($vm in $vms) {
  Add-VMScsiController -VMName $vm
}
```

Now create the virtual disks your cluster will use for its storage pool.

```
New-VHD -Path 'C:\Virtual Storage\HVCO1data01.vhdx' -Dynamic -SizeBytes 1TB
New-VHD -Path 'C:\Virtual Storage\HVCO1data02.vhdx' -Dynamic -SizeBytes 1TB
New-VHD -Path 'C:\Virtual Storage\HVCO2data01.vhdx' -Dynamic -SizeBytes 1TB
New-VHD -Path 'C:\Virtual Storage\HVCO2data02.vhdx' -Dynamic -SizeBytes 1TB
```

Notice that we created the virtual disks as dynamic! It's the only way to create 4TB of storage on our test system, which has a 500GB disk. You can then add the virtual disks to the correct node.

```
Add-VMHardDiskDrive -VMName W19HVC01 -ControllerType SCSI `
-Path 'C:\Virtual Storage\HVC01data01.vhdx' -ControllerNumber 1

Add-VMHardDiskDrive -VMName W19HVC01 -ControllerType SCSI `
-Path 'C:\Virtual Storage\HVC01data02.vhdx' -ControllerNumber 1

Add-VMHardDiskDrive -VMName W19HVC02 -ControllerType SCSI `
-Path 'C:\Virtual Storage\HVC02data01.vhdx' -ControllerNumber 1

Add-VMHardDiskDrive -VMName W19HVC02 -ControllerType SCSI `
-Path 'C:\Virtual Storage\HVC02data02.vhdx' -ControllerNumber 1
```

You've used controller number 1 for the new disks; it's the one you created earlier in this section. The original SCSI controller is number 0.

```
PS> Get-VMScsiController -VMName W19HVC01

VMName     ControllerNumber Drives
------     ---------------- ------
W19HVC01 0                  {DVD Drive on SCSI controller n...
W19HVC01 1                  {Hard Drive on SCSI controller ...
```

Your VM configurations should now look something like those in Figure 10-2.

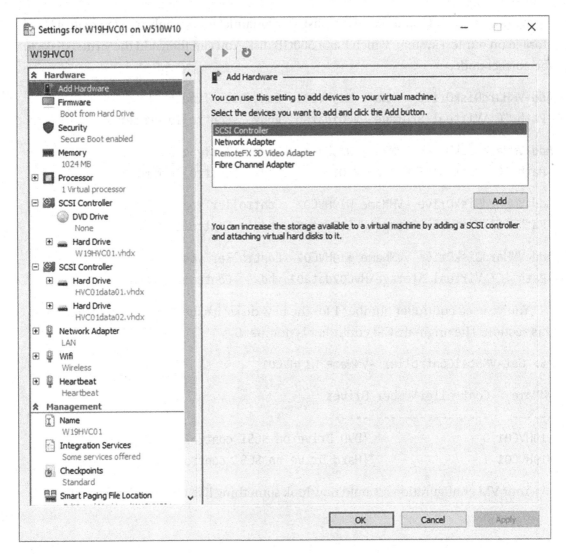

Figure 10-2. *Configuration of the VM after addition of storage and the heartbeat network adapter*

You can see the two SCSI controllers in Figure 10-2. The first one (number 0) has the DVD drive and the system disk. The second SCSI controller has the two data disks you just created.

The LAN and heartbeat network adapters are visible toward the bottom of the Hardware list. Ignore the network adapter named Wifi; it's an artifact of our test lab.

TRY IT YOURSELF

Use the instructions in this section to configure the storage for your cluster.

The storage is ready to use, so it's time to configure the cluster nodes.

Configure Cluster Nodes

Once the storage is ready, it's time to configure the cluster nodes, which involves a number of steps.

- Enabling nested virtualization

- Installing the required Windows features

The VMs must be shut down, so you can enable nested virtualization. If you're proceeding directly from the preceding section, the VMs should already be shut down, but it never hurts to check.

```
PS> Get-VM -Name W19HVC01, W19HVC02

Name      State CPUUsage(%)
----      ----- -----------
W19HVC02 Off   0
W19HVC01 Off   0
```

To configure nested virtualization:
```
$vms = 'W19HVC01', 'W19HVC02'

foreach ($vm in $vms) {
  Set-VMProcessor -VMName $vm -Count 4 `
  -ExposeVirtualizationExtensions $true

  Set-VMMemory -VMName $vm -DynamicMemoryEnabled $false -StartupBytes 4GB

  Get-VMNetworkAdapter -VMName $vm |
  where SwitchName -eq 'LAN' |
  Set-VMNetworkAdapter -MacAddressSpoofing On
}
```

An array containing the VM names is created. A `foreach` loop iterates through the names and, for each NM, performs the following tasks:

- Increases the virtual processors in the VM to 4

- Exposes the virtualization extensions—enables nested virtualization

- Disables dynamic memory

- Increases the memory allocated to the VM to 4GB

- Switches on MacAddressSpoofing for the virtual network adapter connected to the LAN VMswitch. This enables VMs hosted on the VM to communicate with other machines on the network that are on other Hyper-V hosts or are physical machines.

The last step is to add the failover clustering and Hyper-V roles to the nodes, so that they are ready to join the cluster. Just before you do that, you must start the VMs.

```
Start-VM -Name 'W19HVCO1'
Start-VM -Name 'W19HVCO2'
```

TRY IT YOURSELF

Use the instructions in this section to configure the nodes for your cluster.

Your cluster nodes are now configured, so it's time to create the cluster.

Create Cluster

Just before we create the cluster, there's one thing left to do: install the failover clustering role on the two nodes.

```
$vms = 'W19HVCO1', 'W19HVCO2'
foreach ($vm in $vms) {
$cred = Get-Credential "$vm\Administrator"
$s = New-PSSession -VMName $vm -Credential $cred
```

```
$sb = {
  $FeatureList = "Hyper-V", "Failover-Clustering", "FS-FileServer"
  Install-WindowsFeature $FeatureList -IncludeManagementTools
}
Invoke-Command -Session $s -ScriptBlock $sb

## and clean up
Remove-PSSession -Session $s
}
```

For each of the nodes, create a credential for the administrator on the node. The credential is used to create a PowerShell remoting session (in this case, using PowerShell Direct, as you're using the VM name to identify the target). Use the Install-WindowsFeature cmdlet, to add the failover clustering, Hyper-V, and file server features to the machine. You'll have to restart each node after the installation is complete.

ABOVE AND BEYOND

Creating and configuring two nodes, as you're doing in this chapter, can be accomplished quite easily by a series of PowerShell commands and GUI actions.

What if you had to create a cluster with 10, 20, 30, or even more nodes? Or what if you had to add nodes to your cluster on a regular basis as your environment grew.

You have two choices. Create a series of scripts that will perform the work for you. Automation will make this task much easier and less error-prone.

The better approach would be to use a configuration management approach, such as Desired State Configuration (DSC), which enables you to define a standard configuration for your nodes and apply it as you create the node. DSC and other DevOps-related topics are discussed in Chapter 19.

You can create a cluster using the Failover Cluster Manager or Windows PowerShell. Our preference is to use the GUI tool, as it supplies better feedback during the process. We'll show you how to use the PowerShell cmdlets in Chapter 12 The steps to create your cluster follow:

1. Open Failover Cluster Manager (Start-Windows Administrative Tools) on W19HVC01 or W19HVC02. You can also perform this from an external administration machine.

2. Click Create Cluster in the Actions pane.

3. Click Next, to skip the Before You Begin page.

4. Enter W19HVC01 on Select Servers page.

5. Click Add.

   a. You'll see a message about verifying server settings before the server is added to the Selected Servers box, which may take some time, depending on your network.

   b. Note that the Fully Qualified Domain Name (FQDN) is shown in the Selected Servers box.

6. Enter W19HVC02 on the Select Servers page.

7. Click Add. You'll see the same message as in step 5, then the server FQDN will be added to the Selected Servers box.

8. Click Next.

9. On the Validation Warning page, click No.

   a. This bypasses cluster validation. In production, you would want to click Yes, so that the cluster could be validated and would, therefore, be supported by Microsoft.

   b. If you haven't seen the validation tests, it's worth running them to see what is tested. Be warned that they take a few minutes to run.

   c. The only issue that was reported when we ran the validation on this configuration was that a default gateway wasn't defined on any of the network adapters. As the lab is a single machine, that is expected.

10.   Click Next.

11.   Type a cluster name. Use HVCL01.

12.   Click Next.

13.   On the Confirmation page, check that the information is correct. If not, use the Previous button, to navigate to the appropriate page, and correct the information.

14.   Unselect the Add all eligible storage to the cluster check box. You'll be configuring storage in the next section.

15.   Click Next.

16.   The cluster is created.

17.   Click View Report, if required. The report shows the steps performed during creation.

18.   Close the report.

19.   Click Finish.

Congratulations! You now have a working cluster. Expand the HVCL01 entry in Failover Cluster Manager, so that you can examine the cluster details. The following occurred automatically during the cluster creation process:

- The cluster is created.

- An entry for the cluster is created in AD in the Computers container. It has the failover cluster virtual network name account as the description.

- An entry for the cluster is made in DNS, if an IP address was allocated during the creation. If not, it'll be created later.

- Any attached disks are marked as Reserved (if attached to both nodes) or Unallocated (if attached to a single node), in the Disk Management tool on the cluster nodes.

There's still some configuration work to perform on the cluster.

Cluster Configuration

Before you can use your cluster, you must perform a few additional configuration tasks.

- Configure networks

- Configure storage

- Configure witness

Let's start with the network.

Configure Cluster Networking

Your cluster nodes have two network adapters:

- LAN, on the 10.10.54.0 network. This should be configured for client access and used by the cluster.

- Heartbeat, on the 192.168.40.0 network. This should be configured for use only by the cluster.

You also need to allocate an IP address for the cluster.

Configure Networks

The current state of the networks in the Hyper-V cluster can be accessed as follows:

1. Open Failover Cluster Manager.

2. Expand HVCL01.

3. Click Networks.

A display similar to Figure 10-3 will be visible.

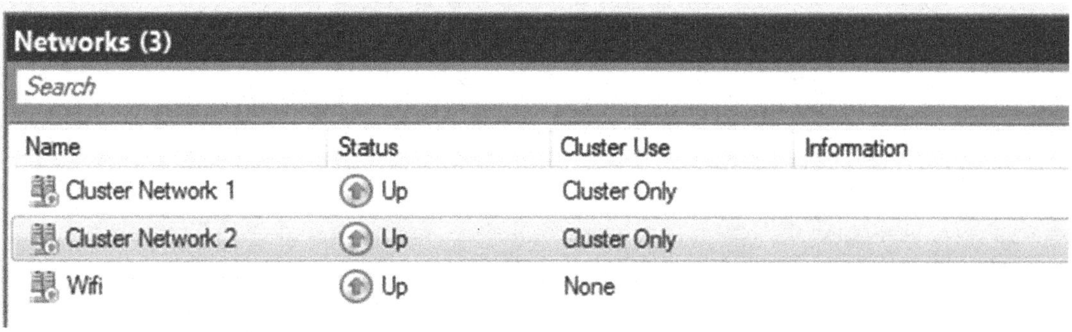

Networks (3)			
Search			
Name	**Status**	**Cluster Use**	**Information**
Cluster Network 1	Up	Cluster Only	
Cluster Network 2	Up	Cluster Only	
Wifi	Up	None	

Figure 10-3. *Cluster networks after creation. Ignore the Wifi network.*

The networks are named consecutively, and unless you can remember the IP subnet associated with each of the networks and what you intended that network to do, the display isn't very meaningful.

You can change the names in the display, to show the network's purpose, and configure how the cluster uses the network.

Change Network Name and Purpose

Allocating descriptive names to the networks will aid you when administering the cluster in the future. Six months from now, you won't remember which network was meant to do what, so having a descriptive name will save you having to consult the documentation (you did document your cluster, didn't you?).

To change the network name,

1.   Open Failover Cluster Manager.

2.   Expand HVCL01.

3.   Click Networks.

4.   Right-click the required network. You may have to click through the networks to determine which subnet they are on.

5.   Click Properties.

6.   Based on the subnet, change the name, as shown in Figure 10-4.

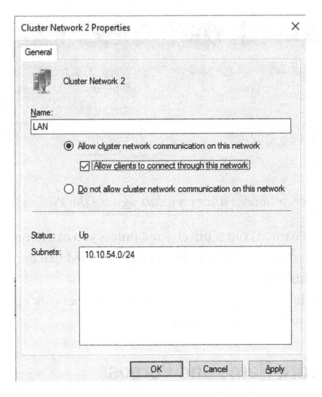

Figure 10-4. *Setting the network name and purpose*

7. Depending on the network, configure if cluster network traffic is allowed on the network, as shown in Table 10-5.

Table 10-5. *Traffic Allowed on the Cluster Networks*

Network	Traffic Setting
Heartbeat Network	Allow cluster network communication on this network.
LAN Network	Allow cluster network communication on this network. Allow clients to connect through this network.

TRY IT YOURSELF

Change the network names to match those in Table 10-5 and check the subnets against your design documentation.

Check whether the traffic settings match those in Table 10-5.

Set Cluster IP Address

Your cluster nodes were configured with an IP address, so that they can be on the network. Your cluster itself also needs an IP address.

To configure the cluster's IP address, do the following:

1. Open Failover Cluster Manager.

2. Expand HVCL01.

3. Under Cluster Core Resources (at the bottom in the center), right-click Name: HVCL01.

4. Select Properties.

5. Remove any network and IP address information by selecting it and clicking Remove.

6. Click Add.

7. Select the network and set an IP address, as shown in Figure 10-5.

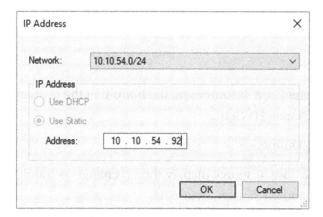

Figure 10-5. *Setting the cluster IP address*

8. Click OK.

9. You should see something like Figure 10-6.

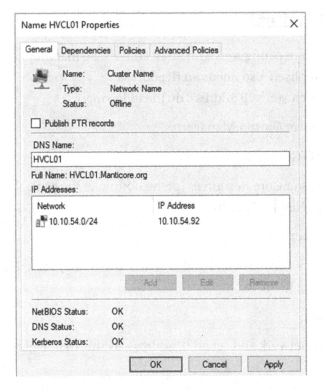

Figure 10-6. *Cluster IP address setting*

10.   Click OK.

11.   Under Cluster Core Resources (at the bottom in the center),
      right-click Name: HVCL01.

12.   Click Bring Online.

13.   The Cluster Core Resource display should change to show that the
      IP address and the cluster are online.

14.   Check that the new IP address for the cluster is present in DNS.

TRY IT YOURSELF

Set the cluster IP address for your cluster. Check that a record exists in DNS and AD.

With the cluster networks configured, it's time to finish configuring the storage.

Configure Storage Spaces Direct

Your cluster nodes each have two 1TB disks allocated for storage. They will be combined into a storage pool from which volumes will be created. First, though, you must enable Storage Spaces Direct. In an elevated PowerShell console on W19HVC01, run

```
PS> Enable-ClusterStorageSpacesDirect

Confirm
Are you sure you want to perform this action?
Performing operation 'Enable Cluster Storage Spaces Direct' on Target
'HVCL01'.
[Y] Yes  [A] Yes to All  [N] No  [L] No to All  [S] Suspend  [?] Help
(default is "Y"): Y
WARNING: 2018/06/30-16:40:02.641 Node W19HVC01: No disks found to be used
for cache
WARNING: 2018/06/30-16:40:02.667 Node W19HVC02: No disks found to be used
for cache

Node    EnableReportName
----    ----------------
W19HVC01 C:\Windows\Cluster\Reports\EnableClusterS2D
        on 2018.06.30-16.40.02.htm
```

You'll be asked to confirm the action. The creation of the storage pool takes a little while. Once the creation has finished, you'll see that a 10GB Cluster Virtual Disk has been created (look in Failover Cluster Manager ➤ HVCL01 ➤ Disks) for the cluster performance history, and a 4TB storage pool has been created (Failover Cluster Manager ➤ HVCL01 ➤ Pools).

You can view the storage pool information, as shown in Figure 10-7.

```
Administrator 64 bit C:\scripts                                    —    □    ×
PS> Get-StoragePool

FriendlyName  OperationalStatus HealthStatus IsPrimordial IsReadOnly   Size AllocatedSize
------------  ----------------- ------------ ------------ ----------   ---- -------------
Primordial    OK                Healthy      True         False     4.12 TB          4 TB
Primordial    OK                Healthy      True         False     4.12 TB          4 TB
S2D on HVCL01 OK                Healthy      False        False        4 TB       21.5 GB


PS> ■
```

Figure 10-7. *Newly created storage pool*

Create two volumes.

```
New-Volume -FriendlyName 'Vol1' -FileSystem CSVFS_NTFS `
-StoragePoolFriendlyName "S2D*" -Size 0.5TB
```

```
New-Volume -FriendlyName 'Vol2' -FileSystem CSVFS_NTFS `
-StoragePoolFriendlyName "S2D*" -Size 0.5TB
```

Remember that the data will be mirrored across both nodes, so your usable capacity in the storage pool is effectively halved. Allocating a 0.5TB volume effectively uses 1TB. Your cluster disks should now look something like Figure 10-8.

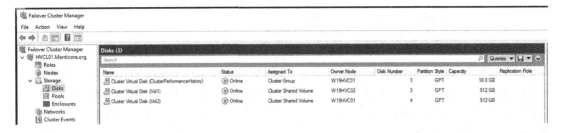

Figure 10-8. *The cluster has three disks: Vol1, Vol2, and ClusterPerformanceHistory*

Vol1 and Vol2 are automatically configured as CSV. They are accessible through the filesystem on each node at C:\ClusterStorage. Within C:\ClusterStorage is a mount point for each volume you created.

TRY IT YOURSELF

Configure the storage on your cluster, following the instructions in this section. Check that the newly created volumes are visible from both nodes and that mount points exist for the CSV on each node.

The last job you have to do is to configure the witness.

Configure Witness

As we stated earlier, the cluster witness or quorum can be disk-, file share-, or cloud-based. For the current cluster, you'll configure a file share witness.

Do the following, to create a file share witness:

1. Open Failover Cluster Manager and select HVCL01.

2. Under Actions (right-hand side) select More Actions.

3. Select Configure Cluster Quorum Settings...

4. Click Next, to bypass the Before You Begin page.

5. Select Advanced quorum configuration.

6. Click Next.

7. Ensure that All Nodes is selected and click Next.

8. Select Configure a file share witness.

9. Click Next.

10. Enter the file and share path. If you click Browse, you can select the server and share, or even create, a new share. Ensure that the cluster HVCL01 has full control of the folder used for the share.

11. Click Next.

12. Check information on Confirmation screen and click Next.

13. The witness will be created.

14. Click Finish, to exit wizard.

You've created the witness for your cluster and have finished the initial configuration work. This has been a long chapter, so we'll leave you to complete the lab. In the next chapter, we'll show you how to manage the cluster and create VMs.

Lab Work

The lab is very straightforward.

1.   Complete the Try It Yourself sections in this chapter.

2.   Complete all steps in the section "Creating a Hyper-V HA Cluster" to create a cluster.

3.   Complete the actions in the section "Cluster Configuration," to configure the cluster.

ABOVE AND BEYOND

If you want to extend your knowledge, try creating Hyper-V clusters, using different storage options. You may want to read Chapters 11 and 12 before attempting this task.

If you've created a virtual Hyper-V cluster, try creating a physical cluster and vice versa.

CHAPTER 11

Using Failover Cluster Manager to Manage Hyper-V Clusters

In the previous chapter, you saw how to create a Hyper-V cluster. As with anything in IT, creating the cluster is the easy bit. You've then got to manage it. You've already seen how to manage Hyper-V hosts using Hyper-V Manager, which is an excellent tool for managing one or more stand-alone hosts. When you cluster Hyper-V hosts, you manage them as a cluster, using Failover Cluster Manager.

Caution   If you're using external storage in your cluster (iSCSI, SAN, etc.), and you have to shut your cluster down, you should shut down the nodes first and then the storage server. If you shut down the storage first, you could lose the connections to your storage and potentially lose data. When starting the cluster, reverse this, so that the storage is online before you start any of the nodes. You can bring the nodes up in any order.

This chapter is a continuation of Chapter 10. A Hyper-V cluster isn't of much use if you don't have any VMs, so you'll start by learning how to create and manage VMs on your cluster. You'll learn how to manage the cluster's networking and storage. Eventually, you'll have to add extra nodes into the cluster (or move nodes out of the cluster), which will be explained toward the end of the chapter.

© Andy Syrewicze, Richard Siddaway 2018
A. Syrewicze and R. Siddaway, *Pro Microsoft Hyper-V 2019*, https://doi.org/10.1007/978-1-4842-4116-5_11

Note   Migrating virtual machines (VMs) between hosts won't be covered in this chapter. We'll postpone migrations until Chapter 14.

Before getting into the technical topics of the chapter, we should say something about *how* you manage your cluster. Many administrators see a cluster with two, four, or many nodes and just see it as that many servers. That is a big mistake!

When you're managing a cluster, especially large clusters, you have to think about the whole environment, not just the individual servers. You must keep three things firmly in mind:

1. People

2. Processes

3. Technology

The people who manage your cluster must understand the technologies they're working with. They must understand, use, and be committed to the processes that are put in place to manage the cluster. Most of all, they have to be people that are trusted to manage a critical piece of your organization's environment.

When you make a change to a cluster, very often that change, such as creating a new VMswitch, has to occur on all nodes in the cluster. If your administrators have a process to follow, the chances of something going wrong are minimized, even more so if the process is backed by automation of some kind. The vast majority of major problems we've seen with Hyper-V environments can be traced back to human error, often because people have stepped outside the process and just done stuff! Set up automated processes for as many administration tasks as you can, to ensure that administration is efficient and safe. Don't forget your change control processes. They protect you and your administrators as well as the organization.

Technology is the third thing to consider. Make sure you're using the correct technology to get the job done. A failover cluster is only created to protect some vital aspect of your organization's IT environment. Make sure you have the right technology to do the job, including hardware, software, and management tools.

Hyper-V clusters are managed with Failover Cluster Manager rather than Hyper-V Manager. This includes the management of VMs, which is our cue to investigate that topic.

Managing Virtual Machines

Managing VMs means managing their life cycle.

- Creation

- Modification

- Destruction

The first step in this process is creating a VM.

Creating Virtual Machines

In early chapters of this book, you learned how to create VMs, using Hyper-V Manager or PowerShell, when working with a single Hyper-V host. You use Failover Cluster Manager to create VMs when your Hyper-V hosts are clustered.

ANTIVIRUS SOFTWARE

It's very important to the performance of your Hyper-V hosts, whether they are physical hosts or you're using nested virtualization, as in this chapter, that you *exclude* the files used for the VMs from your antivirus (AV) scanning.

Scanning a .vhdx file every time you do something in the VM will slow performance dramatically. Your VMs should have AV protection, which will catch any malicious actions on the VM, but you shouldn't impose AV scanning on your VMs (or their files) from the host.

To create a VM on your cluster,

1. Open Failover Cluster Manager.

2. Expand HVCL01.

3. Click Roles.

4. Under Actions, click Virtual Machines...

5. Click New Virtual Machine...

6. Select the target node, as shown in Figure 11-1. In this case, you'll use W19HVC01.

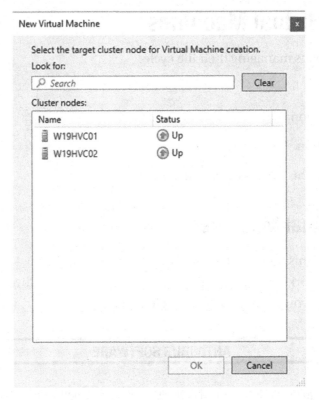

Figure 11-1. *Selecting the node to host a new VM*

7. A check will be made to determine if the Hyper-V management
    tools are installed on the machine you are using. You need
    Hyper-V Manager as well as the PowerShell tools.

8. The New Virtual Machine Wizard will be displayed. This is the
    same wizard you've used through Hyper-V Manager.

9. Click Next, to skip the Before You Begin page.

10. Provide a name for the new VM and the location on the disk to
    store the VM, as shown in Figure 11-2.

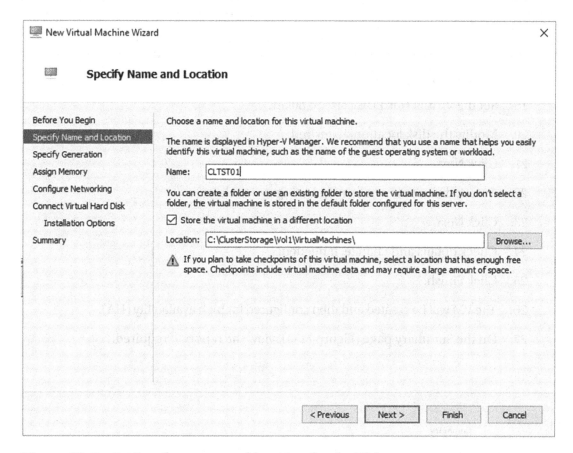

Figure 11-2. *Setting the name and location for the VM*

11. The location should be on one of the Clustered Shared Volumes
     (CSV) you have created; otherwise, the other nodes in the cluster
     can't access the VM. In this case, you're using Vol1, which was
     created in Chapter 10. In Vol1, a folder called `VirtualMachines`
     has been created to house all VMs on that volume. A folder with
     the same name has also been created on Vol2.

12. Click Next.

13. Select Generation 2.

14. Click Next.

15. Leave Startup memory as 1024MB.

16. Select Use Dynamic Memory.

17.   Click Next.

18.   Click Next, to skip configuring the network. You'll configure the VMswitches on the cluster nodes later.

19.   Set the Virtual Hard Disk size to 80GB.

20.   Modify the disk location, if desired.

21.   Click Next.

22.   Accept default of Install an operating system later.

23.   Click Next.

24.   Check details and change, if needed.

25.   Click Finish.

26.   The VM will be created and then configured for high availability (HA).

27.   On the Summary page (Figure 11-3), view the report, if required.

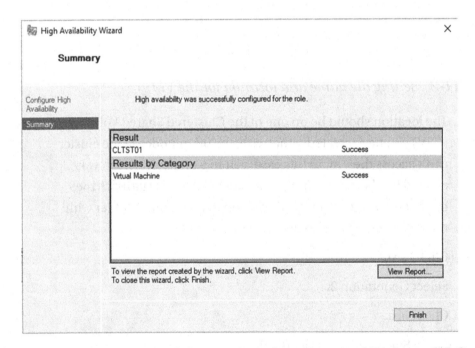

Figure 11-3. *Summary page after New Virtual Machine and High Availability Wizard have completed*

28.   Click Finish.

29.   The new VM is visible in the Roles pane, as shown in Figure 11-4.

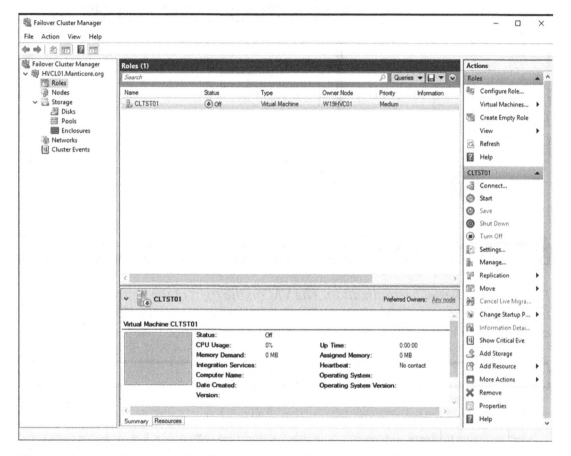

Figure 11-4.   *A high-availability VM viewed in Failover Cluster Manager. Notice the standard VM actions in the Actions pane. Additional actions, such as Move, will be explained in later chapters.*

TRY IT YOURSELF

Create a VM, CLTST01, on the Hyper-V cluster, using the steps in this section. You should also install an OS onto the VM.

If you've created your Hyper-V cluster using nested virtualization, you should see something like Figure 11-5, once your VM is created and the OS has been installed.

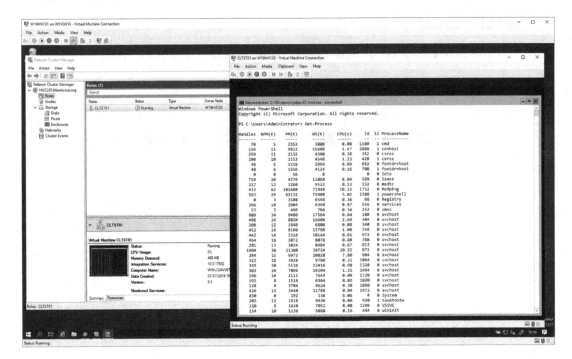

Figure 11-5. *Nested virtualization. The VM on the right of the figure (CLTST01) is a Windows Server 2019 instance of Server Core running on the VM that is the cluster node HVC01, also running on Windows Server 2019.*

ABOVE AND BEYOND

When you create a Hyper-V cluster, give some thought as to where you're going to store the tools you need to create and manage your VMs. Your tool set will include, but not be limited to, the following:

- ISO images for operating installation

- Other software installation packages

- Utility tools

- Scripts

These items should be stored on cluster-shared storage, so that they are available from all nodes. We created a 100GB volume called Images on our test cluster for this purpose.

```
New-Volume -FriendlyName 'Images' -FileSystem CSVFS_NTFS `
-StoragePoolFriendlyName "S2D*" -Size 100GB
```

The need for a volume containing your tool set will become more important if you use System Center Virtual Machine Manager (SCVMM) in your environment. You'll need a volume to store the templates SCVMM can use when creating VMs.

Once you've created a VM, how do you administer it?

Virtual Machine Administration

You use Failover Cluster Manager for VM administration on a Hyper-V cluster, because it exposes the VM migration tools for moving VMs between cluster nodes and storage locations.

It is possible to use Hyper-V Manager to manage the VMs on your cluster, but you can only view and manage the VMs on a single node at a time. If you want a view of all of the VMs on the cluster, you need to use Failover Cluster Manager.

You can run Failover Cluster Manager from one of the cluster nodes or an administration machine.

TRY IT YOURSELF

Connect to the cluster using Failover Cluster Manager from a remote administration machine (not part of the cluster). Compare with using Failover Cluster Manager on a cluster node. Any differences?

Add Network Adapter to Virtual Machine

If you've worked through the practical sections, including creating a VM on the cluster, as in the previous section, you'll realize that the VM can't communicate on the network, because there isn't a virtual switch to which the network adapter that's automatically created when you build a new VM can connect.

We stated earlier that you should automate the creation and configuration of the nodes in your Hyper-V cluster. This ensures that all nodes are configured in an identical manner. This will become even more important when you look at the implications of migrating VMs between hosts, in Chapter 14.

Creating identical virtual switches on all the nodes in your cluster is best performed by a script. If you use Hyper-V Manager, you'll have to connect to each node in turn, to perform the action. The code to add a switch to all your nodes is

```
$vms = 'W19HVC01', 'W19HVC02'

foreach ($vm in $vms) {
  $cred = Get-Credential "$vm\Administrator"
  $s = New-PSSession -VMName $vm -Credential $cred

  $sb = {
     New-VMSwitch -Name 'CLAN' -NetAdapterName 'LAN'
  }
  Invoke-Command -Session $s -ScriptBlock $sb
}
```

Using PowerShell Direct, you connect to each node in turn and run the New-VMSwitch cmdlet. The switch type will automatically be set to External, because you've specified to connect the switch to a network adapter.

Note   You'll probably have to restart the nodes when you make these changes, as Windows moves the IP address from the physical network adapter to the switch.

TRY IT YOURSELF

Create the virtual switches on all of the nodes in your cluster. Which is quicker and more efficient: using Hyper-V Manager or running a script?

Your two nodes are configured identically, so now you can connect the network adapter to your virtual switch.

```
Get-VM -Name CLTST01 |
Get-VMNetworkAdapter |
Connect-VMNetworkAdapter -SwitchName CLAN
```

Get the VM and pipe the object into Get-NetworkAdapter (there's only one on the VM at this stage), then pipe into Connect-VMNetworkAdapter, supplying the switch name you want to use, in this case, CLAN.

TRY IT YOURSELF

Connect the VM's automatically created network adapter to the virtual switch you just created. How would you modify the script, if the VM had multiple network adapters?

Your VM now has a connected network adapter, so you can perform any final configuration work.

One common task you'll need to perform is adding storage to a VM.

Add Virtual Disk to Virtual Machine

You've seen how to manage VMs in previous chapters, so we're not going to repeat all of that material. But as a quick example, to show that managing a VM on a cluster isn't that different from doing so on a stand-alone host, let's add a virtual disk to the VM we've just created.

To add a disk to a VM on a Hyper-V cluster,

1. Open Failover Cluster Manager.

2. Expand HVCL01.

3. Click Roles.

4. Click on a VM—CLTST01.

5. Click Settings in the Actions pane.

6. Click SCSI Controller.

7. Click Hard Drive.

8. Click Add.

9. Select Virtual hard disk.

10. Click New.

11. Click Next, to bypass the Before You Begin page.

12. Click Dynamically expanding.

13. Click Next.

14. Change name to Data01.vhdx.

15. Change location to match the VM (clustered shared volume).

16. Select Create new blank virtual hard disk.

17. Set the size to 100GB.

18. Click Next.

19. Click Finish.

TRY IT YOURSELF

Add a new virtual hard disk to the VM you created on the cluster.

The new disk is a raw partition and must be initialized and formatted. Use the Windows Disk Management tools, if you've created a VM with a GUI. If your VM is Server Core, then you can use PowerShell to initialize and format the disk.

```
Get-Disk |
where PartitionStyle -eq 'RAW' |
Initialize-Disk -PartitionStyle GPT -PassThru |
New-Partition -DriveLetter 'E' -UseMaximumSize |
Format-Volume -FileSystem NTFS -NewFileSystemLabel 'Data disk 01' `
-Confirm:$false
```

You start by getting the new disk, which has the partition style of RAW, meaning that it hasn't been formatted. You must initialize the disk. We've used a partition style of GPT to match the default in modern Windows systems. You could use the older MBR style, if preferred. A partition is created on the disk, using all of the available space. A drive letter of E has been assigned. If you already have a number of disks in the machine and want the system to allocate the drive letter, change -DriveLetter 'E' to -AssignDriveLetter. The final step is to format the disk to NTFS and supply a system label for the disk.

The examples you've seen in this section show that you can use all of the knowledge and skills you've built up so far to manage VMs on stand-alone Hyper-V hosts, to also manage VMs on clusters. You just have to be aware that you're working on a cluster and that some things are slightly different.

When you created the cluster in Chapter 10, you added two 1TB disks to each node. The universal constant in IT is the need for more storage, so how can you expand the storage in your cluster?

Managing Storage

Managing the storage for your cluster includes two main areas. First, you must plan your storage. When you created the cluster in Chapter 10, the instructions said to create four 1TB disks, to be used as shared storage. In reality, you must plan how much storage you'll need and how it might grow.

Second, you must be able to add storage to your cluster. In this chapter, we'll show you how to increase the storage available through Storage Spaces Direct. Other storage technologies will be covered in Chapter 12, when you learn about guest clusters.

Planning your cluster's storage is a multistep process.

Planning Storage Needs

In Chapter 1, you learned about the steps involved in moving an organization from a physical to a virtual environment. One of the steps in that process was calculating the amount of storage used by the physical storage. That is the starting point for the cluster storage requirements. On top of that figure, you'll have to allocate space—for either existing VMs will grow or new VMs will be required, and they'll all need storage.

Note   Always, always, always err on the side of caution when deciding the amount of storage you'll need. Storage is relatively cheap, and it's easier (and often cheaper) to buy more than you think you'll need, rather than rush to add extra capacity later.

Having determined the amount of disk space your VMs will consume, you must determine how that storage will be configured. You'll have to ask yourself a number of questions.

- Which technology will you use, for example, SAN, iSCSI, or Storage Spaces Direct?

- What level of redundancy do you want? Mirroring doubles the required storage, and RAID 5 will take one disk out of the array for parity.

- How many volumes do you need?

- What level of free space do you want to keep on the disks?

Once you've determined your storage needs, you must think about capacity planning.

The art of capacity planning for your storage consists of three steps:

1. Determine the threshold at which you require extra disk space.

2. Measure how much of your storage is used on a regular basis.

3. Graph the results to determine a trend.

Note   Remember that there can be significant, sudden jumps in the amount of storage used, owing to new projects, so be sure to include those in your planning.

Once you have determined a trend, you can predict when you'll run out of storage. This allows you start the discussions about acquiring new storage in sufficient time to prevent a lack of storage becoming a problem.

Assume that you've been performing the capacity planning discussed above and have seen the need for new storage. How do you add the storage to the cluster?

Add Storage to Cluster

The cluster you created in Chapter 10 uses Storage Spaces Direct for storage. Microsoft recommends that you use one (1) storage pool per cluster. A storage pool can contain up to 416 disks, which don't have to be of the same size.

Let's add two more disks to each node and then incorporate them into the storage pool. First create the disks.

```
New-VHD -Path 'C:\Virtual Storage\HVC01data03.vhdx' -Dynamic -SizeBytes 1TB
New-VHD -Path 'C:\Virtual Storage\HVC01data04.vhdx' -Dynamic -SizeBytes 1TB
New-VHD -Path 'C:\Virtual Storage\HVC02data03.vhdx' -Dynamic -SizeBytes 1TB
New-VHD -Path 'C:\Virtual Storage\HVC02data04.vhdx' -Dynamic -SizeBytes 1TB
```

Each node in the cluster will get an additional two disks: HVC0Xdata03 and HVC0Xdata04. Add the disks to the relevant nodes.

```
Add-VMHardDiskDrive -VMName W19HVC01 -ControllerType SCSI `
-Path 'C:\Virtual Storage\HVC01data03.vhdx' -ControllerNumber 1

Add-VMHardDiskDrive -VMName W19HVC01 -ControllerType SCSI `
-Path 'C:\Virtual Storage\HVC01data04.vhdx' -ControllerNumber 1

Add-VMHardDiskDrive -VMName W19HVC02 -ControllerType SCSI `
-Path 'C:\Virtual Storage\HVC02data03.vhdx' -ControllerNumber 1

Add-VMHardDiskDrive -VMName W19HVC02 -ControllerType SCSI `
-Path 'C:\Virtual Storage\HVC02data04.vhdx' -ControllerNumber 1
```

The new disks will be automatically added to the storage pool. The disks will automatically rebalance their contents to give the most even distribution possible.

You can view the disks in the storage pool.

1. Open Failover Cluster Manager.

2. Expand HVCL01.

3. Select Storage.

4. Select Pools.

5. Select the Physical Disks tab at the bottom of the GUI.

Alternatively, you can run the following code:

```
Get-StoragePool -FriendlyName s2D* |
Get-PhysicalDisk |
foreach {
```

```
$node = $psitem | Get-StorageNode -PhysicallyConnected |
        select -ExpandProperty Name

$size = [math]::Round( ($psitem.Size / 1GB), 2)
$free =
[math]::Round( ( ($psitem.Size - $psitem.VirtualDiskFootprint) / 1GB), 2)

$props = [ordered] @{
  Node = ($node -split '\.')[0]
  DeviceID = $psitem.DeviceId
  Type = $psitem.MediaType
  'Size(GB)' = $size
  'Free(GB)' = $free
  FreePerc = [math]::Round( ( ($free / $size) * 100 ), 2)
}

New-Object -TypeName PSobject -Property $props
} |
sort Node, DeviceID |
Format-Table
```

This code, adapted from https://blogs.technet.microsoft.com/
filecab/2016/11/21/deep-dive-pool-in-spaces-direct/, gets the physical disks
in the storage pool and for each disk determines the node, calculates the size and free
space in GB, and calculates the percentage of free space available. When the percentage
of free space available drops to a value that's too low (40% is a good starting point), it's
time to think about adding more disk.

TRY IT YOURSELF

Use the procedure in this section to add one or more disks to the nodes in your cluster and
add them into the storage pool.

If you think the disks need to be rebalanced, you can perform that yourself.

```
Optimize-StoragePool -FriendlyName "S2D*"
```

The progress of the optimization can be followed using

```
PS> Get-StorageJob | Format-List Name, ElapsedTime, JobState,
PercentComplete, BytesProcessed, BytesTotal

Name            : S2D on HVCL01-Optimize
ElapsedTime     : 00:32:48
JobState        : Running
PercentComplete : 99
BytesProcessed  : 2437393940480
BytesTotal      : 2445983875072
```

You've added extra disks to the cluster, but the CSV are still the original size. To utilize the new storage capacity, either create new volumes (see Chapter 10) or extend the current volumes.

Extending a Cluster Shared Volume

Extending the CSV to use additional storage capacity is a multistep process. After adding the additional disks, and once the rebalancing has completed, the first step is to extend the virtual disks you created on the storage pool.

```
Get-VirtualDisk -FriendlyName Vol1 | Resize-VirtualDisk -Size 768GB
Get-VirtualDisk -FriendlyName Vol2 | Resize-VirtualDisk -Size 768GB
```

The next task is to increase the partition size, so that the new area of the disk is available. You could create a new partition with the space, but that would be wasteful, as you'd end up with lots of small bits of disk that had too much wasted space. To increase the partition size, use this code:

```
Get-Disk -FriendlyName Vol? |
foreach {

  $part = Get-Disk -FriendlyName ($_.FriendlyName) |
  Get-Partition | where Type -eq 'Basic'

  $size = $part |
  Get-PartitionSupportedSize |
  select  -ExpandProperty SizeMax

  $part | Resize-Partition -Size $size
}
```

This is where a consistent naming convention comes in handy. Get the disks name Vol1?—Vol1 and Vol2, in this case—and extract the partition information for the CSV. Find the maximum possible size of the partition, based on the new disk size, and resize the partition to that size.

TRY IT YOURSELF

Use the procedure in this section to extend the virtual disks created from the storage pool on your cluster.

CSV are accessible by each node in the cluster. Each volume (virtual disk in Storage Spaces Direct terminology) has an owner node. You may have to change the owner node, for example, if you plan to take a node offline.

Change a Node That Owns a Disk

Clusters are used to provide resiliency, so you expect the nodes to be online most, if not all, of the time. If you take down a node, any disks owned by that node will failover to another node. This is the expected behavior of the cluster. It's a better practice to manually failover any disks owned by a node rather than relying on the automatic failover, because the failover is under your control and happens *before* the current owner goes offline.

ABOVE AND BEYOND

Automatic failover of resources is usually very reliable. Very occasionally, you may see problems. A couple of examples we've seen may help, if you ever have to troubleshoot failover issues.

First, if the nodes aren't all patched to the same level, there was a known bug in automatic failover that caused the cluster to lose contact with the storage when the node went offline.

The second example involves moving a cluster between datacenters and changing the IP addresses of the nodes and the cluster. This can cause problems with the storage failing over between nodes.

To perform a manual failover, do the following:

1. Open Failover Cluster Manager.

2. Expand HVCL01.

3. Expand Storage.

4. Select disks.

5. Right-click the disk, or disks, to failover.

6. Click Move.

7. Click Select Node…

8. Select the node in the dialog box.

9. Click OK.

10. The failover will occur within a few seconds. The Owner Node in the Disks pane will change to match the node you selected.

TRY IT YOURSELF

Select one of the data disks and initiate a failover to the other node in the cluster, using the procedure in this section.

You can also use PowerShell, as follows:

```
Move-ClusterSharedVolume -Name 'Cluster Virtual Disk (Vol1)' `
-Node W19HVC02
```

You performed most of the networking configuration when you created the cluster in Chapter 10, but you must think about adding a migration network.

Create Migration Network

Migrating VMs between the nodes in the cluster can involve significant network traffic. Microsoft recommends configuring a specific network for migration, so that migrations don't impact user access to the VMs. A 1GB NIC provides sufficient bandwidth for migration traffic in a small environment with low migration requirements. In larger networks, you may look at using a number of teamed network adapters on the migration network, but you should throttle the migration VLAN to 2GB, as a starting point.

Adding a network to the cluster specifically for the traffic involved in migrating VMs between nodes is a good idea, as it removes the traffic from the other cluster networks, especially the network over which users access the VMs.

You saw how to add networks to the cluster in the section "Creating a Hyper-V HA Cluster," so this is another recap. We'll use 192.168.30.0/26 for the network. That'll supply sufficient IP addresses for the cluster.

To add a migration network, perform the following tasks on each node:

1.   Create a new private switch on your Hyper-V host (or create a new VLAN, if use physical hosts).

     ```
     New-VMSwitch -Name Migration -SwitchType Private
     ```

2.   Add an adapter to each node using the new switch.

     ```
     Add-VMNetworkAdapter -VMName W19HVC01 -SwitchName
     Migration
     Add-VMNetworkAdapter -VMName W19HVC02 -SwitchName
     Migration
     ```

3.   On W19HVC01, rename the new adapter to Migration. Set the IP address to 192.168.30.1, with a subnet mask of 255.255.255.192. Remember: New adapters are always named Ethernet.

4.   On W19HVC02, rename the new adapter to Migration. Set the IP address to 192.168.30.2, with a subnet mask of 255.255.255.192.

5.   In Failover Cluster Manager ➤ Networks, rename the new network to Migration network. Ensure it's configured to allow cluster traffic only.

6.   In the Actions pane, click Live Migration Settings...

7.   Unselect all networks except the Migration network.

8.   Click OK.

TRY IT YOURSELF

Create and configure a migration network for your Hyper-V cluster.

These instructions can be used to create other networks for your cluster. Remember to configure the VMswitch to be of type Internal or External, if you require the cluster nodes to communicate with just the VM host or external clients, respectively.

TRY IT YOURSELF

Configure a management network for your Hyper-V cluster.

So far in this chapter, you've seen how to create and manage VMs on the cluster, how to manage the cluster's storage, and how to manage the networking aspects of the cluster. One last thing must be covered in this chapter: how to add and remove nodes from the cluster.

Managing Cluster Nodes

Servers use their resources—CPU, memory, disk, and network—to support workloads. Clusters can be thought of in the same way, except that the resources are provided through the individual nodes. We've stated before that you should put as much memory as possible in your Hyper-V hosts, as it's usually the resource that controls the number of VMs that you can run on the host.

A cluster of Hyper-V hosts will eventually run out of resources and can't support any further increase in the number of VMs it's running. You've seen how to add disk to the cluster. If your nodes are at capacity, as far as CPU and memory are concerned, your only option is to add one or more nodes to the cluster.

Add a Cluster Node

The new node should be configured in exactly the same way as the existing nodes, including any virtual switches. We keep saying that you should automate your node creation with scripts, but once you've had to build a few nodes, and spent the time correcting configuration mistakes, you'll appreciate why we repeat the message.

If you're using Storage Spaces Direct, decide if you're going to add more disk storage capacity with this node and, if so, how much. This isn't a real issue when adding nodes, but it could become one when removing nodes.

Once your new node is built and configured, you can add it to the cluster. The procedure to add a node is as follows:

1. Open Failover Cluster Manager.

2. Expand HVCL01.

3. Select Nodes.

4. In the Action pane, click Add Node...

5. Click Next, to bypass the Before You Begin page.

6. Supply the name of the new node and Click Add. The node will be verified, which may take some time.

7. Click Next.

8. On the Validation Warning page, select Yes to run the validation report and No to skip the report.

9. Click Next.

10. On the Confirmation page, click Next.

11. The node will be added to the cluster.

12. View the report, if required.

13. Click Finish.

Note   If you don't run the validation report while adding the node and get an error, then go back and repeat the exercise, but this time, run the validation report, to help determine the reason for the failure.

You'll recognize that the wizard is similar to the one you used to create the cluster initially.

If you want to add the cluster node using PowerShell rather than the GUI, use the following:

```
PS> Add-ClusterNode -Name W19HVC03 -Type Node -NoStorage
```

Use -NoStorage to prevent the addition of any shared storage on the new node to the cluster, during the process of adding the node to the cluster.

```
┌─────────────────────────────────────────────────────────┐
│                    TRY IT YOURSELF                       │
└─────────────────────────────────────────────────────────┘
```

Create a machine to be an extra node for your cluster and add it to the cluster.

Sometimes, it's necessary to remove a node from the cluster, for example, if the node has experienced a motherboard failure or must be retired.

Remove a Cluster Node

Before you remove a cluster node from your Hyper-V cluster, you should ensure that

- All VMs have been migrated to other nodes.

- Any shared storage attached to the node, especially, using Storage Spaces Direct has been removed. If you have multiple disks attached to the node that are used in Storage Spaces Direct, remove them one at a time, to allow the storage pool to reconfigure itself. If you remove multiple disks at the same time, you risk corrupting your storage pool.

Removing a node from the cluster is also referred to as evicting a node. To evict a node,

1. Open Failover Cluster Manager.

2. Expand HVCL01.

3. Select Nodes.

4. Right-click the node to be evicted.

5. Select More Actions from the context menu.

6. Click Evict.

7. Click Yes on the confirming dialog box.

8. The node will be evicted from the cluster and will no longer be displayed under Nodes in Failover Cluster Manager.

You can evict a node from the cluster using PowerShell, as follows:

```
PS> Remove-ClusterNode -Name W19HVC03
```

You'll be prompted to confirm the removal of the node.

TRY IT YOURSELF

Remove the new node from the cluster.

That brings you to the end of the chapter, and the techniques you've learned in it will enable you to successfully manage your Hyper-V cluster. All that remains is for you to complete the lab, to consolidate your knowledge.

Lab Work

1. Complete all of the Try It Yourself sections in this chapter. In particular, you should practice the techniques using the GUI and PowerShell. The ability to use both will make you a better administrator.

2. You will also have to install an OS into the VM you created on the cluster.

3. If you have time, create a second virtual machine, CLTST02, on the cluster. Use a different CSV for the storage.

CHAPTER 12

Clustering Hyper-V Guests

You've seen, in Chapter 10, how to cluster Hyper-V hosts to provide high availability to your virtual machines (VMs). In this chapter, we'll look at clustering Hyper-V guests. Rather than clustering the hosts, we'll cluster the VMs running on your hosts. Clustering at the level of the guest machines provides an additional level of resiliency and protection for your VMs. Just as you can't have too much protection when rock climbing, your business-critical applications can never be overprotected.

The chapter opens with an explanation of Hyper-V guest clusters, including an examination of why you might have to use them. You've clustered your hosts; isn't that enough? In some circumstances it isn't, as we'll explain.

There are some specific requirements for Hyper-V guest clustering. You may not be able to meet those requirements in your lab, so we'll explain how you can experiment with guest clusters, using a minimum of hardware.

Let's start by looking at what we mean by "guest clustering."

Hyper-V Guest Clustering Explained

A few years ago, a failover cluster would imply racks full of very expensive equipment. Technology has moved on, and it's now possible to create those clusters on your virtual environment. You're still supporting, and protecting, your critical business applications, only in a cheaper and easier way.

Use Cases for Hyper-V Guest Clustering

The reasons for implementing a guest cluster are similar to those for implementing a Hyper-V host cluster. You want to provide high availability to your applications.

Note   Not all applications are suitable for clustering. Some vendors don't support their applications when clustered, and there are applications that aren't "cluster aware" and, so, can't be clustered.

If you cluster your Hyper-V hosts, you provide high availability to the VM, *but* there are still cases in which downtime could occur, for instance:

- Sudden, unexpected failure of a Hyper-V host. The VM should failover, but it may be slow, depending on workloads and priority, relative to other VMs.

- Operating system (OS) patching often requires at least one restart of the VM. This would cause application downtime, which could be unacceptable to the business.

- Failure occurs in the guest OS, for instance, owing to running out of disk space or a corrupted virtual disk file.

- Application issues cause a VM to crash.

Having identified that your application requires the use of guest clustering so that it remains available even if the problems listed above do occur, what do we need to implement it?

Requirements for Hyper-V Guest Clustering

The requirements for clustering Hyper-V guest machines are the same as for clustering physical machines. Figure 12-1 illustrates a simple two-node cluster.

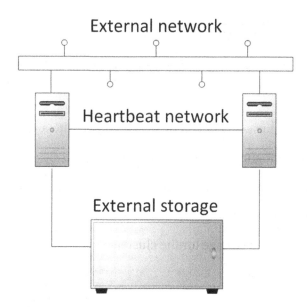

Figure 12-1. *Guest cluster requirements*

You need two or more guest machines. A guest cluster can contain a maximum of 64 members or nodes (Windows Server 2019 extends this through the use of cluster sets that allow for the aggregation of clusters). The cluster nodes need network connectivity to the external network. This is how your users reach the applications hosted on the cluster.

A heartbeat network is used by the cluster nodes for internal communication. You can run the heartbeat over the external network, but it's best practice to separate the two types of traffic.

The cluster nodes also require access to shared storage. This includes the storage used for the cluster witness and the data. In a production environment, this will be external to the Hyper-V hosts.

Clustering at the level of the guest machines provides an additional level of resiliency for your VMs. If you implement guest clustering in your production environment, the underlying Hyper-V hosts should be clustered, and each guest machine that is in the cluster should be on a different host. A single host or multiple members of the guest cluster residing on the same host will reduce the level of resiliency in your environment, as you could lose the whole cluster if the host fails.

You also must ensure that the storage used for the guest cluster has a sufficient level of resiliency to match the needs of your cluster.

Guest Cluster Specification

In this chapter, you'll create a clustered file server. This illustrates the concepts and is an example that you can re-create in your lab to experiment with clustering techniques and administration.

Creating a Hyper-V guest cluster can be broken down into a number of steps.

1. Create and configure VMs to be cluster members.

2. Create the cluster.

3. Create external storage.

4. Configure external storage for the cluster.

5. Configure the cluster.

Note   In reality, the external storage can be created and configured at the same time as the cluster nodes are created. When explaining the process, it's easier to show it as a sequential process.

The cluster will be created to match the configuration shown in Figure 12-2.

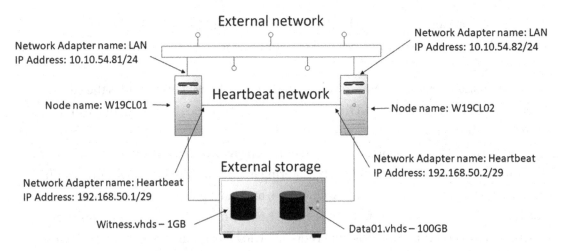

Figure 12-2. *Cluster configuration*

Additional configuration information is supplied in Table 12-1.

Table 12-1. *Cluster Configuration Data*

Item	Value
Cluster name	GC01
Cluster IP address	10.10.54.80
File server name	CFS01
File server IP address	10.10.54.160

We're going to cheat a little (as we did in Chapter 10), because this time, we want to demonstrate using the converged infrastructure (compute and storage) that you created and configured in Chapters 10 and 11, as well as using an iSCSI target. Choose the Hyper-V cluster or stand-alone host. Don't try to mix the two options. You'll follow these steps to create your guest cluster:

1. Create the VMs that will form the cluster on the Hyper-V cluster you created in Chapter 10 *or* on a stand-alone Hyper-V host. Create a third VM to function as the iSCSI target, if required.

2. Create the cluster, using the name and IP address in Table 12-1.

3. Use VHD sets for the witness disk and the first data disk *or* create the witness disk and data disk on the iSCSI target.

4. Configure the witness and data disk.

5. Create the file server on the cluster, using the name and IP address in Table 12-1.

6. Create an additional VHD set *or* create additional storage on the iSCSI target. Allocate the extra storage to the cluster.

Note   You don't have to use the names and IP addresses we've used. If you use other values, document the changes you're making, to avoid confusion during the practical work.

You created a cluster in Chapter 10, so we'll just provide abbreviated instructions in this chapter. Refer back to Chapters 10 and 11, if you're unsure of any details.

Create Cluster Nodes

The following steps will create the cluster nodes for the cluster:

1. Create a VM named W19CL01. The initial disk in the machine needs only to be sufficient for the OS. You could use a 50GB disk or if your organization has a standard size, then use that. If you're creating the VM on a Hyper-V cluster, ensure that the VM is created on the shared storage, so that both nodes of your Hyper-V cluster can administer it.

2. Configure networking in the VM. Set a static IP address. This isn't strictly necessary. You can create a cluster with the IP addresses set by DHCP, but best practice is to assign static addresses. Our lab used 10.10.54.81/24.

3. Rename the network adapter; the new name is LAN.

4. Join W19CL01 to your domain.

5. Add a second network adapter and rename; the new name is Heartbeat. Network adapters can be hot-added to VMs. There is no need to stop the machine. You can create a separate virtual switch for the heartbeat network, if you prefer.

6. Set the IP address of the heartbeat network adapter to 192.168.50.1, with a subnet mask of 255.255.255.248. (This is a 29-bit subnet mask [or prefix length], which allows for a maximum of 6 nodes in the cluster. If you need more, recalculate the subnet mask. See www.subnet-calculator.com for an online subnet calculator.)

    Repeat these steps for W19CL02 but use 10.10.54.82 as the LAN IP address and 192.168.50.2 as the IP address on the heartbeat adapter.

7. Modify the firewall rules on W19CL01 and W19CL02, to enable ping.

8. Test heartbeat connectivity:

    a. From W19CL01, ping 192.168.50.2.

    b. From W19CL02, ping 192.168.50.1.

9. Add the Clustering feature to W19CL01 and W19CL02 using Server Manager or PowerShell. If you use PowerShell, it has to be from an elevated session (run as administrator).

    ```
    Install-WindowsFeature -Name Failover-Clustering
    -IncludeManagementTools
    ```

TRY IT YOURSELF

Use the instructions in this section to create the VMs to function as nodes in your cluster.

The nodes are created, so your next task is to create the cluster.

Create Cluster

You can create a cluster, using the Failover Cluster Manager or Windows PowerShell. You used the GUI to create the cluster in Chapter 10, so this time it's PowerShell's turn. You use the New-Cluster cmdlet, as you might expect.

```
PS> New-Cluster -Name GC01 -NoStorage `
-IgnoreNetwork 192.168.50.0/29 -Node W19CL01, W19CL02
```

Note   You must run the New-Cluster cmdlet from a PowerShell console with elevated privileges. It won't work if you don't (yes, that is the voice of experience).

Congratulations, you now have a working guest cluster on your Hyper-V server! You must check, and configure, if necessary, the IP address allocated to the cluster. Rename the networks to have sensible names. A few things happened during the cluster creation.

- The 10.10.54.0/24 network is assigned to Cluster and Client use.

- The 192.168.50.0/29 network is assigned to Cluster use only.

- An entry for the cluster is created in Active Directory (AD) in the Computers container. It has `Failover cluster virtual network name account` as the description.

- An entry for the cluster is made in DNS.

TRY IT YOURSELF

Create a cluster, using the nodes you created in the previous section.

You now have a cluster, but it doesn't do anything. The next step is to configure the external storage required by your cluster.

Create VHD Set

Clusters can use a number of options for external storage.

- Chapter 9 showed you how to configure storage, using iSCSI to an external device.

- Chapter 10 showed you how to use Storage Spaces Direct and create converged infrastructure.

One option in this chapter is to use VHD sets, which are a shared virtual disk model for guest clusters in Windows Server 2016 and later versions. In earlier versions of Windows Server, you'd have to use shared virtual disks instead. VHD sets are an improvement on shared VHDX files, in that VHD sets support

- Hot resizing

- Backup from the host

- Hyper-V replica

A VHD set consists of two files:

- A VHDS file to which the VMs in the cluster connect

- An AVHDX file where the data is actually stored

You start by creating the files. First, is the witness (also known as quorum) disk. We recommend a 1GB disk for this.

```
PS> New-VHD `
-Path 'C:\ClusterStorage\Vol1\Virtual Storage\GC01witness.vhds' `
-Dynamic -SizeBytes 1GB
```

```
ComputerName              : W19HVC01
Path                      : C:\ClusterStorage\Vol1\Virtual
                            Storage\GC01witness.vhds
VhdFormat                 : VHDSet
VhdType                   : Dynamic
FileSize                  : 4194304
Size                      : 1073741824
MinimumSize               :
LogicalSectorSize         : 512
PhysicalSectorSize        : 4096
BlockSize                 : 33554432
ParentPath                :
DiskIdentifier            : 0A869DCE-D8D9-48C7-AAB5-AC4886F5CC0F
FragmentationPercentage   : 0
Alignment                 : 1
Attached                  : False
DiskNumber                :
IsPMEMCompatible          : False
AddressAbstractionType    : None
Number                    :
```

Then create the data disk. 500GB is an arbitrary figure. You may choose any figure you wish. Ensure that the disk is dynamic; otherwise, you may fill your volume!

```
PS>  New-VHD `
-Path  'C:\ClusterStorage\Vol1\Virtual Storage\GC01data01.vhds' `
-Dynamic -SizeBytes 500GB
```

Now add the virtual disks to *both* cluster nodes.

```
PS> Add-VMHardDiskDrive -VMName W19CL01 `
Path 'C:\ClusterStorage\Vol1\Virtual Storage\GC01witness.vhds' `
-SupportPersistentReservations
```

```
PS> Add-VMHardDiskDrive -VMName W19CL01 `
Path 'C:\ClusterStorage\Vol1\Virtual Storage\ GC01data01.vhds' `
-SupportPersistentReservations
```

```
PS> Add-VMHardDiskDrive -VMName W19CL02 `
Path 'C:\ClusterStorage\Vol1\Virtual Storage\GC01witness.vhds' `
-SupportPersistentReservations
```

```
PS> Add-VMHardDiskDrive -VMName W19CL02 `
Path 'C:\ClusterStorage\Vol1\Virtual Storage\ GC01data01.vhds' `
-SupportPersistentReservations
```

The parameter -SupportPersistentReservations indicates that the disk is a shared disk to be used by multiple VMs, in this case, the cluster nodes. You may see -ShareVirtualDisk used as an alternative, as it's a parameter alias of -SupportPersistentReservations.

TRY IT YOURSELF

If you're using VHD sets in your cluster, create the VHD sets and add them to the cluster nodes. Bring the disks online on both nodes. Format the disks on one node *only*. Add to the cluster, if necessary. If you're unsure of these procedures, follow the instructions in the following iSCSI section.

If you want to use iSCSI as your external storage, you must create and configure a storage server. In your production environment, you may be using iSCSI to connect to the storage underpinning your Hyper-V environment.

Configure iSCSI Storage

You've seen how to use VHD sets to supply the storage to your guest cluster. Now it's time to create the iSCSI target server and use that to supply storage to your cluster. The VM W19ST01 will be configured as an iSCSI target server. Figure 12-3 explains conceptually how this works.

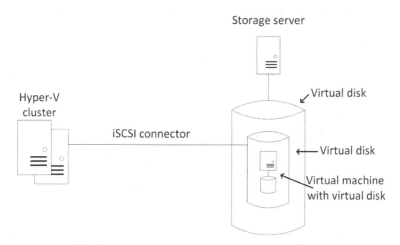

Figure 12-3.   *The nesting of virtual disks for the iSCSI server*

The storage server has virtual disks for data. There is also the system disk, but it is separate to this discussion. Within that virtual disk, the iSCSI target server stores one or more virtual disks that are presented to the cluster as external storage.

You end up with virtual disks inside virtual disks inside virtual disks. If your head hasn't exploded, you're doing well. In production, you would create this on a cluster, but to reduce complexity, we'll use a single machine.

Note   The GUI tools mentioned in the following steps are standard tools that you should be familiar with. New tools will be explained and illustrated with screenshots, where appropriate.

Create iSCSI Server and Target

The following steps should be performed to configure the cluster storage:

1. Create and configure a VM—W19ST01. Join the VM to your domain.

2. On your Hyper-V host(s), create a virtual switch for the storage network.

    ```
    New-VMSwitch -Name Storage -SwitchType Internal
    ```

    An internal switch enables network connectivity between the host and the VMs and between virtual hosts. No traffic is sent outside of the Hyper-V host.

3. Add a network adapter to W19ST01, using the storage virtual switch created earlier. Use Hyper-V Manager or PowerShell.

    ```
    Get-VM W19ST01 |
    Add-VMNetworkAdapter -SwitchName Storage -Name Storage
    ```

4. Configure the adapter with an address on the storage network. Use Network and Sharing Center or PowerShell.

    ```
    Get-NetAdapter -Name Ethernet | Rename-NetAdapter
    -NewName Storage

    $index = Get-NetAdapter -Name Storage |
    select -ExpandProperty ifIndex

    New-NetIPAddress -InterfaceIndex $index -IPAddress
    172.16.0.2 `
    -AddressFamily IPv4 -PrefixLength 24
    ```

5. On W19CL01, add a network adapter for the storage network and set its address to 172.16.0.11.

6. On W19CL02, add a network adapter for the storage network and set its address to 172.16.0.12.

7. Install the iSCSI target feature, using Server Manager or PowerShell.

```
Add-WindowsFeature -Name FS-iSCSITarget-Server `
-IncludeAllSubFeature -IncludeManagementTools
```

8. Add a virtual disk to W19ST01. In this example, we're only using 500GB. Production disks would be in the multi-terabyte range. Use Hyper-V Manager or PowerShell.

```
New-VHD -Path C:\VirtualMachines\W19ST01\iscsi01.vhdx
-SizeBytes 500GB
```

```
Add-VMHardDiskDrive -VMName W19ST01 `
-Path C:\VirtualMachines\W19ST01\iscsi01.vhdx
```

9. Initialize and format the disk. Use Disk Management or PowerShell.

```
Initialize-Disk -Number 1 -PartitionStyle GPT
New-Partition -DiskNumber 1 -UseMaximumSize -DriveLetter F
```

```
Get-Volume -DriveLetter F |
Format-Volume -FileSystem NTFS -NewFileSystemLabel Data01
```

10. Create the witness disk iSCSI target. The process can be viewed best by using Server Manager.

    a.   On W19ST01, open Server Manager.

    b.   Click File and Storage Services.

    c.   Click iSCSI.

    d.   Above the iSCSI Virtual Disks pane, click Tasks.

    e.   Click New iSCSI Virtual Disk.

    f.   In the Type a custom path: field at the bottom of the page, type "F:\GC01" (without quotes). See Figure 12-4.

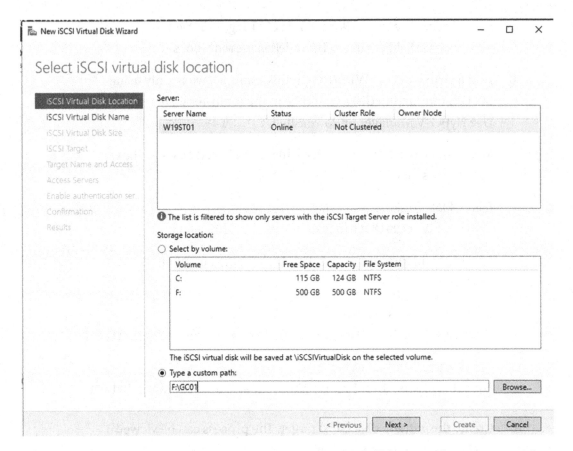

Figure 12-4. *Defining the path for the iSCSI virtual disk. Notice the custom path at the bottom of the page.*

    g.   Click Next.

    h.   In the name field, type "Witness" (without quotes).
        See Figure 12-5.

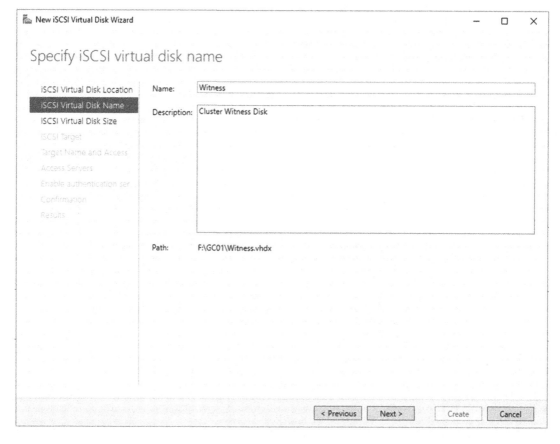

Figure 12-5. *Supplying a name and description for the virtual disk*

    i.   Add a description, if required.

    j.   Click Next.

    k.   In size field, type "1."

    l.   Leave units as GB and disk type as Dynamically expanding. See Figure 12-6.

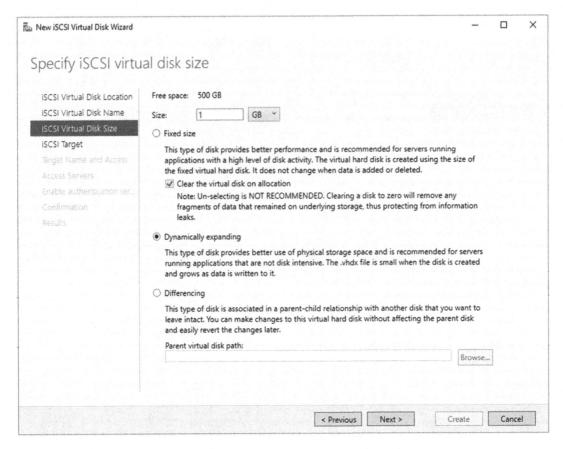

Figure 12-6. *Setting disk size and type*

m. Click Next.

n. On Assign iSCSI target page, leave New iSCSI target selected.

o. Click Next.

p. In the Name field, type "GC01."

q. Supply description, if required.

r. Click Next.

s. On the Specify Access servers page, click Add.

t. Select Enter a value for the selected type.

u. Select type IP Address.

v. Type "172.16.0.11" in the value field. See Figure 12-7. This is the IP address on the storage network for cluster node W19CL01.

Figure 12-7. *Supplying IP address of servers that will use the iSCSI target*

w. Click OK.

x. Click Add and repeat for 172.16.0.12. This address is the IP address on the storage network for cluster node W19CL02.

y. Click Next.

z. Click Next, to skip Enable Authentication page.

aa. On Confirm selections page, review details and correct, if necessary.

bb. Click Create.

cc. Virtual disk and iSCSI target will be created. See Figure 12-8.

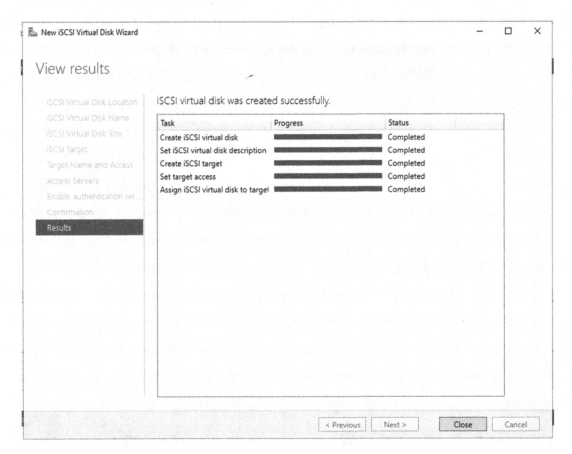

Figure 12-8. *Completion of the creation of the iSCSI virtual disk and iSCSI target*

dd. Click Close.

11. Use PowerShell to create a data disk and add it to the iSCSI target.
The new disk is automatically configured to be dynamic.

```
New-IscsiVirtualDisk -Path F:\GC01\Data01.vhdx
-SizeBytes 500GB
Add-IscsiVirtualDiskTargetMapping -TargetName GC01 `
-DevicePath F:\GC01\Data01.vhdx
```

12. Click Refresh in Server Manager. Your display should be similar to
that shown in Figure 12-9. Make a note of the iSCSI target name,
as you'll be seeing it again when you connect the storage to the
cluster nodes.

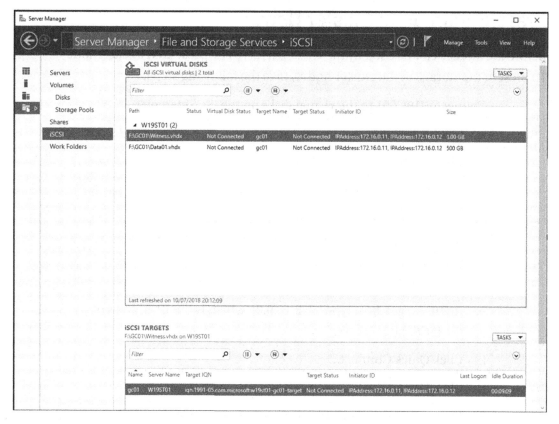

Figure 12-9. *iSCSI virtual disks in the upper pane, and iSCSI target displayed in the lower pane*

TRY IT YOURSELF

Use the instructions in this section to create the iSCSI storage for your cluster.

The iSCSI storage is ready to use, so it's time to add it to the cluster nodes.

Present Storage to Cluster Nodes

Before the storage can be used by the cluster, it has to be presented to each node. To present the storage to the cluster nodes, take the following steps:

1. Connect W19CL01 to the virtual disks on the iSCSI target.

    a. Open Server Manager on W19CL01.

    b. Click Tools.

    c. Click iSCSI Initiator.

    d. If this is the first time you've used the iSCSI initiator on the server, you may be prompted to start the iSCSI service (MSiSCSI) and set it to automatically start when Windows starts. Click Yes.

    e. In the Target box, type "172.16.0.2," which is the IP address of the iSCSI target server.

    f. Click Quick Connect...

    g. Click Done.

    h. In the Discovered targets, you'll see the name of the iSCSI target you created, as shown in Figure 12-10.

Note   Once iSCSI is configured, you should reopen the iSCSI initiator and check the Favorite Targets tab, to ensure the configuration you're making is recorded. If it isn't, the node won't reconnect to the iSCSI target after it's restarted. If your node can't see the storage for some reason, checking the Favorite Targets tab is a good first troubleshooting step.

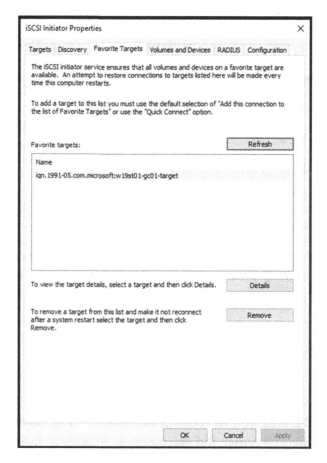

Figure 12-10. *Connecting the cluster node to the iSCSI target*

  i.   Click OK.

  j.   Click File and Storage Services.

  k.   Click Disks. Refresh, if necessary.

  l.   Confirm that the two virtual disks from the iSCSI target are
       connected.

2. Repeat for W19CL02.

3. Bring the disks online on W19CL01.

    a. Right-click the first of the iSCSI disks: disk number 1.

    b. Click Bring Online.

    c. Repeat for other disks, to bring all disks online.

4. Repeat for W19CL02.

5. Format disks on W19CL01 *only*.

    a. Right-click disk number 1. It should be the 1GB disk.

    b. Click New Volume...

    c. Click through the standard disk formatting wizard. Accept maximum size for volume. Select Don't assign a drive letter of folder. Select NTFS as file system. Type "Witness" as volume label.

    d. Repeat for disk 2. Use Data01 as the volume label.

Caution   Perform this task on *only one of the nodes*. If you attempt to initialize and format on both nodes, you *will* corrupt the disks. This is a common mistake made by many admins who rush the cluster creation without reading the instructions fully. You have been warned!

TRY IT YOURSELF

Use the instructions in this section to present the iSCSI storage to the nodes in your cluster.

You can view the disks in the Disk Management tool as well as Server Manager, as shown in Figure 12-11.

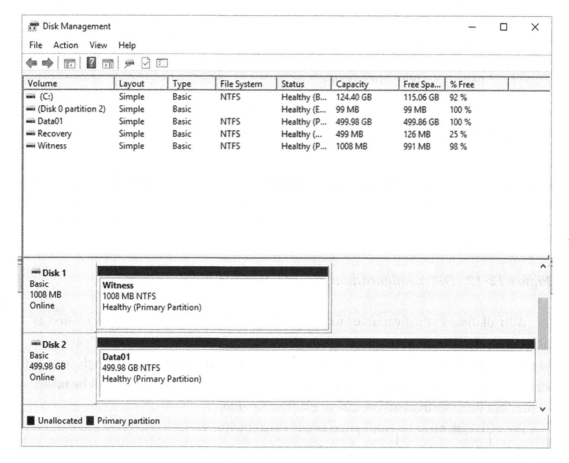

Figure 12-11. *Disk configuration after initialization and formatting. The top pane shows the summary information, and the lower pane shows the format details.*

- Disk 0 is the disk allocated to the VM when it was created and contains the OS.

- Disk 1 is the 1GB shared disk that will be the cluster witness.

- Disk 2 is the 100GB shared disk that will be the cluster data disk.

You must now enable the cluster to see the disks.

1. In Failover Cluster Manager, expand the cluster name.

2. Expand Storage.

3. Select Disks.

4. Click Add Disk, in the Actions pane.

5. You should see the two iSCSI attached disks.

6. Ensure that both are selected.

7. Click OK.

8. The disks pane should look like Figure 12-12.

Disks (2)								
Search							🔍 Queries ▼ 🔲 ▼ ⊙	
Name	Status	Assigned To	Owner Node	Disk Number	Partition Style	Capacity	Repli
📇 Cluster Disk 1	⊙ Online	Available Storage	W19CL02	1	GPT	1.00 GB	
📇 Cluster Disk 2	⊙ Online	Available Storage	W19CL02	2	GPT	500 GB	

Figure 12-12. *Disk configuration after presentation to the cluster*

With all disks in the Available Storage pool, this means that the storage is treated as one unit and is associated with a single node. In the following section, you'll learn how to create a witness disk, which will add to the cluster's stability, and separate the storage, so that disks can be moved independently between nodes, so that a node can be taken offline, but the resources on the disk are still accessible.

The 1GB disk must be configured as the cluster witness.

Configure Witness Disk

In Chapter 10, you used a file share as the witness. In this chapter, you'll use the 1GB disk that you specifically created to act as the witness.

Note   The witness disk should be small. 512MB is the minimum recommended by Microsoft. We prefer to use a 1GB disk, so that we don't deal with fractions of a gigabyte. You won't need more than 1GB.

This is the disk you'll configure as the witness. Do the following, to configure the witness:

1. On W19CL01, open Failover Cluster Manager.

2. Right-click GC01 cluster.

3. Click More Actions.

4. Click Configure Cluster Quorum Settings…

5. Click Next.

6. Click Select the quorum witness.

7. Click Next.

8. Click Configure a disk witness.

9. Click Next.

10. Select the required disk. Expand the disk details, to check, if required, as shown in Figure 12-13.

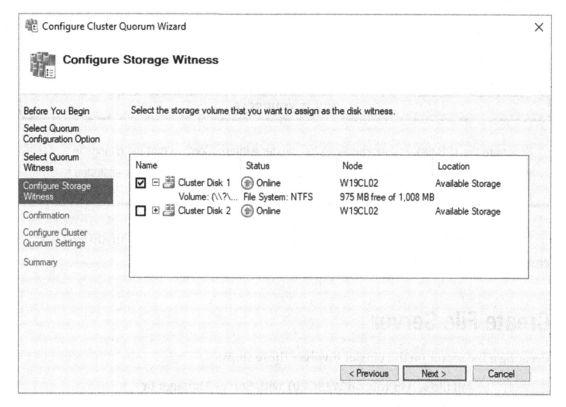

Figure 12-13. *Selecting the witness disk*

11. Click Next.

12. On Confirmation page, check disk to be used as witness.

13. Click Next.

14. On Summary page, click Finish.

15. Expand Storage.

16. Click Disks in Failover Cluster Manager.

17. Assigned To for the disk should now read "Disk Witness in Quorum."

18. Right-click the disk.

19. Click Properties.

20. Overtype Name field with Cluster Witness.

21. Click OK.

TRY IT YOURSELF

Configure the 1GB disk in your cluster as the cluster witness. Confirm that the change is visible in Failover Cluster Manager on both nodes of the cluster and the disk is assigned to Disk Witness in Quorum.

You now have a cluster with storage attached, but it still doesn't do anything. Let's create a file server on the cluster.

Create File Server

Creating a file server on the cluster involves these steps:

1. Install file server role on W19CL01 with Server Manager or PowerShell, as follows:

```
Install-WindowsFeature File-Services `
-IncludeAllSubFeature -IncludeManagementTools
```

2. Install file server role on W19CL02.

a. Restarts are not required for these features.

3. Open Failover Cluster Manager.

4. Expand Cluster GC01.

5. Select Storage

6. Determine Owner Node in Disks pane or run.

   `Get-ClusterResource -Name 'Cluster Disk 2' | Select OwnerNode`

7. On node identified in step 6, open Disk Management tool.

8. Right-click Disk 2.

9. Select Change Drive Letter and Path.

10. Click Add.

11. Select Assign the following drive letter.

12. Select F.

13. Click OK.

14. Click OK.

    a. The drive and drive letter will only be visible to the owning node.

15. Return to Failover Cluster Manager.

16. Select Roles.

17. Click Configure Role... in Actions pane.

18. Click Next, to skip the Before You Begin page.

19. Select File Server on Select Role page.

20. Click Next.

21. Select File Server for general use.

22. Click Next.

23. On the Client Access Point page, do the following:

    a. Supply a name for the file server: use CFS01.

    b. Supply a network address from the client access network: 10.10.54.160, in our lab.

24. Click Next.

25. Click the check box for Cluster Disk 2 on Select Storage page.

26. Click Next.

27. Check information on Confirmation page; if incorrect, use Previous key, to move back through wizard and correct entries. Return to Confirmation page.

28. Click Next.

29. Role is configured.

30. Click View Report... on Summary page, if required.

    a. AD and DNS entries are automatically created.

31. Click Finish.

32. On the node owning CFS01, open Failover Cluster Manager.

33. Expand GC01.

34. Select Roles.

35. Select CFS01 on Roles pane.

36. Click Add File Share from Actions pane.

37. Select SMB Share—Quick, on New Share Wizard.

38. Click Next.

39. Click Next, to skip the selecting server and path.

40. Supply Share Name: use GeneralData.

41. Supply description, if required.

42. Share paths are automatically created.

43. Click Next.

44. On Configure share settings page, configure, as required. Leave defaults selected.

45. Click Next.

46. Click Next, to skip permissions page.

47. Confirm data is correct and click Create.

48. Share is created.

49. Click Close.

50. From your Hyper-V host, or another VM, map a network drive in File Explorer to \\CFS01\Generaldata. Create a text document with Notepad and save to the drive. Confirm creation on the node owning CFS01, with File Explorer.

TRY IT YOURSELF

Create a file server on your cluster.

Once you have created the file server role, you can set the preferred owners. This restricts the nodes to which a resource will automatically failover and in which order the nodes are preferred as a failover target. Open the properties for the CFS01 role and view the General tab, as shown in Figure 12-14.

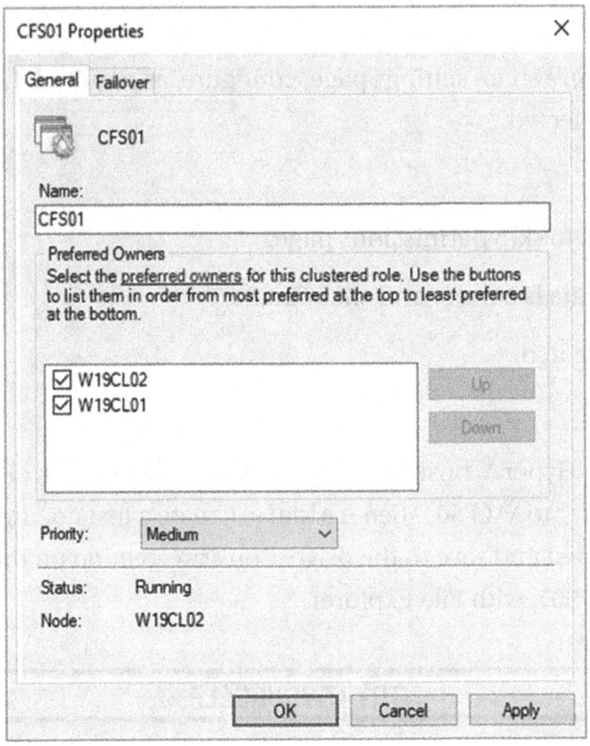

Figure 12-14. *Setting a preferred owner for CFS01*

Select the nodes that you want to be a preferred owner of the resource. You can use the Up and Down buttons to set the order in which the nodes will be used. If you don't set preferred owners, any node can be a failover candidate.

TRY IT YOURSELF

Set the preferred owner for the file server.

You should now have a working clustered file server in your lab environment. The following lab gives you a chance to put this into practice and work through the practical aspects of this chapter.

Lab Work

It's a simple lab for this chapter.

1. Work through the chapter to create a guest cluster in your Hyper-V environment. It may take some time, but don't worry, as there are a number of points at which the work can be logically—and sensibly—paused.

2. Once you have a working file server, use the instructions in the chapter to add more storage to the cluster.

3. If possible, perform the exercise using both VHD sets and iSCSI for storage. You could use VHD sets for the initial storage and iSCSI for additional storage.

CHAPTER 13

Monitoring Hyper-V and Associated Guest VMs

It's one thing to set up and install a new workload, it's another thing entirely to *keep* it running. Any workload that's been in production for some time requires a bit of attention now and then. Maybe resources configured for a virtual machine (VM) at installation are no longer sufficient for the running workload. Maybe a new driver was installed on the host, and now it's causing issues with the storage. Maybe every single VM on the host is running slow, but you're not entirely sure why. These examples are possible issues you'll run into while maintaining a virtualization environment. How are you, the administrator, going to locate those issues and resolve them, once you've found them. That's the question we'll be answering in this chapter.

In This Chapter and Beyond

You should know your way around a Hyper-V host at this stage of the book. We've covered how to set up and cluster one or more Hyper-V hosts. We've talked about how to set up and configure VMs. Additionally, we've discussed how to modify those VMs to suit the needs of the workloads they host.

© Andy Syrewicze, Richard Siddaway 2018
A. Syrewicze and R. Siddaway, *Pro Microsoft Hyper-V 2019*, https://doi.org/10.1007/978-1-4842-4116-5_13

In short, you're at a point now where you understand the basics of running a Microsoft virtualization solution. Looking ahead, the next several chapters are going to fill in some knowledge gaps and teach you some skills and techniques that make managing and maintaining a Hyper-V environment easier and stress-free. We'll start with troubleshooting and performance-tuning tips.

What Monitoring Tools Are Available?

One big question that always comes up: "What tools do I have available to help me manage Hyper-V?" When we're asked that question, we politely remind people that even though it's serving up VMs, it's still Windows Server at its core.

That means you have the same tool sets that you use for Windows Server management. This throws a lot of people off, as it is a bit unexpected, especially if you've worked with the products of any of the other virtualization vendors. However, it does have one large advantage. You don't have to learn a new tool set to monitor Hyper-V, so the learning curve is quite shallow, if you've been a Windows Server administrator for any length of time.

Before we really get started on how we use all these utilities, we'll list the various tools that are available, with a brief description to act as a reference.

Task Manager

Task Manager is just as useful for Hyper-V as for Windows Server. When you suspect resource contention, this is one of the first places to look. It's a valuable tool for looking into resource utilization on both the Hyper-V host itself and the guest VMs.

Event Viewer

Event Viewer is one of the first tools you should be consulting when troubleshooting a Hyper-V issue. Microsoft has created some excellent logging capabilities in Event Viewer. There are a number of Hyper-V logs you should be aware of, listed in Table 13-1.

Table 13-1. *Hyper-V Event Log Subsections*

Partial Hyper-V Log Name	What It Tracks
Hyper-V-Compute	Used by the host container service in Windows Server 2016
Hyper-V-Config	Issues having to do with VM configuration files, including missing or corrupt paths
Hyper-V-Guest-Drivers	Guest VM driver logs
Hyper-V-Hypervisor	Hypervisor layer-specific events
Hyper-V-StorageVSP	Virtualization service provider storage logging
Hyper-V-VID	Virtualization infrastructure driver logging
Hyper-V-VMMS	VM management service logs
Hyper-V-VmSwitch	Logs pertaining to virtual switching
Hyper-V-Worker	Log used by the work process that is used when running a VM

These aren't the traditional logs, such as System or Application, that you have used before. These logs are the newer types of logs introduced with Windows Vista. You can find the full list of available Hyper-V logs using

```
PS> Get-WinEvent -ListLog *Hyper-V*
```

The results of the command are shown in Figure 13-1.

```
Administrator 64 bit C:\Scripts

PS> Get-WinEvent -ListLog *Hyper-V*

LogMode   MaximumSizeInBytes RecordCount LogName
-------   ------------------ ----------- -------
Circular             1052672          16 Microsoft-Windows-Hyper-V-Compute-Admin
Circular           134217728         674 Microsoft-Windows-Hyper-V-Compute-Operational
Circular             1052672           0 Microsoft-Windows-Hyper-V-Config-Admin
Circular             1052672           0 Microsoft-Windows-Hyper-V-Config-Operational
Circular             1052672           0 Microsoft-Windows-Hyper-V-Guest-Drivers/Admin
Circular             1052672             Microsoft-Windows-Hyper-V-Guest-Drivers/Operational
Circular             1052672           0 Microsoft-Windows-Hyper-V-Hypervisor-Admin
Circular             1157939         266 Microsoft-Windows-Hyper-V-Hypervisor-Operational
Circular             1052672          26 Microsoft-Windows-Hyper-V-StorageVSP-Admin
Circular             1052672           0 Microsoft-Windows-Hyper-V-VID-Admin
Circular             1157939         296 Microsoft-Windows-Hyper-V-VMMS-Admin
Circular             1052672          19 Microsoft-Windows-Hyper-V-VMMS-Networking
Circular             1052672         153 Microsoft-Windows-Hyper-V-VMMS-Operational
Circular             1052672          10 Microsoft-Windows-Hyper-V-VMMS-Storage
Circular             1052672             Microsoft-Windows-Hyper-V-VMSP-Admin
Circular             1052672           0 Microsoft-Windows-Hyper-V-VmSwitch-Operational
Circular             1157939        1619 Microsoft-Windows-Hyper-V-Worker-Admin
Circular             1052672           0 Microsoft-Windows-Hyper-V-Worker-Operational


PS>
```

Figure 13-1. *List of Hyper-V logs*

In Figure 13-1, note the full name of the logs. They are a bit too long to remember, so a quick search using `get-WinEvent` is the quickest way to find them. Looking into the log records, you'll see something like this:

```
PS> Get-WinEvent -LogName Microsoft-Windows-Hyper-V-Hypervisor-Operational
| select -First 1 | Format-List *

Message              : Hyper-V successfully deleted a partition (partition 6).
Id                   : 16642
Version              : 0
Qualifiers           :
Level                : 4
Task                 : 0
Opcode               : 0
Keywords             : 2305843009213693952
RecordId             : 266
```

```
ProviderName           : Microsoft-Windows-Hyper-V-Hypervisor
ProviderId             : 52fc89f8-995e-434c-a91e-199986449890
LogName                : Microsoft-Windows-Hyper-V-Hypervisor-Operational
ProcessId              : 4
ThreadId               : 11204
MachineName            : W510W10
UserId                 : S-1-5-18
TimeCreated            : 10/07/2018 21:56:59
ActivityId             :
RelatedActivityId      :
ContainerLog           : Microsoft-Windows-Hyper-V-Hypervisor-Operational
MatchedQueryIds        : {}
Bookmark               : System.Diagnostics.Eventing.Reader.EventBookmark
LevelDisplayName       : Information
OpcodeDisplayName      : Info
TaskDisplayName        :
KeywordsDisplayNames   : {}
Properties             : {System.Diagnostics.Eventing.Reader.EventProperty}
```

In addition to the Hyper-V logs, there are a number of Failover Clustering Event Viewer subsections that you should be aware of as well. Failover Clustering Event Viewer subsections can be found in Table 13-2.

Table 13-2. *Failover Event Log Subsections*

Failover Cluster Log Name	What It Tracks
FailoverClustering	Main clustering log containing informational clustering events
FailoverClustering-CsvFlt	Logging for the CSV Filter Driver
FailoverClustering-CsvFs	Logging for the CSV File System Driver
FailoverClustering-Manager	Logging for errors, dialog boxes, and pop-ups shown in Failover Cluster Manager
FailoverClustering-WMIProvider	Logging for the failover clustering WMI provider

Again, use `Get-WinEvent`, to view the full names of the logs and their contents.

The System Log on both the host and guests also can be used for troubleshooting of issues at the operating system (OS) level.

Performance Monitor

It's hard to beat Performance Monitor for troubleshooting performance bottlenecks and resource contention. You can start Performance Monitor and remotely connect to your Hyper-V hosts. You'll find a large number of Hyper-V focused counters that can be used to troubleshot issues.

PowerShell

PowerShell is at least as powerful as the UI when it comes to working with Hyper-V. That applies to monitoring and performance statistics as well, especially `Get-Counter` and `Get-EventLog`.

Now we know about the various tools we have at our disposal for monitoring Hyper-V related workloads. Let's actually put them to use.

Reviewing the State of Host and Guest VM Resources

A common situation you might find yourself in when managing a virtualized environment is the business need to add additional workloads. Companies, and even departments, are continually adding new applications and, therefore, new VMs. How do you make sure your Hyper-V host has enough resources to accommodate workload X?

There are a number of steps to take to answer this question. First, we must gather some resource utilization information. Let's do so now.

Determining Host Resource Utilization

These steps can be used to determine the current resource utilization on the host system:

1. Log in to your Hyper-V host.

2. Use Hyper-V Manager, to ensure there are VMs running.

3. Open a command prompt, type "taskmgr" (without quotes), and press Enter.

4. Open the Performance tab.

5. Review CPU and Memory Utilization. Are there any resources left?

6. Take note of CPU and Memory Utilization.

7. Review Storage and Networking performance. Note their current status.

8. Open Performance Monitor from Administrative Tools in the Control panel and add the following counters, as shown in Figure 13-2.

    a. Memory: % Committed Bytes in Use

    b. PhysicalDisk: % Disk Time

    c. PhysicalDisk: Current Disk Queue Length

    d. Processor: % Processor Time

    e. Network Interface: Bytes Total/sec

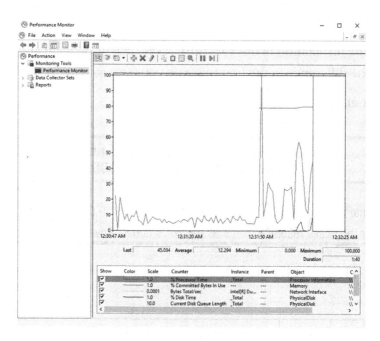

Figure 13-2. *General Performance Monitor counters for Hyper-V host*

9. Take note of the counter values for each added counter.

10. Open a PowerShell Prompt, type "Get-Counter" (without quotes), and press Enter.

11. Note the counter samples for CPU, Memory, Networking, and Storage.

12. Within that same PowerShell Prompt, type "Get-Volume" (without quotes) and note the volume size on the storage location that is used to house your VMs.

13. Build a new Windows Server VM on the host. Give the VM the following:

    a. CPU: 1 Virtual CPU

    b. Memory: 1GB of memory (disable Dynamic Memory)

    c. Storage: A 20GB dynamically expanding VHDX

    d. Networking: A single virtual NIC

14. As you start the new VM and begin installing the OS, using the tools mentioned above, take note of how the resource utilization on the host changes.

15. After the installation of the VM, run Get-Volume once again and note the difference in the free space on your storage volume.

16. Power off the new VM.

**TRY IT YOURSELF—MONITORING HOST RESOURCE
CHANGES AS WORKLOADS ARE ADDED**

Add an additional VM to your Hyper-V host. The VM should use an OS and resources of your choice. Monitor the host's resource usage as the VM is added. Power off the VM once done.

ABOVE AND BEYOND

What percentage of resources should be free on a Hyper-V host? The answer will ultimately depend on your organization's budget and IT staff, but a good rule of thumb is that you want no more than 60% to 70% utilization.

This gets a bit more complicated in a Hyper-V cluster. You want to ensure that there are enough free resources across the cluster, so the cluster can tolerate a single host failure. One of the reasons for recommending multi-node Hyper-V clusters is that if you have to take a node down, you can easily spread the load across the remaining nodes. The free resources across your cluster should always be able to accommodate the VMs running on one node, or you'll have to shut down VMs in the event of a node being taken down.

Determining Virtual Machine Resource Utilization

So now we know how to determine resource usage on the Hyper-V host. What about the VMs running on it? Is there anything special that needs to be done to determine the amount of resources a VM is using? The answer is yes, and it's quite simple. Let's dig in a bit further.

The nice thing about trying to determine the resource usage of a particular VM is that you can make the determination just as if it were a physical stand-alone server.

PHYSICAL VS. VIRTUAL RESOURCES

In practice, the apparent resource usage of a VM isn't 100% identical to that of a physical server. If your VM is using Dynamic Memory, the memory allocated to the VM will change, depending on the VM's workload.

Virtual disks are usually expanding, so the underlying file will grow. You may have allocated a 200GB virtual disk, but if you're only using 50GB, you have to ensure that you have sufficient disk space on the host for the full disk.

CPU utilization within the VM isn't the same as the host utilization, as the VM only has a share of the host CPU.

> When you're looking at the resource usage of a VM, keep these thoughts in mind. If you have 20 VMs on a host, and 2 VMs are working very hard, it doesn't necessarily mean the other VMs are working equally hard or that the host is stressed. If in doubt, check the host resource utilization as well as the VM.

Remember that the VM's OS has no idea that it's running in a virtualized state, and, as such, if you allocated 8GB of memory to the VM, it thinks it has 8GB of memory. You can use all the usual Windows tools, such as Task Manager and Performance Monitor from within the guest VM, to see how the guest OS is performing. Additionally, Hyper-V Manager provides some metrics within the UI as well. Let's use this time-saver now.

1. Open Hyper-V Manager and connect to your Hyper-V host.

2. Power on the VM we created in the previous section.

3. Select the VM from the center pane in Hyper-V Manager and note the VM Summary tab at the bottom-center of the screen.

4. Click the Memory tab and note the memory statistics. It should look similar to Figure 13-3, with the exception of Dynamic Memory.

ANDO-JN-DC01			
Startup Memory:	768 MB	**Assigned Memory:**	768 MB
Dynamic Memory:	Enabled	**Memory Demand:**	307 MB
Minimum Memory:	386 MB	**Memory Status:**	OK
Maximum Memory:	1024 MB		

| Summary | Memory | Networking | Replication |

Figure 13-3. Memory statistics view for a VM in Hyper-V Manager

5. Power off the VM and modify the VM's memory settings.

    a. Enable Dynamic Memory.

    b. Set Startup Memory to 768MB.

    c. Set Minimum Memory to 386MB.

    d. Set Maximum Memory to 1024MB.

6. Power on the VM. Give the VM a couple minutes to boot and for the memory status in the Memory tab (Figure 13-3) to show as OK.

7. Begin to start and stop processes and programs within the VM and note how Dynamic Memory modifies the Memory Demand and Memory Status fields, as needed.

8. Log in to the Guest VM and, using Task Manager, Performance Monitor, and PowerShell, take note again of the guest's resource utilization.

9. Log out of the VM and power it off when done.

Did you notice how the guest VM only shows the resources that you've allocated it in Hyper-V Manager? Remember this, as you begin troubleshooting performance issues in Hyper-V, as this can come in handy when trying to determine the troubleshooting order. For example, you may receive from a department a report that a particular application is running slow. You know that the application in question has an underlying SQL Server database that resides on a VM. You need to answer the following question: Is the VM running slow, or is it the host? The troubleshooting steps to answer the question would be the following:

1. Verify that the VM isn't suffering from resource contention, by using Hyper-V Manager and/or logging into the guest and running Task Manager, PowerShell, or Performance Monitor.

2. If the VM is tight on resources, allocate more from the host. You may need to shut down the VM, to allocate the extra resources.

3. If the VM is fine, review other VMs for similar issues and review the resource utilization on the Hyper-V host itself, using Task Manager, PowerShell, and Performance Monitor.

4. If the Hyper-V host itself is experiencing resource contention, either

    a. Shutdown unneeded VMs.

    b. Reduce resources on oversized VMs.

    c. Move VMs to other hosts that have more available resources.

    d. Add additional hardware to the Hyper-V host.

TRY IT YOURSELF—TROUBLESHOOTING RESOURCE CONTENTION

Modify two of the VMs in your lab on a single Hyper-V host, to enable Dynamic Memory and have slightly more memory allocated between them than the host has. Start the VMs and begin to start some heavy workloads within the VMs. Once the memory is consumed and you start to notice some slowdowns, review resources on both the host and guests. Take note that the guest VMs will likely show available resources, because they think those resources are available, while performance tools on the host will show resources to be topped out.

Troubleshooting Error Messages

No matter how carefully you deploy a technology, at some point, you will have to troubleshoot error messages. So, how do you troubleshoot a cryptic error message in Hyper-V? The process follows these steps:

1. Read the error message, including the detailed information.

2. Refer to the relevant logs in Event Viewer on the host system.

3. Refer to Technet and/or MSDN for more information about a specific error message.

It may seem odd that step 1 is reading the error message. We say this because the error messages and logging in Hyper-V are *very* well done, and most issues can be resolved simply by reading the error messages. In most cases, the error message will tell you exactly what's wrong, but in those rare cases it doesn't, what do you do next?

Event Viewer then becomes your best friend. Hyper-V has a whole slew of event logging going on behind the scenes. You'll spend a great amount time looking at the Hyper-V-VMMS log, as many Hyper-V Manager events about VMs are logged to this location. Let's examine what this process looks like.

Troubleshooting a VHDX Pathing Issue—An Example

1. Log in to your Hyper-V host and open Hyper-V Manager.

2. Select one of the VMs you've been working with throughout the book and power it off.

3. Locate the VM's VHD file using Hyper-V Manager and File Explorer.

4. Append the word TEST into the file name. For example: VMStorage.VHDX is renamed VMStorageTEST.VHDX.

5. Attempt to start the VM. You'll get an error like that in Figure 13-4.

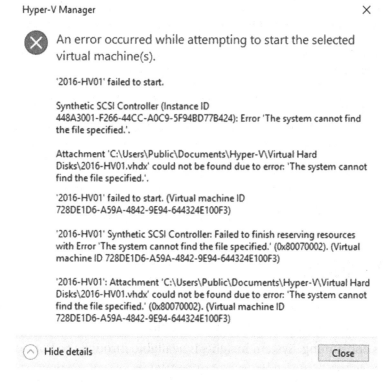

Figure 13-4. *Hyper-V error generated when the specified virtual disk cannot be found*

6. Expand the Details of the error message and read through the error.

7. Take particular note of "Cannot Find the File Specified" text and the associated path.

8. Open Event Viewer, either locally on the host itself or remotely from another machine.

9. Navigate to the Hyper-V-VMMS Admin Log located at "Application and Services Logs\Microsoft\Windows\Hyper-V-VMMS\Admin."

10. Review the latest logs in the list, and you'll notice EventID 32902.

11. Open EventID 32902. It states the VM is attempting to use a file that does not exist.

12. Close Event Viewer.

13. Navigate back to the location of the VHDX file and rename it its original name.

14. Power the VM back on and verify that it starts.

Tools needed to diagnose the error condition are built into the Windows Server OS. Keep this troubleshooting order in mind when you encounter error messages in Hyper-V.

Now, what do you do when the error message and Event Viewer are of no help? You'll want to consult with either TechNet or MSDN. These are official Microsoft sources and are useful when you want to check for a known issue or dig into some official documentation regarding a problem.

System Insights

Windows Server 2019 includes a new feature, System Insights, which is designed to help you monitor your environment, such as disk capacity, amount of memory, and CPU a Hyper-V host is consuming. System Insights is available through the Windows Admin Center (WAC), which means you have to deploy WAC to gain the benefits.

System Insights uses local predictive analysis and machine learning to analyze your system, to provide predictions for when you need more disk, memory, or CPU. As well as providing predictions regarding capacity trends, you can also enable remedial jobs that will mitigate the issue. PowerShell can be used to aggregate predictions from a set of remote machines, so that you can easily monitor your whole server estate.

This a new feature that is only available on Windows Server 2019 and presumably won't be ported to older versions of Windows Server. Until Windows Server 2019 is released and in widespread use, it's difficult to predict how useful this feature will be.

Enterprise Monitoring Applications

You'll have noticed that so far, we've not said anything about enterprise-level monitoring applications, such as System Center Operations Manager (SCOM) or IBM's Tivoli suite. And we're not going to say much about them.

If your organization has an enterprise-monitoring suite in place, talk to the people running it, to ensure that your Hyper-V hosts and VMs are being monitored correctly. The monitoring team understands its product; it doesn't necessarily understand Hyper-V and VMs. Our experience shows that if you don't have the conversations about what you need, you'll get the generic-level of monitoring that is either useless for your needs or triggers too many alerts to be useful. Be aware that you'll have to put in a lot of work to refine the monitoring solution.

You've reached the end of the chapter on monitoring and, as usual, we'll finish with some practical work.

Lab Work

Pretend you're managing a production Hyper-V environment. You've just received a request for a new File Server VM and a new Database VM with the following requirements:

VM Name: FS01

CPUs: 1

RAM: 1GB

Storage: 50GB

NICs: 1

VM Name: DB01

CPUs: 2

RAM: 2GB

Storage: 20GB

NICs: 1

Verify that your environment has enough resources to accommodate the VMs, build them, and then, using performance-monitoring utilities, take note of how they affect the resource utilization on your Hyper-V hosts. Remember: You'll need baseline readings from before the introduction of the new VMs, to determine the changes.

CHAPTER 14

Migrating Virtual Machines Between Hosts

Eventually, you'll have to move virtual machines (VMs) from one Hyper-V host to another. With stand-alone hosts, this could be owing to the physical server requiring an upgrade or even being retired. If your Hyper-V hosts are clustered, you may have to move the VMs, so that you can reboot a server that's been patched, or you must balance the workloads on the servers.

In this chapter, we'll introduce you to the various options you have for moving a VM between hosts, show you how the techniques work, and make recommendations as to when it's best to use each approach.

Introduction to Virtual Machine Mobility

Table 14-1 summarizes the options for migrating VMs between Hyper-V hosts.

Table 14-1. *Hyper-V Migration Approaches*

Migration Type	Requires Cluster	Downtime	Perform With
Cold migration	No	Yes	Hyper-V Manager
Quick migration	Yes	Short	Failover Cluster Manager
Live migration	Yes	None	Failover Cluster Manager
Shared nothing migration	No	None	Hyper-V Manager
Storage migration	No	None	Hyper-V Manager or Failover Cluster Manager

© Andy Syrewicze, Richard Siddaway 2018
A. Syrewicze and R. Siddaway, *Pro Microsoft Hyper-V 2019*, https://doi.org/10.1007/978-1-4842-4116-5_14

The slowest option is a cold migration, which is performed with the VM switched off and can require significant downtime, depending on the speed at which you can copy files across your network. A quick migration requires a small amount of downtime (usually about one minute), while a live migration can be performed safely with the VM running. Users attached to the VM won't notice any impact to their service.

A shared nothing migration also doesn't require downtime and can be performed between non-clustered hosts. The final migration type is a storage migration, which moves the VM's files from one location to another on the same host and can be performed with the VM running.

We'll work through the migration types, show you how to use them, and explain when each should be used. Before we get to that topic, we must consider the configuration version of the VMs in your environment.

Configuration Version

The configuration version of a VM is set when the VM is created. It represents the compatibility of the VM's configuration, saved state, and snapshot files with the version of the Hyper-V host. Each new version of Hyper-V brings changes to the configuration version. Table 14-2 summarizes the configuration versions associated with recent versions of Windows.

Table 14-2. *Summary of Hyper-V Configuration Versions*

Configuration Version	Introduced With
8.3	Windows Server 2019 previews Windows Server 1803 Windows 10 1803 (April 2018 Update)
8.2	Windows Server 1709 Windows 10 1709 (Fall Creators Update)
8.1	Windows 10 1703 (Creators Update)
8.0	Windows Server 2016
7.1	Windows Server 2016 Technical Preview

(*continued*)

Table 14-2. (*continued*)

Configuration Version	Introduced With
7.0	Windows 10 builds 10565 or later
6.2	Windows 10 builds prior to 10565
5.0	Windows Server 2012 R2 Windows 8.1

A given version of Hyper-V can run a VM with a configuration version that is equal to or less than the configuration version associated with that version of Hyper-V. For example, Windows Server 2016 can run any VM with a configuration version of 8.0 or less. Windows Server 1803 can run a VM with a configuration version of 8.3 or less. You can think of the configuration versions given in Table 14-2 as the maximum configuration versions that the host can support.

Note   When Windows Server 2019 is finally released, it may well have a configuration version of 8.4 (or higher).

If you upgrade the Hyper-V host or migrate the VM to a host running a later version of Hyper-V, your VM won't get the benefit of any new features associated with the later version of Hyper-V until you upgrade the VM's configuration version. The features available with each configuration version can be viewed at `https://docs.microsoft.com/en-gb/windows-server/virtualization/hyper-v/deploy/Upgrade-virtual-machine-version-in-Hyper-V-on-Windows-or-Windows-Server`. The configuration version doesn't upgrade automatically; you must explicitly perform the upgrade action.

Note   You can upgrade (increase) the configuration version of a VM. You can't downgrade (decrease) the configuration value.

Some examples may help you to understand configuration versions. If you create a VM on a Windows Server 2016 version of Hyper-V, its configuration version is 8.0. This VM can be moved to a host with a higher configuration version number, and it will run, *but* it won't be able to access any new features.

If you leave the configuration version at 8.0, you can move the VM back to a Windows Server 2016 Hyper-V host, but you can't move it to a Windows Server 2012 R2 Hyper-V host, as that can't support a VM with a configuration version higher than 5.0.

If you move the VM from Windows Server 2016 to a Windows Server 1803 Hyper-V host and upgrade the configuration version to 8.3, you won't be able to move it back to the Windows Server 2016 host or any host that can't support a configuration version of 8.3.

You can view the configurations supported by your Hyper-V host, with the following:

```
PS> Get-VMHostSupportedVersion | sort Version -Descending
```

Name	Version	IsDefault
Microsoft Windows 10 Update/Server 1803	8.3	True
Microsoft Windows 10 Fall Creators Update/Server 1709	8.2	False
Microsoft Windows 10 Creators Update	8.1	False
Microsoft Windows 10 Anniversary Update/Server 2016	8.0	False
Microsoft Windows Server 2016 Technical Preview 5	7.1	False
Microsoft Windows 10 1511/Server 2016 Technical Preview 4	7.0	False
Microsoft Windows 10 1507/Server 2016 Technical Preview 3	6.2	False
Microsoft Windows 8.1/Server 2012 R2	5.0	False

The default configuration version is used when a VM is created. Note the IsDefault property output by Get-VMHostSupportedVersion. You can view the default version directly.

```
PS> Get-VMHostSupportedVersion -Default
```

Name	Version	IsDefault
Microsoft Windows 10 Update/Server 1803	8.3	True

You can create a VM with a configuration version lower than the default:

```
New-VM -Name 'TestConfigV' -Version 8.0
```

This creates a VM with a configuration version of 8.0, meaning you could run it on Windows Server 2016.

You can view the current configuration version of a VM in Hyper-V Manager.

- In the Virtual Machines pane, the configuration version is in the left-hand column.

- The configuration version for a VM you've selected is visible in the Summary pane.

You can also use PowerShell to discover the configuration version.

```
PS> Get-VM | select Name, Version

Name       Version
----       -------
Lin01      8.0
W10PRV01   8.0
W16AS01    8.0
W16CN01    8.2
W16DC01    8.0
W16DSC01   8.0
W16ND01    8.0
W19CL01    8.3
W19CL02    8.3
W19ST01    8.3
```

Upgrading the configuration version can be accomplished in Hyper-V Manager.

1. Stop the VM to be upgraded, if it's running.

2. Right-click the VM to be upgraded.

3. Select Upgrade Configuration Version...

4. Click Upgrade in the Confirmation dialog.

You can't choose the configuration version you're going to upgrade to. It's automatically the default configuration version of the host. You can also perform the upgrade from the VM's action pane.

PowerShell offers the ability to perform an upgrade.

```
PS> Update-VMVersion -VMName W16AS01 -Confirm:$false
```

The following code will upgrade all of the VMs on your host:

```
PS> Get-VM |
where Version -lt (Get-VMHostSupportedVersion -Default).Version |
Update-VMVersion -Confirm:$false -Passthru

Name       State Uptime    Status             Version
----       ----- ------    ------             -------
Lin01      Off   00:00:00  Operating normally 8.3
W16CN01    Off   00:00:00  Operating normally 8.3
W16DC01    Off   00:00:00  Operating normally 8.3
W16DSC01   Off   00:00:00  Operating normally 8.3
W16ND01    Off   00:00:00  Operating normally 8.3
```

Get the VMs on your host and only accept those that have a version that is less than the default configuration version. Pass those into Update-VMVersion. Once you've performed the upgrade, remember that you can't downgrade, and you can't move the VM to a Hyper-V host that only supports lower configuration versions.

Now that you understand configuration versions, we can move on to migration techniques. We'll start with the slowest migration option: a cold migration.

Cold VM Migrations

A cold migration involves moving a VM's files from one host to another. The hosts don't have to be on the same network, as files can be migrated via removable storage.

Export VM

You can cold migrate a VM that's running or stopped. A running VM could be exported as a rough backup. For a migration, you'd want the VM to be stopped, so you can guarantee the state of the VM.

The migration process starts by exporting the stopped VM.

1. To export the VM, right-click the VM in Hyper-V Manager and select Export...

2. Confirm the location for export files.

3. Click Export.

The VM's status in Hyper-V Manager will change to Exporting with a percentage figure that changes to show progress. A folder with the same name as the VM will be created in the location you specified. This folder has three subfolders:

- *Snapshots*: Contains any current snapshots of the VM

- *Virtual Hard Disks*: Contains the VHD or VHDX files for the VM

- *Virtual Machines*: Contains the VM configuration information

---

Note   Exporting a VM does *not* delete the VM on the original host. If you're going to move the VM to another host, we recommend you complete the move, verify the VM is working correctly, and only then delete the original instance of the VM.

You can also perform an export with PowerShell.

```
Export-VM -Name CLTST01 -Path C:\Export2\
```

TRY IT YOURSELF

Export a VM and copy the files to another Hyper-V host.

After the export is complete, move the exported files to the new host. It's recommended that you put the files on the new host directly into the correct location, to save further copying during the import process.

Note   If you don't have a second host available, delete the VM you've exported.

Now you can import the VM into its new host.

Import VM

Importing the VM is the reverse of exporting. The process is as follows:

1. In Hyper-V Manager, click Import Virtual Machine… in the Actions menu.

2. Click Next, to bypass the Before You Begin page.

3. On the Locate Folder page, use the Browse button to locate the folder with VM export files.

4. Click Next.

5. Select VM to import—usually, only one is available. Click Next.

6. Choose Import Type, as follows:

   a. Register VM in place (use existing ID)—the default

   b. Restore VM (use existing ID)

   c. Copy VM (create new ID)

7. In this case, use the Rdefault. Click Next.

8. If the virtual switches on the new host are different from the original host's, you'll have to connect the VM's virtual NIC to the correct switch. Click Next.

9. On the Summary page, click Finish, and the import will be performed.

Once the import has completed, you can start the VM and let your users connect to the workload.

VIRTUAL MACHINE CONFIGURATION FILES

Remember: The VM folder that's created when you export a VM holds the configuration files.

```
PS> Get-ChildItem -Path 'C:\VirtualMachines\CLTST01\Virtual Machines\' |
select Name

Name
----
1351AC66-B664-4BC6-8A31-32A4C5E48527.vmcx
1351AC66-B664-4BC6-8A31-32A4C5E48527.vmgs
1351AC66-B664-4BC6-8A31-32A4C5E48527.VMRS
```

In Windows Server 2016 Hyper-V and later versions, the .vmcx file stores the VM configuration, and the .vmrs file stores the VM state. In earlier versions of Hyper-V, there would be an .xml file for the configuration plus .bin and .vsv files for the state.

You can also import a VM using PowerShell.

```
PS> Import-VM -Path 'C:\VirtualMachines\CLTST01\Virtual Machines\1351AC66-
B664-4BC6-8A31-32A4C5E48527.vmcx'

Name     State CPUUsage(%) MemoryAssigned(M) Uptime   Version
----     ----- ----------- ----------------- ------   -------
CLTST01 Off   0           0                 00:00:00 8.3
```

Note   The output has been truncated to fit the display.

If you place the files in the correct location for the VM, the import will be easier and less error-prone.

TRY IT YOURSELF

Import the VM you exported earlier either to its current host (after deleting the original VM) or a new host.

Cold migrations should only be used when moving VMs between hosts, and you can't use shared nothing migrations. They are also useful if you are migrating to a different infrastructure, for example, a third-party hosting company.

Let's move on to quick migrations, which drastically reduce downtime.

Quick VM Migrations

Quick migrations enable you to move a running VM from one host to another with *minimal* downtime. You *will* have downtime. If you can't afford downtime, perform live migration. Quick migrations have been available since the first version of Hyper-V (Windows Server 2008).

When you initiate a quick migration, the following occurs:

- The VM is put into a saved state.

- Information in the VM's memory is transferred to the new host.

- The VM is started on the new host.

The Hyper-V hosts involved in a quick migration must be clustered, and the storage on which the VM is hosted must be visible to both nodes involved in the migration.

A quick migration is performed using Failover Cluster Manager.

1. Open Failover Cluster Manager and connect to your Hyper-V cluster.

2. Select Roles within your cluster.

3. Select the VM to migrate in the Roles pane.

4. Click Move in the Actions pane.

5. Click Quick Migration.

6. Click Select Node... The dialog shown in Figure 14-1 appears.

7. Select the cluster node to which you'll move the VM. Click OK.

8. VM status changes to Saved. Information shows the migration progress.

9. After migration, the VM will restart.

10. Notice the VM uptime is reset, as the machine was effectively restarted.

TRY IT YOURSELF

Use the Failover Cluster Manager to perform a quick migration of a VM between nodes on your Hyper-V cluster.

Quick migrations work, but a better solution is to use live migrations.

Live VM Migrations

Live migrations were introduced with Windows Server 2008 R2. The advantage of a live migration is that there is no downtime for the VM. Your users can keep working while the migration occurs.

To perform a live migration, do the following:

1. Open Failover Cluster Manager and connect to your Hyper-V cluster.

2. Select Roles within your cluster.

3. Select the VM to migrate in the Roles pane.

4. Click Move in the Actions pane.

5. Click Live Migration.

6. Click Select Node... The dialog shown in Figure 14-1 appears.

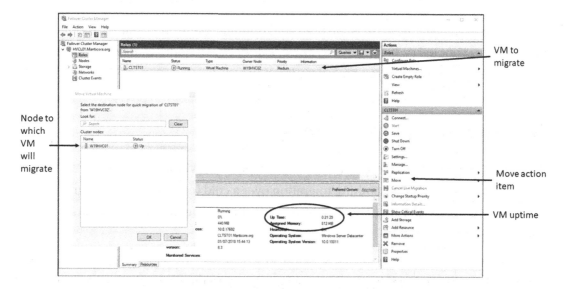

Figure 14-1. Performing a quick migration. The VM to migrate and the node to which it will migrate are indicated by the arrows.

7. Select the cluster node to which you'll move the VM. Click OK.

8. VM status changes to Live Migrating. Information shows the migration progress.

9. Post-migration VM status changes back to Running.

10. Users may have to log back in, but their session and work will be preserved during the migration.

If you have many VMs to migrate, for example, you're moving all VMs from a host, so that it can be patched, then use PowerShell to perform the moves. To move a single VM when you're connected to the cluster node hosting the VM, supply the VM name and the destination host.

```
Move-VM -Name CLTST01 -DestinationHost W19HVC02
```

TRY IT YOURSELF

Use the Failover Cluster Manager to perform a live migration of a VM. Note the difference from when performing a quick migration.

Performing a live migration is the preferred option, whenever possible, as there is no downtime for your users. If you have to move VMs between nodes that aren't in the same cluster, a new option is a shared nothing migration.

Shared Nothing Migrations

Shared nothing migrations were introduced to Hyper-V in Windows Server 2012. The advantage of using a shared nothing migration over a cold (export/import) migration is that the VM keeps running. The disadvantage is that the procedure is a lot more complicated.

Note   Using shared nothing migrations isn't a replacement for clustering, as it doesn't supply high availability, only mobility.

There are a number of requirements for shared nothing migrations.

- Two or more Hyper-V hosts running Windows Server 2012 or later versions that are in the same Active Directory (AD) domain and have network connectivity

- Each host has its own storage configured.

- Hyper-V hosts should have the same processor type and should be configured with the same Hyper-V switches.

- VMs to be migrated don't use pass through storage.

- The Hyper-V hosts must be configured for Live Migrations (see Figure 14-2). Ensure the Enable incoming and outgoing live migration check box is checked and that the IP range for migrations is configured, if required.

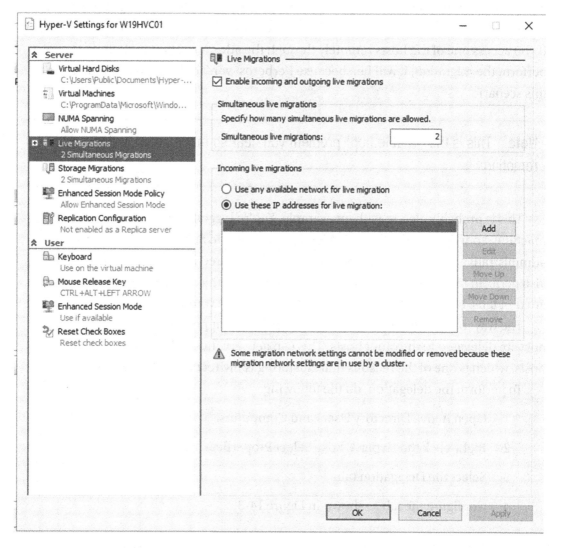

Figure 14-2. *Configuring a Hyper-V host for live migration*

One last problem remains—authentication.

Authentication for Shared Nothing Migrations

When you perform a live migration on a cluster, you're using the cluster account to perform the migration under the covers. In a shared nothing environment, you are using your own administrator account. During a shared nothing migration, actions are performed on the original and new hosts. These actions require authentication. If you log on to either the source or target hosts and perform a shared nothing migration, your credentials are delegated to the other host by Kerberos—the AD authentication protocol. If you access one of the hosts remotely through the administration tools and attempt to perform the migration, it will fail, because Kerberos won't delegate your credentials in this scenario.

Note   This is the "double hop" problem you hear so much about in PowerShell remoting.

This is probably clearer with an example. You're logged on to your administration machine. Your instance of Hyper-V Manager connects to ServerA. You can perform administrative tasks on ServerA perfectly well. In a shared nothing migration, you must also perform tasks on ServerB. ServerA attempts to do this on your behalf, and the attempt fails, because ServerA isn't allowed to delegate your credentials.

The way to solve this is to create a delegation. The appropriate credentials for each host are delegated to the other hosts. This can get very messy if you have a number of hosts, which is one of the reasons that clustering is the recommended solution.

To perform the delegation, do the following:

1. Open Active Directory Users and Computers.

2. Right-click the Hyper-V host. Select Properties.

3. Select the Delegation tab.

4. Configure the tab as shown in Figure 14-3.

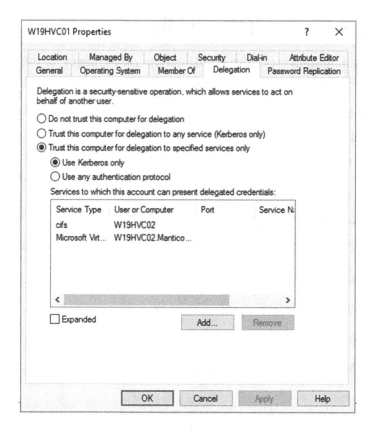

Figure 14-3. *Configuring the Kerberos delegation*

You're constraining the delegation by specifying the exact *services* for which you want authentication to be delegated. Selecting Use Kerberos only ensures that you're secure. The Add button on the Delegation tab is used to specify the computer (standard AD computer picker dialog) and the services to delegate. If you don't recognize CIFS, it's the filesystem.

In Figure 14-3, you've delegated your credentials from the server to W19HV02 for CIFS and Microsoft Virtual System Migration Service only. No other services are delegated.

You must repeat the delegation on the other host, so that it works both ways—on host A delegate to host B and on host B delegate to host A.

You're now in a position to migrate VMs between the two hosts.

TRY IT YOURSELF

Configure two stand-alone Hyper-V hosts for shared nothing migrations. Perform a migration.

Performing a Shared Nothing Migration

A shared nothing migration is performed using Hyper-V Manager. To perform the migration, do the following:

1. Open Hyper-V Manager and connect to the server currently hosting the VM.

2. Select the VM.

3. In the Actions pane for the VM select Move...

4. Click Next, to bypass the Before You begin page.

5. Select Move the virtual machine.

6. Click Next.

7. Supply the name of the destination host.

8. Click Next.

9. Select Move the virtual machine's data to a single location.

10. Click Next.

11. Select the folder on the destination host to which the VM will be moved.

12. Click Finish.

13. A progress bar will be displayed, and the Status field in Hyper-V Manager will display a message with a percentage completion.

The speed of a shared nothing migration is constrained by the network links between the Hyper-V hosts. We recommend that clustering is used whenever possible, as it provides more protection for the VM.

TRY IT YOURSELF

Perform a shared nothing migration for a VM between the two hosts you configured in the previous section.

If you want to try a shared nothing migration without building two new Hyper-V hosts, use the two cluster nodes you created in Chapter 10 and also used for the quick and live migrations in this chapter.

Create the VM you want to migrate on storage that isn't seen by the cluster, for example, the C: drive.

The last migration option we want to consider is storage migration.

VM Storage Migrations

So far, you've seen how to move a VM between hosts. An export/import or shared nothing migration implies that you're changing the storage on which the VM resides. A live migration or a quick migration on a Hyper-V cluster may or may not change the VM's storage location.

It's also possible just to migrate the VM to another storage location. You may need to do this if your storage is filling up, or if you add storage and have to balance the load across the sets of storage.

Note   A pure storage migration is performed live. The VM keeps on running during the migration, with no impact to your users.

To perform a storage migration with Hyper-V Manager,

1.   In Hyper-V Manager, select the VM to move.

2.   Click Move in the Actions pane.

3.   Click Next, to bypass the wizard's opening page.

4.   Select Move the virtual machine's storage.

5. Click Next.

6. Select the movement option (see Figure 14-4), in this case, move all data to a single location. Click Next.

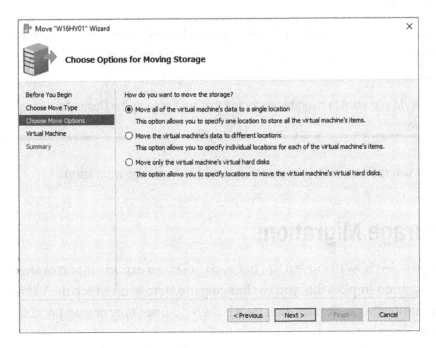

Figure 14-4. *Options for moving storage*

You have three options:

- Move all data to a single new location.

- Move the VM's data to different locations. Virtual disks, configuration, checkpoints, and smart paging can all be moved independently.

- Move only the virtual disks. The disks can be moved independently.

We normally recommend keeping all of the VM's data together. It makes administration and troubleshooting easier, if you have everything available in one place. Spreading a VM's data across multiple storage locations increases the risk of a storage failure affecting your VM.

There is a case for splitting the virtual disks across different physical storage, if the VM hosts an application with high I/O requirements. A high-end SQL Server or Exchange system could be a good candidate, but you have to measure the risk against any performance improvements.

1. Specify the new location for the VM.

2. Click Next.

3. Inspect the information and click Finish.

4. Watch the move information in the Status column of Hyper-V Manager.

5. A success message will flash in the Status column of Hyper-V Manager.

Note   The folder the VM used to occupy will still be present. It'll be empty. You'll have to delete it manually, if required.

You can also use PowerShell to perform storage migrations.

```
Move-VMStorage -VMName W19HV01 `
-DestinationStoragePath 'E:\Virtual Machines\W19HV01\'
```

Specify the name of the machine and the new storage location. The Move-VMStorage cmdlet also has the option of moving individual components, as discussed previously.

TRY IT YOURSELF

Select a test VM in Hyper-V Manager and move all of its data to a new location. Use PowerShell to move it back. Has anything changed in the way the data is organized?

It's your responsibility to ensure that the target storage location when using Hyper-V Manager or PowerShell has sufficient space for the VM.

If your VM is on a cluster, you must use Failover Cluster Manager to perform the storage migration. The procedure is as follows:

1. Open Failover Cluster Manager.

2. Expand your cluster.

3. Select Roles.

4. Select the VM that will have its storage migrated.

5. Click Move in the VM's Action pane.

6. Click Virtual Machine Storage.

7. Select the disk to move.

8. Drag and drop the selected disk into the destination folder in the lower pane, as shown in Figure 14-5.

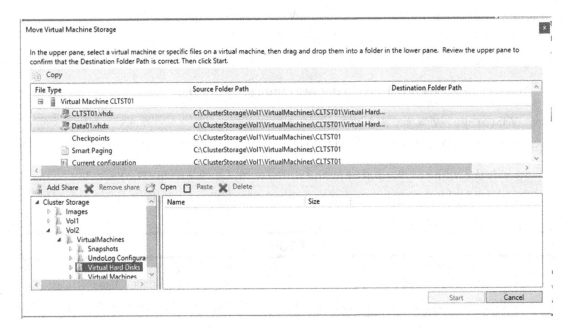

Figure 14-5. Performing a storage migration with Failover Cluster Manager

9. Repeat for any other disks or VM components to be migrated.

10. Click Start.

11. The Information field in Failover Cluster Manager changes to show that the VM storage migration has started.

12. There is no message to state that the migration has completed. The Information field will go blank.

TRY IT YOURSELF

Use Failover Cluster Manager to perform a storage migration on the disks attached to your test VM.

Let's close the chapter with lab work.

Lab Work

These exercises will provide an opportunity to practice migrations:

1. Complete the Try It Yourself sections, if you haven't done so.

2. Perform a cold migration where the Hyper-V switches don't match on the hosts. What happens? How can you repair the VM?

3. Take down one of the nodes in your Hyper-V cluster while VMs are running. What happens to the VMs?

4. Start a live migration and crash the target node while it's happening. Can you repair the VM?

5. Perform a storage migration. In each case, examine the VM properties.

   a. Move just the disk or disks.

   b. Move each component to a different location.

6. Automate moving all your VMs to a new storage location.

CHAPTER 15

Moving Existing Workloads to Hyper-V

Now that you've built this nice, shiny brand-new Hyper-V environment, how do you use it to its full potential? Like most administrators, you're most likely not planning on only provisioning new workloads on this environment. You have existing workloads on physical servers that are providing services on your network, and for most of those, it doesn't make sense to rebuild them from the ground up. You have to migrate them into your virtualized environment. This is known as a physical-to-virtual (P2V) conversion.

Alternatively, you may have an existing virtualization platform from which you want to move VMs onto your Hyper-V platform. If the existing platform is Hyper-V, you can use the techniques you learned in Chapter 14. Techniques for migrating workloads from other platforms will be covered in this chapter.

How do you go about moving those workloads (operating system [OS] included) into VMs on your new Hyper-V solution? This is the question that this chapter will answer. While the migration story centered on Hyper-V has always been something of a moving target, there are native Microsoft tools that will get the job done, even if they all have their own problems, issues, and caveats.

In This Chapter and Beyond

At this stage in the game, you're able to create new Hyper-V hosts, clustered or stand-alone, and manage new and existing hosts. You know how to provision and manage virtual machines (VMs).

Now we're filling out your knowledge with some final topics and information to make your transition into Hyper-V administration easier. This chapter will focus on migrating existing workloads into your Hyper-V environment. Topics to come in later chapters include Hyper-V Replica, Containers, and System Center Virtual Machine Manager. Let's get started.

© Andy Syrewicze, Richard Siddaway 2018
A. Syrewicze and R. Siddaway, *Pro Microsoft Hyper-V 2019*, https://doi.org/10.1007/978-1-4842-4116-5_15

What Workloads Are Candidates for Migration into Hyper-V

Before we get too far into the "how to perform a migration" question, let's first talk about what workloads are a good fit for migration. While most existing physical servers can be virtualized, there are those that just don't make sense, from an operational perspective.

A common source of concern, for many administrators, is Active Directory (AD). We find that many administrators are often very timid when it comes to making any changes regarding the domain controllers (DCs) in their environments. AD is a critical part of a modern Windows environment and is not fully understood by many administrators. When people start migrating their DCs into a virtualized environment, their knee-jerk reaction is to use a conversion utility to turn the DC into a VM.

Converting a workload into a Hyper-V VM isn't a destructive process by any means, but it can be time-consuming, and you may have to take the workload offline, depending on the utility you're using to do the conversion. This is the primary reason we always steer administrators away from using conversion utilities with DCs. Remember: AD is designed to be a replicated highly available service.

If you have more than one DC in a domain (and if you don't, we recommend you stop reading and create a second one immediately), all DCs will talk to each other and replicate AD data among themselves—automatically. Not only is this useful as a high-availability mechanism, it can also be used for migrations.

When it comes to DCs, we always recommend that administrators simply create a new DC on the virtualized solution, let the information replicate from the old DCs to the new virtualized one, and then decommission the old DCs once you're happy that the new DC is working correctly and your users can log on. The specifics are a bit more complicated but are outside the scope of this book.

As a rule of thumb, if the workload you're attempting to convert has its own built-in replication and migration technology, the best approach is to build a new server on the Hyper-V infrastructure and allow the workload's replication system to transfer the needed data. Not only is this method cleaner, it's also less prone to issues and errors. AD was simply used as an example in this case; other similar situations would include Microsoft SQL Server, Microsoft Exchange, and DNS.

Another factor to consider when performing a physical-to-virtual conversion is the hardware in the original server. If the hardware isn't available as a virtual component in Hyper-V, for example, fax boards or licensing dongles, you won't be able to perform a straight conversion.

What Tools Are Available?

We mentioned earlier that Microsoft's story around migrating workloads into Hyper-V has always been a moving target. The tool set has changed many times, and the information coming from Microsoft hasn't always been consistent. There are a number of different tools that support different situations and budgets. Microsoft's support for these tools has changed, as they've been removed and then added back into the tool set a number of times over the last several years. It can be difficult to know the currently supported tool set and what works best in your situation. There are a number of tools readily available to move your workloads onto Hyper-V.

Note   If the disks you want to convert are encrypted, or the data is encrypted, we recommend that you perform an un-encryption *before* undertaking the migration to Hyper-V. You can re-encrypt the data once your new VM is up and running on Hyper-V.

It's not possible for us to supply you with a complete listing of the available tools for migrating workloads onto Hyper-V. The tools in the rest of the section provide a good selection of possibilities, and one of them should meet your needs. An Internet search will enable you to discover other tools, if these don't meet your needs.

Microsoft Virtual Machine Converter

Microsoft Virtual Machine Converter (MVMC) is a free utility that can be downloaded and used to migrate live workloads into your Hyper-V environment. It's a decent tool; has PowerShell support, which lends itself well for automating the process; and has a high degree of success. MVMC will convert an existing VM, for example, a VM running on VMware, to a Hyper-V VM.

However, there are some things to be aware of. Officially, this tool was deprecated as of June 2017. MVMC is often the best method for moving workloads into Hyper-V. This is one of the main tools we'll be covering in this chapter, so you'll hear more about it shortly.

Disk2VHD

Disk2VHD is a free Sysinternals command-line tool that has been around for some time. This tool is designed to create a virtual disk from an existing workload. Disk2VHD takes a copy of a running machine and copies it into one or more VHD files—one per existing disk. You can control which disks are converted. The VHD file is attached to a new VM on your Hyper-V host.

As with MVMC, this tool also has a history of a high degree of success. Unlike MVMC, this tool has to be run on the machine that it is actually converting. This tool can be downloaded from https://technet.microsoft.com/en-us/sysinternals/ee656415.aspx.

System Center Virtual Machine Manager or Virtual Machine Manager

There's a chapter later in the book covering the basics of Virtual Machine Manager (VMM). With VMM, you have the ability to convert physical workloads to Hyper-V VMs, and it works pretty well. However, VMM is not a free tool. In order to gain access to VMM, you have to purchase the entire System Center suite, which could be costly and, often, not within the reach of small and medium-size businesses.

If you do happen to have VMM available to you, you can access a how-to on converting workloads to Hyper-V at https://technet.microsoft.com/en-us/library/hh427286(v=sc.12).aspx.

Azure Site Recovery

As far as age is concerned, this tool is the youngest of the bunch. Azure Site Recovery (ASR) is a service providing disaster recovery to the cloud. ASR takes a running copy of your targeted machines and places a copy in Microsoft's Azure public cloud. Then, if something happens to your on-premises location, you can start those workloads inside Azure, for business continuity.

ASR can also be used for workload conversions to Hyper-V, with a few caveats. When Microsoft said that MVMC was being deprecated, they targeted ASR as its successor. However, ASR requires a pretty significant footprint in your datacenter, so it's not without significant hardware and monetary costs. It's not easy to set up, and all conversions go straight to Azure (as of the time of this writing).

If you want to have that workload in your on-premises infrastructure, you must download the virtual disk and attach it to a new VM in Hyper-V. So now you have to wait for that workload to traverse your external network—twice—before you can fire it up in Hyper-V. It is hoped that Microsoft will continue to make improvements to this product.

Issues with Physical-to-Virtual Conversions

A physical-to-virtual migration is probably a rare occurrence these days, but there will be organizations that haven't embraced virtualization, for whatever reason. If you do get involved in a P2V migration, you must be aware of a number of issues.

We've already mentioned potential issues with hardware that isn't matched by a virtual component. Other possible hardware-related issues include

- *Hard drives*: If the source machine is using RAID drives, you may have disk errors when trying to boot the VM. You'll have to try and repair Windows to surmount the errors.

- *Drivers*: Windows will hide drivers for which it can't find matching hardware. You'll have to be sure you move the drivers and ensure that any corresponding devices are removed.

- You'll almost certainly have to reactivate Windows, as the machine's hardware signature will have changed. Moving an OEM copy of Windows breaks the licensing agreement.

You may also have issues with support from software vendors. Some vendors still won't support their application in virtual environments, and some won't support software that's been through a physical-to-virtual migration.

Note   Back up. Before you even think of performing a migration—P2V or virtual-to-virtual—make sure that you have a backup of the source machine. You should have at least one backup and also verify that the backup can be read and that data can be recovered from it. Having to explain to senior management why its critical application isn't available, because the server broke during a conversion, and you don't have a usable backup, will not be a comfortable experience. Always make sure you have a usable backup!

Performing a P2V migration is a difficult lab to create, so we're concentrating on walking you through using MVMC, for the practical work in this chapter. It's important to know how to do this, as you'll want as many of your existing workloads virtualized as possible. When all your workloads are running within Hyper-V, it allows you to lower your administrative overhead and take advantage of the full range of all the various Hyper-V features we've been talking about throughout the book. Let's take a little time and take a closer look at MVMC.

Using the Microsoft Virtual Machine Converter

As mentioned, MVMC was deprecated as of June 2017. So, one of the first questions you're going to ask is why you should waste time learning a tool that was going to be deprecated, and following is our answer.

Even though Azure Site Recovery (ASR) has been named the official successor for this functionality, it is nowhere near ready as of this writing. It has a hefty footprint, and moving things to Azure and then back is just not viable, especially if you have a lot of machines to convert.

Additionally, learning how MVMC works will help you to understand how the workload conversion/migration procedure works. You'll have a strong understanding of how the process should work, which can be transferred to other tools, if required.

Let's start by taking a look at what host and guest OSs are officially supported (see Table 15-1).

Table 15-1. *Microsoft Virtual Machine Converter–Supported Operating System Types for Host and Guest*

Supported Destination Hyper-V Host Operating Systems	Windows Server 2008 R2
	Windows Server 2012
	Windows Server 2012 R2
Supported Source Host Operating Systems	Windows Server 2008 R2
	Windows Server 2012
	Windows Server 2012 R2
	VMware vCenter/ESXi 4.1, 5.1, 5.5
Supported VMware Hardware Versions	4, 7, 8, 9, and 10
Supported Guest Operating Systems	Windows Server 2008, 2008 R2, 2012, 2012 R2
	Microsoft Windows Vista and newer versions
	Red Hat Enterprise Linux 5/6
	CentOS 5/6
	Ubuntu 10.04/12.04
	SLES 11
	Debian 7
	Oracle Linux 5/6

As you can see, there is no mention in the list of Windows Server 2016 (or later versions) being supported. That doesn't mean it doesn't work, it's just not supported. It goes without saying that when attempting to convert to an unsupported host, or attempting to convert an unsupported guest OS, you'll want to test, test, test, before allowing the machine to be placed into production using this tool. And don't forget your backups!

ABOVE AND BEYOND

If you want more information on MVMC, the best source is the article available at `https://docs.microsoft.com/en-us/previous-versions/windows/it-pro/windows-server-2012-R2-and-2012/dn873998(v=ws.11)`.

The article and download are labeled as MVMC 3.0 but are really MVMC 3.1.

MVMC is a fairly simple tool to use, but there are a few things you must be aware of. It's best to install and run this tool from an independent "worker machine" that is separate from the target and the destination workloads. This machine has to have enough free space to accommodate the size of the workload you're converting. For example, if you have a file server that has a 40GB C: volume and a 600GB E: volume, your worker machine must have roughly 650GB of free space, so plan accordingly.

Another thing to note is that MVMC will make a new virtual disk for each volume, not disk. So, if you have a single disk that has three volumes on it, MVMC will create three virtual disks during the conversion process, all of which will have to be attached to the new VM prior to booting it. Let's do this now on a test machine.

Note   For this exercise, you'll need an operating system (OS) installed somewhere outside of your Hyper-V lab that can be used for the conversion process. This could be your management workstation or another server you have running in the lab. Keep in mind that after the conversion, the target workload will still be there and functional. This is a nondestructive process, and the newly virtualized instance will be removed afterward.

Follow these steps to perform a conversion:

1. Download MVMC from the following link: `https://www.microsoft.com/en-us/download/details.aspx?id=42497`.

2. Install MVMC on an independent workstation, separate from the target or the destination.

3. Launch the utility after installation. You'll be greeted with a screen very similar to that shown in Figure 15-1.

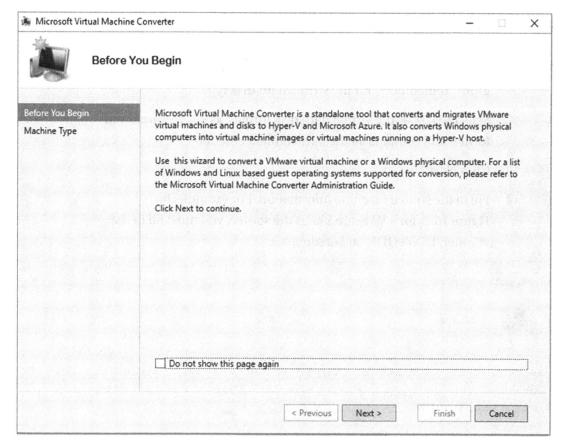

Figure 15-1. *MVMC beginning window*

4. Click Next to Continue.

5. Select whether this is a Virtual Machine Conversion (in the case of VMware VMs or some other hypervisor) or a physical machine conversion.

6. Click Next.

7. Select Migrate to Hyper-V and click Next.

8. Enter in the fully qualified domain name (FQDN) of the destination Hyper-V host, followed by the credentials for your Hyper-V host, or use your Windows User Account, by clicking the check box.

9. Click Next.

10. Select the path on the Hyper-V host on which you would like to store the converted virtual disk.

11. Select Dynamically Expanding (which consumes disk space as it grows, remember?) for the virtual hard disk type.

12. Select VHDX as the virtual hard disk format, as it is the preferred format and contains all the latest enhancements.

13. Click Next.

14. Fill in the source machine information. For example, in Figure 15-2, for a VMware VM as the source, you must fill in the vCenter/ESXi FQDN and credentials.

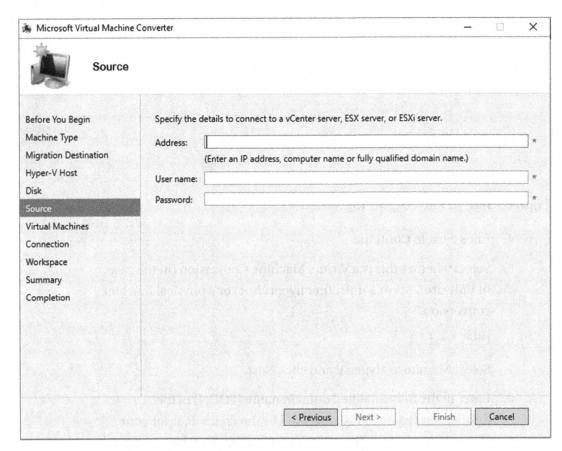

Figure 15-2. MVMC Source window information screen

15. If connected to an ESXi or vCenter server, select the source VM and click Next. If you selected a physical machine, you will not have this step.

16. Click Next.

17. On the Virtual Machine Connection window, enter the credentials for the source OS, then determine the final state of both the source and destination machines, so that they can be powered on or off after the operation.

18. Click Next.

19. Define a location on the machine running MVMC where you would like to have the disk conversion take place. Remember: This has to be a location that is large enough to accommodate the size of the workload that is being converted.

20. Click Next.

21. Review the Summary Screen and then click Finish.

22. Monitor the Job to Completion and take note of the files being created in the workspace you defined on the machine running MVMC.

23. Review the results and click Close.

24. Log in to Hyper-V Manager, connect to the target host, and verify that the newly converted machine is shown in the list.

25. Using the Virtual Machine Properties UI, make sure the NIC is disconnected for the new VM, and power it on.

26. Verify the OS boots and note that it's the same machine now running within a Hyper-V VM.

27. If the machine was a VM, remove any hypervisor guest software, such as VMware Tools.

28. If you're doing an official cutover, you'll want to shut down the source machine and then attach the newly converted VM to a vSwitch that can talk with the production network.

TRY IT YOURSELF—CONVERTING A PHYSICAL MACHINE USING MVMC

Convert a physical machine in your environment. This could be a workstation or a server. Additionally, you could set up a small VM on top of Hyper-V and use MVMC to target it as if it were a physical server.

The process was fairly straightforward. You configured MVMC to connect to the source machine, made a copy of it in a new VHDX on the worker machine, and then pushed those files to the defined Hyper-V and used them to make a new VM.

It's pretty simple and works most of the time; however, there are a few things that can create failures. Applications that create high amounts of disk IO are often the main culprits. Heavy SQL Server or Exchange workloads are common issues, and antivirus software has been known to create issues for MVMC from time to time. In those situations, if you get a failure on the first attempt, it's best to disable any services that are likely to create high amounts of disk activity and then re-enable them, once the conversion is completed.

Once you have successfully converted a workload, it's highly recommended that you test it extensively prior to using it for production. You want to make sure that all software packages on the newly converted machine continue to work correctly.

If you need to convert several machines, you should consider using PowerShell. If you're looking for more information on using MVMC in this way, the PowerShelldocumentation can be found alongside the download for MVMC.

Lab Work

Being comfortable with the conversion process is a matter of practice, but it's best to get a feel for how different OSs behave when going through the process. For your lab work, we recommend that you try the following:

1. Complete the Try It Yourself sections in the chapter.

2. Create a VM on your Hyper-V host with a different OS. This could be a different version of Windows, or it could be a version of Linux (Ubuntu, for example).

3. Once that VM is running, use MVMC and target it as if it were a physical machine.

4. Once converted, test the new VM and simulate performing an official cutover to it.

CHAPTER 16

Preparing for Disaster with Hyper-V Replica

Thus far, you've learned about setting up new workloads and migrating existing ones. You've learned methods to make your VMs resilient to failure and about configuration and troubleshooting methods. There is another handy feature that is baked into Hyper-V, namely, Hyper-V Replica. While failover clustering does a fantastic job of keeping your workloads running, by using the built-in high-availability features of Microsoft clustering, what if you're in a situation in which you don't have a failover cluster? Maybe you're at a location with a single host and no cluster, but you still want some level of built-in redundancy. What if something were to happen to your main production location? In that situation, you'd likely have to rely on your backup software, to get back up and running, but that can take some time, depending on the vendor. These are situations in which Hyper-V Replica can help.

In This Chapter and Beyond

Though we've covered the bulk of what you need to know to successfully manage a Hyper-V environment, we want to introduce you to a few more features that will make your life a bit easier. Hyper-V Replica is one of these, and while it doesn't have a direct correlation with any of the previous chapters, it has a similar goal to failover clustering: to provide additional resiliency to your virtual machines (VMs). In this chapter, we talk about the differences between these two and how to configure and use Hyper-V Replica. Then, in Chapters 17 and 18, we show you two additional useful features: Windows Hyper-V containers and System Center Virtual Machine Manager (CVMM).

© Andy Syrewicze, Richard Siddaway 2018
A. Syrewicze and R. Siddaway, *Pro Microsoft Hyper-V 2019*, https://doi.org/10.1007/978-1-4842-4116-5_16

What Is Hyper-V Replica?

Hyper-V Replica is a technology that's baked into the Hyper-V stack and designed to provide additional resiliency to your Hyper-V environments. While failover clustering protects your VMs from a host failure, Hyper-V Replica is designed for a couple of different scenarios.

The first scenario is that of a small deployment. Let's say your company has two small Hyper-V hosts, but they either lack the needed licensing or don't meet all the requirements of Microsoft clustering (such as shared storage). Consequently, the company requires an alternate method for providing some resiliency to their VMs. Hyper-V Replica can help in this situation.

The second scenario is a disaster recovery situation. Let's say your company has all their workloads virtualized and running at a primary location. Let's then say that the building containing your datacenter is struck by a meteor. In this situation, you'd likely have to recover your VMs from offsite backups (if you have any). This is a time-consuming process, because the data must be written to disk from the backups before the VMs can be spun up again to start serving your end users. Hyper-V Replica can reduce the time required for recovery in situations such as this, by acting as a supplemental tool to your backup procedures.

Caution   With the preceding scenario in mind, it should be noted that Hyper-V Replica is *not* a replacement for backups. Hyper-V Replica cannot be used for file- and object-level recovery from within your VMs, and it is not intended to be used as such. Instead, it is designed to allow you to failover critical workloads to another Hyper-V host, in the event of disaster.

With these situations in mind, you can start to see where Hyper-V Replica fits. But what does it actually do? Essentially, Hyper-V Replica takes a copy of a VM and sends it to a target Hyper-V host. After the initial copy, only the changed data is sent from the source host to the target host, on a periodic basis. How often this happens is configurable So, depending on your recovery time objective, you have some options. Additionally, Hyper-V Replica provides the ability to "failover" the VM to the replicated copy as need be, in a disaster recovery situation. This can be either a test failover or a planned failover, both of which you'll see explained later in this chapter. This is a manual process, and the replicated VM at the target location acts as something of a cold spare of the source VM. You'll see both cases later in the chapter.

Also worth noting is that with Windows Server 2012 R2 Hyper-V and newer versions, the ability to perform extended replication has been added. Extended Replica allows you to replicate the data from the secondary location to yet another Hyper-V host. This allows you to further extend resiliency to those VMs with extra-critical workloads.

Host and Environment Requirements for Hyper-V Replica

There are a few different requirements and considerations to consider prior to setting up Hyper-V Replica. While none of them is overly rigid, they can cause issues, if not properly accounted for. First, here is a list of the more crucial considerations, so you can choose best how to proceed in your own environment. As we step though the process of setting up Replica later, you'll see how these considerations can affect its performance.

>*Authentication mechanisms*: Hyper-V Replica requires an authentication mechanism, to ensure that only the allowed hosts have access to send and receive data. You have two options for this, Kerberos and certificate-based authentication. Kerberos-based authentication is useful in environments in which the replica traffic will *not* be traversing the public Internet. All Replica communication is first authenticated with Active Directory (AD) and then sent to the configured Replica server. The other option is certificate-based authentication, which is best-suited for when the replica data has to be encrypted. The most common scenarios for this are when you are replicating to a Hyper-V host that is offsite, with no secured connection back to the main site.

MORE TO LEARN

We're going to be focusing on the Kerberos option in this chapter. If you're interested in more detailed steps on how to use Hyper-V Replica with certificate-based authentication, you can find more information here: `https://blogs.technet.microsoft.com/virtualization/2013/04/13/hyper-v-replica-certificate-based-authentication-makecert/`.

Firewall rules: The answer to this requirement depends on your choice of authentication mechanism. Port 80 must be open if you chose to use Kerberos authentication, and port 443 needs to be open if you go the certificate route. Again, remember that if the data is going across the public Internet, *you really should use certificate-based authentication and consider a VPN tunnel as well!* Also, if you use Windows Firewall in your environment, there are two pre-created inbound rules, called Hyper-V Replica HTTP Listener and Hyper-V Replica HTTPS Listener, that must be enabled, depending on your configuration.

Data sizes: While not a difficult requirement, the size and frequency of change in your data is something to consider. If you have a server with a large rate of change in its data set, you're going to need more bandwidth available, to be able to replicate the changes. While there isn't a hard-set formula for this, it's something you should keep an eye out for, by using the Replica reporting tools you'll see shortly.

Using Hyper-V Replica and failover clustering together: There are sometimes situations in which you would like to use Replica with a host that is part of a failover cluster. This is a supported configuration, but you have to set up a Hyper-V Replica Broker using Failover Cluster Manager. For the purposes of this chapter, we'll be removing the failover cluster that we set up in previous chapters. Details on setting up a Hyper-V Replica Broker can be found here: `www.altaro.com/hyper-v/hyper-v-replica-broker/`.

SUPPORTING MATERIALS

If you're interested, Microsoft supplies a utility for Replica capacity planning that can make decisions centered on making storage for this feature easier. The tool can be downloaded at `www.microsoft.com/en-us/download/details.aspx?id=39057`.

Configuring Hyper-V Replica

Now that you know what Hyper-V Replica is and what its various requirements are, let's configure it. You're going to start by removing all VM clustered roles, then destroying the cluster. Don't worry, you'll be putting the cluster back together at the start of Chapter 18, and none of the steps we take following will be destructive to our VMs. They'll continue to be available on the hosts themselves. Also, you won't be changing any of the fundamental settings of the hosts, so putting the cluster back together will be quite simple.

To break your cluster, do the following:

1. In Failover Cluster Manager, click on Roles, in the left-hand pane.

2. For any VMs in the Roles list in the center pane, right-click on each VM, then click Remove.

3. Click Yes for each VM on the dialog asking if you are sure.

4. Using Storage Migrations, make sure that no VMs are left on cluster-shared storage (`C:\ClusterStorage\` on each host). You'll want to move these VMs back to local host storage. This is to prevent Clustered Shared Volumes (CSV) volume corruption.

5. In Failover Cluster Manager, right-click the cluster name in the left-hand tree; hover over More Actions; and then click Destroy Cluster...

6. Click Yes on the Confirmation dialog.

Now you have two stand-alone hosts once again. Even though you destroyed the cluster, the VMs contained on your hosts will still run, just not in a clustered state. At this point, you're going to pretend that these two hosts are in different physical locations. You're going to configure Hyper-V Replica to replicate a VM from one host to the other.

To configure Hyper-V replication,

1. Choose a Hyper-V host to act as the source host and one to act as the target.

2. Open Hyper-V Manager and connect to the target host.

3. Click on Hyper-V Settings in the Actions pane and then click Replication Configuration in the left-hand pane. It should look like the window shown in Figure 16-1.

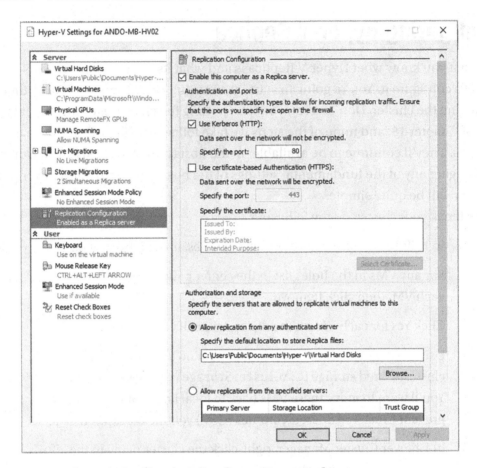

***Figure 16-1.** Hyper-V Replication Configuration window*

4. Click the check box at the top, to enable this server as a replica
    server.

5. Click the check box to Use Kerberos authentication (HTTP) for the
    authentication mechanism and keep the default port 80.

6. Select the radio button to Allow replication from any
    authenticated server.

7. Click Browse and select a location to store the replica files. This
    location must have enough free space to accommodate the VM
    you're going to replicate.

8. Click Apply and then close the UI.

9. Using Hyper-V Manager, connect to your source Hyper-V host.

10. Choose a VM to replicate; select it; and then click Enable Replication in the Actions pane on the right, to open the Enable Replication Wizard.

11. Click Next on the opening screen.

12. Specify the Fully Qualified Domain Name of the target Hyper-V host in the Replica server text box and click Next.

13. On the Specify Connection Parameters screen, as shown in Figure 16-2, make sure the Use Kerberos authentication (HTTP) radio button is selected.

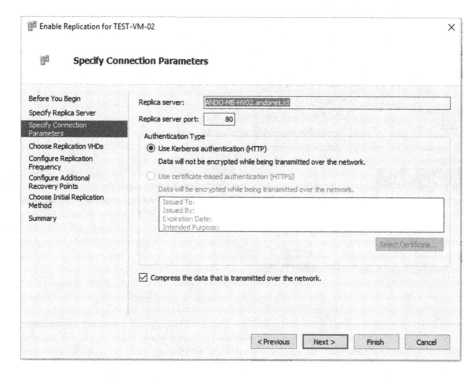

Figure 16-2. *Input the Replica server FQDN and select the Authentication Type*

14. Make sure the check box for Compress the data that is transmitted over the network is checked and click Next.

15. On the Choose Replication VHDs screen, make sure all VHD(X)s are selected and click Next.

16. Choose the replication frequency by clicking the drop-down and selecting 30 seconds. Then click Next.

17.   On the Configure Additional Recovery Points screen, select the
      Maintain only the latest recovery point radio button, then click Next.

18.   You'll see the Choose Initial Replication Method screen, as shown
      in Figure 16-3. Make sure the Send initial copy over the network
      and Start replication immediately radio buttons are selected and
      click Next.

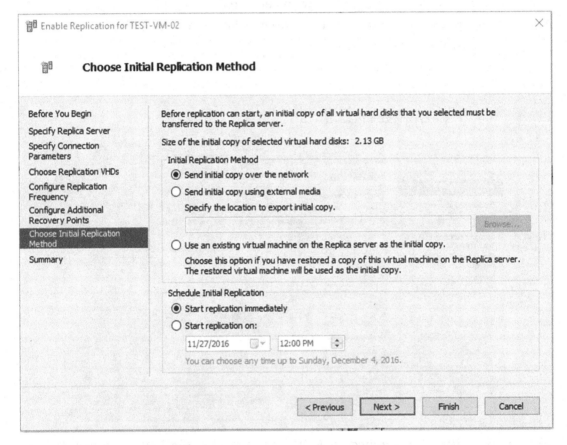

Figure 16-3. *Select the Initial replication type and schedule*

19.   Review the Summary screen for accuracy, then click Finish.

20.   Monitor the initial replication status in the Status column for the
      VM in Hyper-V Manager.

21. Once completed, select the VM, click Replication, in the Actions pane, then click View Replication Health. You'll see a small report much like that shown in Figure 16-4.

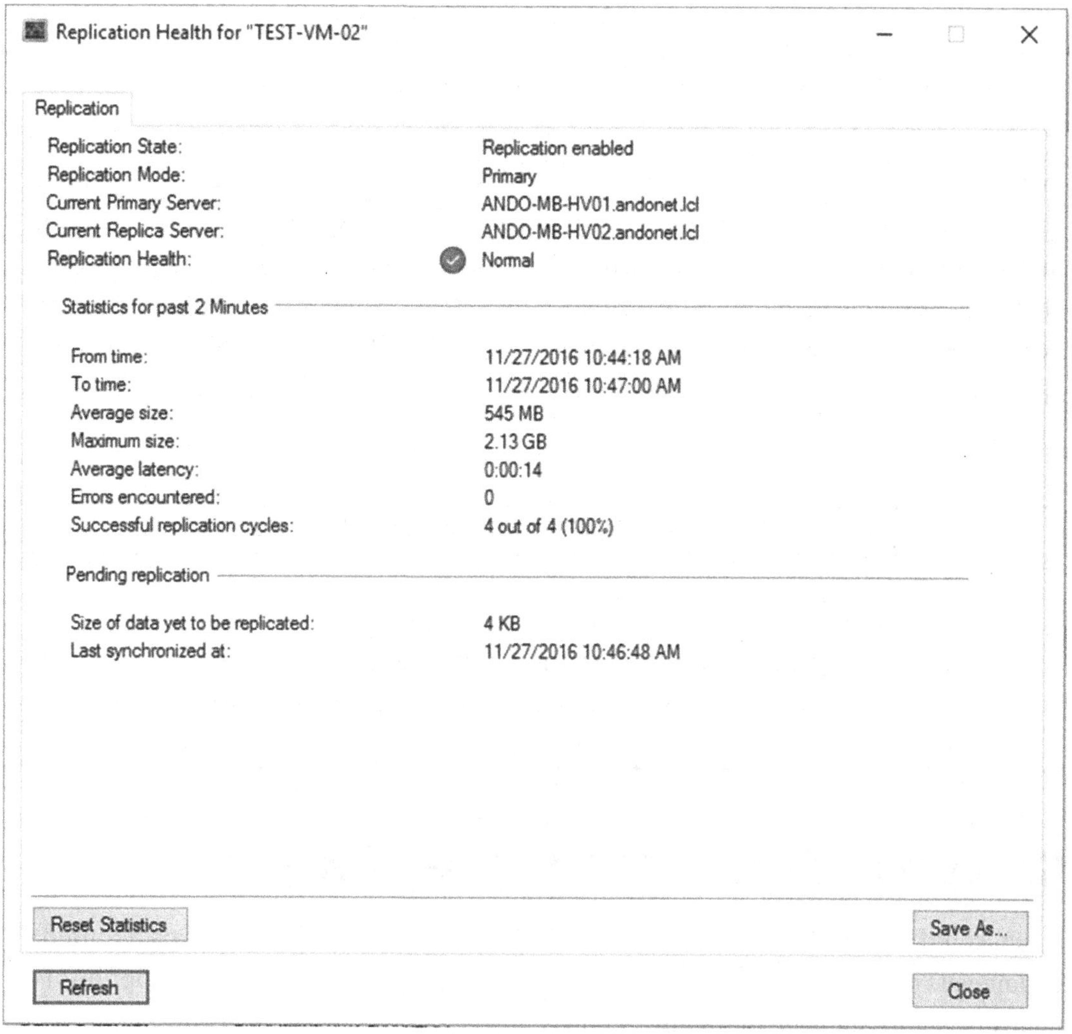

Figure 16-4. *Replication health report*

22. Close the report and, with the newly replicated VM still selected, click the Replication tab, in the VM pane near the bottom of Hyper-V Manager. Take note that the replication mode shows as "Primary."

23. Connect to the Target Hyper-V Host and Refresh the VM List.

24. Take note that the VM now shows in the VMs list in the center pane.

25. With the replicated copy of the VM selected, click the Replication tab in the lower center of Hyper-V Manager in the VM pane. Take note that the Replication Mode shows as Replica. This is how to determine whether a VM is a production VM or a replica.

Once the groundwork is in place, setting up Replica isn't that difficult, and you'll find that as long as the rate of change within the VM is pretty low, replication finishes quite quickly. Also, as you saw throughout the wizard, there are a few other options available that you didn't use. For example, if you wanted to, you could have specified the specific hosts that are allowed to replicate, instead of all authenticated hosts. Additionally, if the initial replication is very large, you have the option of either scheduling the initial copy, or seeding it, using an external disk, to make things quicker. There are lots of options for a variety of situations.

TRY IT YOURSELF—CONFIGURE A VM FOR REPLICATION

If you haven't already, take the steps required to destroy your existing cluster, until you have two stand-alone Hyper-V hosts once again. Choose a source and a target replica host and, using the preceding steps, set up replication for a specified VM and conduct the initial replication.

Conducting Failovers with Hyper-V Replica

A replicated VM doesn't do us any good if we can't recover from it. The steps required to do failovers of the replicated copy are quite simple. There are three different options for failovers, all of which are manually initiated.

Failover: This is done in the event that the source host is offline. A failover is conducted from the target host, and the VM is brought online using one of the replica copies. After the primary host is back online, the administrator must reverse the replication and then do a planned failover (see following) back to the primary host.

Planned failover: This is a graceful failover from the source to the target. The VM has to be powered off, and as part of the wizard, the administrator can failover the VM, reverse the replication, and power on the VM on the target host automatically.

Test failover: Like a failover, this is initiated from the target host. This failover mode simply brings up a replica copy as a new VM, makes sure it's disconnected from the network, and boots it. This is good for testing your replication on a periodic basis.

Now that you know the different failover types, let's talk about what the steps are for conducting them. We'll start with a test failover, then move on to simulating an actual failover event.

1. Using Hyper-V Manager, connect to the target Hyper-V host.

2. Select the replica copy of the VM you configured for replication earlier in the chapter and click Replication in the Actions pane, then click Test Failover.

3. In the Test Failover dialog, select the recovery point you'd like to test and then click Test Failover.

4. Note that a new VM appended with the word *Test* is created in Hyper-V Manager.

5. Open the settings for this test VM and note that the NIC is in a disconnected state, so that this VM cannot interfere with production operations on the network. Close the VM Settings UI.

6. Connect to the VM and power it on. Verify that the operating system (OS) boots and then closes the console window.

7. Select the replica instance of the VM (*not the test one*) and click Replication in the Actions pane, then click Stop Test Failover.

8. Click Stop Test Failover when the verification dialog comes up.

9. Note that the test VM is deleted.

These test failovers are good for incorporating into your backup and disaster readiness testing policies, as they show whether you can failover to one of the replicated copies successfully. It's highly recommended that you do this on at least a quarterly basis, as you don't want to find out that you can't recover when it's too late. Now let's move on to an actual failover situation.

To perform a failover, do the following:

1. Connect to the source Hyper-V Host with Hyper-V Manager and shut down the VM that was selected to be the primary VM in the replica set. Let's pretend now that this Hyper-V host is no longer available.

2. Connect back to the Target Hyper-V host with Hyper-V Manager and select the replica copy of the VM that was configured earlier in this chapter.

3. Click Replication in the Actions pane and then click Failover.

4. Select the recovery point to use, using the drop-down, and then click Fail Over.

5. Verify that the machine boots and that the OS can talk with the network.

6. We'll pretend now that the source host has come back online, and a failover back to the production site must occur, starting with replicating the changes back to the source host.

7. On the target host, select the running replica copy of the VM. Click Replication in the Actions pane, and then click Reverse Replication.

8. Click Next on the first screen of the wizard, which you'll find looks very familiar to the wizard we used to configure the initial replication.

9. Verify that the FQDN of the source Hyper-V host is automatically populated to the Replica server text box and then click Next.

10. Verify that the auto-populated connection parameters all look correct and then click Next.

11. Select 30 seconds' replication frequency, using the drop-down, and then click Next.

12. Select the Maintain only the latest recovery point radio button and then click Next.

13. Make sure the Use an Existing VM and Start replication immediately radio buttons are selected and then click Next.

14. On the summary screen, verify that all the settings look correct and then click Finish.

15. Monitor the initial replication job in Hyper-V Manager and verify that the replication mode for the selected VM on the target host now shows as Primary and as a replica on the original source host.

16. Power off the VM on the target replica host, as a planned failover back to the source host can now occur.

17. Select the replicated VM using Hyper-V Manager on the target host and then click Replication in the Actions pane, then click Planned Failover.

18. In the Planned Failover dialog, make sure both check boxes for Reverse the replication direction after failover and Start the Replica virtual machine after failover are selected, then click Failover.

19. Monitor the failover status using the wizard, and upon success, you'll see a verification window such as that shown in Figure 16-5.

Figure 16-5. Planned Failover verification window

20. Verify that the VM is now running on the original source Hyper-V host and that it is showing replication type primary.

21. Using the replication health report, verify that replication is once again successfully occurring between hosts.

22. Finally, select the replicated VM on the source host and click Replication in the Actions pane in Hyper-V Manager, then click Remove replication.

23. When the confirmation dialog comes up, click Remove Replication.

TRY IT YOURSELF—SIMULATED REPLICA FAILOVER

If you haven't already, using the preceding steps, select a small VM in your environment to replicate from one host to another. Simulate a failover to the target Hyper-V host, reverse the replication back to the source Hyper-V host, and then do a planned failover to get the VM running on the original source host again. Once done, remove the replication.

Lab Work

As with the last chapter, the best way to gain a clear understanding of the material is to practice. With this in mind, do the following:

1. Choose another VM to replicate alongside the original VM.

2. Instead of powering down only the source VM, power down the entire source host, to simulate a host/site failure, and recover it to the target host.

3. Finally, fail things back to the original host after powering it back on and remove all replication configurations going into the next chapter.

CHAPTER 17

Containers

Containers have been available in the Linux world for a number of years. They are a way to virtualize and isolate applications. Windows Server 2016 introduced the technology to the Windows world. Containers are also available on Windows 10 builds post RTM. The container functionality in Windows Server was further enhanced in Windows Server 1709, Windows Server 1803, and Windows Server 2019.

In this chapter, we'll explain what this exciting new technology is and what you can do with it. This includes how to install the containers feature and the configuration steps you must take before you can use containers. We'll look at the networking implications of containers and how you can overcome those issues.

Before you can use a container, you need to know how to create one—and manage its life cycle. Containers are an excellent way to deliver applications and, in a DevOps environment, could be a way to simplify your delivery processes. You use container images to move containers and, therefore, application functionality from one machine to another, as we'll show you toward the end of the chapter.

CHANGES TO CONTAINER TECHNOLOGY ON WINDOWS

Windows Server 2016 Technical Preview 3 (TP3) gave us our first view of containers on the Windows platform. Containers behaved, and were treated, as mini-virtual machines in TP3 through TP5, and you could use Docker or Windows PowerShell to manage your containers.

This suddenly, and surprisingly, changed without warning in Windows Server 2016 RTM, when containers became application isolation objects that matched their implementation on the Linux platform. Docker became the recommended and only practical management technology.

© Andy Syrewicze, Richard Siddaway 2018
A. Syrewicze and R. Siddaway, *Pro Microsoft Hyper-V 2019*, https://doi.org/10.1007/978-1-4842-4116-5_17

There is a PowerShell module for managing containers—`https://github.com/Microsoft/Docker-PowerShell`—but the only release (August 2016) is rated as an alpha release, and so it can't be recommended for use. The module has been deprecated and archived recently, with no further development planned.

Docker is the only practical administration mechanism, unless you want to create your own functionality using Docker.Dotnet—`https://github.com/Microsoft/Docker.DotNet`.

First, though, just what are these containers that you've heard so much about?

Containers Explained

Containers are lightweight virtualized isolation objects for running applications without impacting the rest of your system. The isolation ensures the container has no knowledge of, and no interaction with, other applications or processes that exist on the same host machine.

Note   The Microsoft documentation for containers is available at `https://docs.microsoft.com/en-us/virtualization/windowscontainers/about/`. At the time of writing, this documentation isn't complete and is contradictory in places. Be aware and double-check.

Containers can be easily ported between hosts, as the application in the container has all of the dependencies and configuration data required for its execution.

Container hosts can be physical or virtual machines (VMs). Container portability means that you can create a container for your application on your Windows 10 machine and, when you're sure its performing as required, port the container to a production host or VM.

Containers in the Windows environment are available in two distinct flavors:

- Windows Server containers

- Hyper-V isolation containers

All Windows Server containers share the kernel of their host's operating system (OS) but still provide process and namespace isolation. Windows Server containers aren't a security boundary, so they can't guarantee to isolate untrusted code. The same kernel version and configuration are required for the host and its Windows Server containers.

Hyper-V isolation containers run in a highly optimized "virtual machine." You can't see or interact with this VM; it's a background object to support only the containers. Each Hyper-V container on a host has its own kernel OS. These containers provide the same security assurances as a VM. Different kernel versions and configurations can be run on the host, for example a Windows 10 container host uses Hyper-V isolation to run containers, based on the Windows Server kernel.

The main differences between Windows Server and Hyper-V containers are summarized in Table 17-1.

Table 17-1. *Windows Server and Hyper-V Container Comparison*

Windows Server Containers	Hyper-V Containers
Share Windows kernel	Own Windows kernel
Memory shared through host	Memory assigned directly
OS trusts applications	Applications not trusted by OS
Applications trust each other	Applications don't trust each other
Faster startup	Slightly slower startup
LESS ISOLATION	MORE ISOLATION

The important point to note is that Hyper-V containers provide more isolation at the OS and application level than Windows Server containers.

Before moving on to installing the containers feature, we must spend a moment discussing container management.

Managing Containers

In the Linux world, the de facto standard for managing containers is Docker—www.docker.com/. Containers are often referred to as Docker containers when, in fact, Docker is a management API for containers. Docker itself refers to Docker as a container platform (www.docker.com/what-docker).

Irrespective of its actual definition, Docker is what you will require in order to manage containers in a Windows platform. The documentation for the Docker command-line interface (CLI) is available online at `https://docs.docker.com/engine/reference/commandline/docker/`.

Note   There isn't a GUI option, from Microsoft or Docker, for managing containers in a Windows environment. You have to use the command line. Kitematic is an open source version of a legacy GUI for Windows (and Mac), if you want to try a GUI option. Most Docker-related documentation assumes management via the command line.

The advantage of using Docker is that it is a standard, and there are many books and articles written on the subject. Unfortunately, most of those are written for Linux users and will require some work to "translate" into Windows. You can use Docker from a Linux machine to administer containers on a Windows machine and vice versa.

The disadvantage to using Docker is that it has an arcane syntax typical of traditional Linux or Windows command-line utilities. If you've become accustomed to the (usually) consistent and logical syntax of PowerShell, you'll have to modify your expectations, unfortunately. The Docker-PowerShell module we mentioned earlier could become an alternative, but it'll need a lot of work. Alternatively, you could create a number of functions to wrap Docker functionality that would provide, at least, a basic level of PowerShell functionality. We'll show you some examples of such functions later in the chapter.

So, how do you get containers up and running?

Installing the Containers Feature

The container functionality isn't available on Windows by default. You need to install the feature. The installation steps have some slight variations, depending on the version of Windows with which you're working. We're going to show you how to install containers on the following platforms:

- Windows Server

- Windows Server Insider Previews

- Windows 10

Note   At the time of writing, Windows Server is taken to include Windows Server 2016, Windows Server 1709, and Windows Server 1803. Windows Server Insider Previews is taken to mean the Windows Server 2019 Previews and all future preview releases. Once Windows Server 2019, or future SAC versions, have been officially released, we expect the container feature installation instructions for Windows Server will apply to them as well.

The one option we won't cover is installation of containers on a Nano server machine. Nano server was introduced with Windows Server 2016 as an ultra-low footprint installation option that could perform a number of infrastructure roles, including being a container host. As of Windows Server 1709, Nano server has been relegated to being a container OS only. All of the infrastructure roles have been removed, and you can only use Nano server as the basis of a container. We don't recommend using Nano server as a container host, owing to the change in emphasis from Microsoft. The Nano server documentation is available online at `https://docs.microsoft.com/en-us/windows-server/get-started/getting-started-with-nano-server`, but the container-related documentation has been removed.

Warning   Microsoft is expending a lot of development effort on container-based technology. The installation details have changed a number of times over the last few years. Before starting an installation on a new machine, double-check the documentation, to ensure that things haven't changed. Prime candidates for change include the provider modules and Docker installation package names.

Let's start by discovering how to install the containers feature on Windows Server.

Installing Containers Feature on Windows Server

The procedure for installing and using containers on a Windows Server system consists of the following:

- Install the Docker provider.

- Download and install Docker.

- Download container images.

- Create containers.

You'll learn about the first two parts of the procedure in this section. Finding, downloading, and using container images will be addressed in later sections.

Note   We're going to use the Server Core option for all of our Windows Server container hosts. Containers don't have an administration GUI, and we want to keep the overhead of using containers as low as possible, making Server Core the ideal option. Windows Server 1709 and Windows Server 1803 are only available as Server Core, which is also a powerful driver for using this option.

Usually, you'd just install the appropriate Windows feature to get access to a feature's functionality, but containers are a bit different. The following commands are executed in a PowerShell console running with elevated privileges. First, find the available Microsoft Docker providers in the PowerShell gallery. You should see something like this:

```
PS> Find-Module -Name Docker*prov* -Repository PSgallery

Version Name                        Repository Description
------- ----                        ---------- -----------
1.0.0.4 DockerMsftProvider          PSGallery  PowerShell module…
0.0.0.3 DockerProvider              PSGallery  PowerShell module…
1.0.0.2 DockerMsftProviderInsider   PSGallery  PowerShell module…
```

The version numbers may be different. Even the names may be different, given the rate of change Microsoft is imposing, which is why we urge you to check the documentation.

FIRST-TIME GALLERY USER

If this is the first time you've used the PowerShell gallery from a machine, you'll see a message like this:

```
NuGet provider is required to continue
PowerShellGet requires NuGet provider version '2.8.5.201' or newer to interact
with NuGet-based repositories. The NuGet provider must be available in
'C:\Program Files\PackageManagement\ProviderAssemblies' or
'C:\Users\richard\AppData\Local\PackageManagement\ProviderAssemblies'. You
can also install the NuGet provider by running 'Install-PackageProvider -Name
NuGet -MinimumVersion 2.8.5.201 -Force'. Do you want PowerShellGet to install
and import the NuGet provider now?
[Y] Yes  [N] No  [S] Suspend  [?] Help (default is "Y"):
```

Answer with Y and press Enter, for the install to proceed.

You'll then get your results. Future access to the gallery won't show the message about the NuGet provider, as it's already installed.

The three provider modules should be used as follows:

- *DockerMsftProvider*: Use for production versions of Windows Server—Windows Server 2016, Windows Server 1709, Windows Server 1803, etc.

- *DockerProvider*: Use for Windows Server Insider Previews.

- *DockerMsftProviderInsider*: Ignore. This was the provider to use for Windows Server Insider Previews but has been superseded by DockerProvider. We expect that this provider will be removed eventually.

Install the provider.

```
PS> Install-Module -Name DockerMsftProvider -Repository PSGallery -Force
```

Use -Force to override the messages about the PSGallery being an untrusted source. Then download and install Docker.

```
PS> Install-Package -Name docker -ProviderName DockerMsftProvider
```

```
The package(s) come(s) from a package source that is not marked as trusted.
Are you sure you want to install software from 'DockerDefault'?
[Y] Yes  [A] Yes to All  [N] No  [L] No to All  [S] Suspend  [?] Help
(default is "N"): Y
WARNING: A restart is required to enable the containers feature. Please
restart your machine.

Name    Version     Source        Summary
----    -------     ------        -------
Docker  18.03.1-ee-2  DockerDefault  Contains Docker EE for use with
                                     Windows Server.
```

You must accept the message to install from an untrusted source and press Enter to continue or use the -Force parameter to bypass the message.

Note   If you hit any problems in the download and install of the Docker package, follow the instructions in the "Troubleshooting the Installation Process" section.

You'll have downloaded and installed the latest version of Docker and installed the containers feature. Your machine needs to be rebooted, to finish the installation.

```
PS>  Restart-Computer
```

The containers feature and Docker are now installed on your server. Let's turn to the Windows Server previews for a moment.

Installing Containers Feature on Windows Server Insider Previews

Installing the containers feature on a Windows Server Preview instance is very similar to the installation on Windows Server, except you use the preview provider.

To install the provider, use the following code:

```
PS>  Install-Module -Name DockerProvider -Repository PSGallery -Force
```

Then install the Docker package.

```
PS>  Install-Package -Name docker -ProviderName Dockerprovider
-RequiredVersion Preview

The package(s) come(s) from a package source that is not marked as trusted.
Are you sure you want to install software from 'Docker'?
[Y] Yes  [A] Yes to All  [N] No  [L] No to All  [S] Suspend  [?] Help
(default is "N"): Y
WARNING: A restart is required to enable the one or more features. Please
restart your machine.
```

Next, restart your machine.

```
PS>  Restart-Computer
```

You should be able to install containers on any of the Windows Server versions now. The last installation option to consider is Windows 10.

Installing Containers Feature on Windows 10

The installation procedure on Windows 10 is completely different—isn't consistency a jewel. You'll need to have the Hyper-V feature installed and working on your Windows 10 system before installing Docker.

First, you must download the Docker for Windows installer from `https://download.docker.com/win/stable/InstallDocker.msi`. Installation instructions are available from Docker at `https://docs.docker.com/docker-for-windows/install/`, but they aren't totally consistent with those in the Microsoft documentation at `https://docs.microsoft.com/en-us/virtualization/windowscontainers/quick-start/quick-start-windows-10`.

Our install experience can only be described as awful. Once you've started it, you'll get no feedback—not even when it finishes! You'll have to add your user account into the Docker-users local group. (The installation creates the group but doesn't add you to it!) If you're not in the group, Docker for Windows won't start. Once you've added yourself to the group, either log off and log on or restart the machine. We recommend restarting.

The Docker installation procedure will create a VM switch called DockerNAT with a switch type of Internal.

You'll have to start Docker for Windows manually, the first time you use it. Docker should start automatically on subsequent machine restarts.

Docker for Windows is configured to run Linux containers by default! To switch the default to Windows containers, run this command:

```
PS> & 'C:\Program Files\Docker\Docker\DockerCli.exe' -SwitchDaemon
```

If you then click on the Docker icon (whale shape) in the notification area, you'll see something like Figure 17-1. You can use the switching option on the menu, to switch between Windows and Linux containers, if you don't want to use the command line.

Figure 17-1. *Docker for Windows pop-up from notification area*

Sometimes things go wrong and you may have to become more involved in the installation process.

Troubleshooting the Installation Process

You may experience problems when installing the Docker packages. In our case, we saw the following index download:

```
VERBOSE: Downloading https://dockermsft.blob.core.windows.net/
dockercontainer/DockerMsftIndex.json
```

Then we hit a warning.

WARNING: Cannot verify the file SHA256. Deleting the file.

The install then terminated with an object not found error.

```
Install-Package : Cannot find path
 'C:\Users\Richard\AppData\Local\Temp\2\DockerMsftProviderInsider\Docker-
17-06-0-ce.zip' because it does not exist.
```

You could try to use Save-Package, but we got a similar error. This seems to a be a common issue discussed in the following thread: https://github.com/OneGet/MicrosoftDockerProvider/issues/15.

A modified version of the workaround from that thread resolves the issue. First, download the index file.

```
PS>  Start-BitsTransfer -Source https://dockermsft.blob.core.windows.net/
dockercontainer/DockerMsftIndex.json -Destination c:\source
```

Then convert to a PowerShell object.

```
PS>  $dv = Get-Content -Path  c:\source\DockerMsftIndex.json |
ConvertFrom-Json
```

You can see the versions available.

```
PS>  $dv.versions
```

Extract the required version.

```
PS>  $dv.versions.'17.06.0-ce'
```

```
date   : 2017-07-10T16:35:52
url    : https://dockermsft.blob.core.windows.net/dockercontainer/docker-
         17-06-0-ce.zip
size   : 16277800
notes  : This is the latest CE version of docker
sha256 : 3D27360A11A3A627AAC9C6D73EB32D4A9B6DCCA6BCB4B2C7A5FCD9D2E0EC6C82
```

Now you can download the zip file.

```
PS> Start-BitsTransfer -Source "https://dockermsft.blob.core.windows.net/
dockercontainer/docker-17-06-0-ce.zip" -Destination C:\source\docker.zip
```

Unblock the file, just in case.

```
PS> Unblock-File -Path C:\Source\docker.zip
```

Check the file hash.

```
PS> $dv.versions.'17.06.0-ce'.sha256
3D27360A11A3A627AAC9C6D73EB32D4A9B6DCCA6BCB4B2C7A5FCD9D2E0EC6C82
PS> Get-FileHash -Path C:\Source\docker.zip | Format-List
Algorithm : SHA256
Hash      :
3D27360A11A3A627AAC9C6D73EB32D4A9B6DCCA6BCB4B2C7A5FCD9D2E0EC6C82
Path      : C:\Source\docker.zip
```

They look to be the same, but to save wear and tear on your eyeballs, use the following:

```
PS> $dv.versions.'17.06.0-ce'.sha256 -eq (Get-FileHash -Path C:\Source\
docker.zip).hash
True
```

Now copy docker.zip to the folder Install-Package was trying to use.

```
PS> Copy-Item -Path C:\source\docker.zip -Destination C:\Users\Richard\
AppData\Local\Temp\2\DockerMsftprovider\ -Force
```

Notice the 2 in the path. Not sure why that's there, but it seems to be necessary. Move into the folder.

```
PS> Push-Location -Path C:\Users\Richard\AppData\Local\Temp\2\
DockerMsftProvider\
```

Rename it.

```
PS> Copy-Item -Path .\docker.zip -Destination .\Docker-17-06-0-ce.zip
```

The instructions say to rename the zip file, but use Copy-Item instead of Rename-Item. It's because Install-package will delete the zip file when it's completed. This way, you have the original available, if you need it. You can now install the package.

PS> Install-Package -Name docker -ProviderName DockerMsftProviderInsider
-Verbose -RequiredVersion 17.06.0-ce

Because the download file exists, the save is skipped. The hash verification works, and Docker is installed. The installation of Docker also enables the containers feature. The installation output is shown in Figure 17-2.

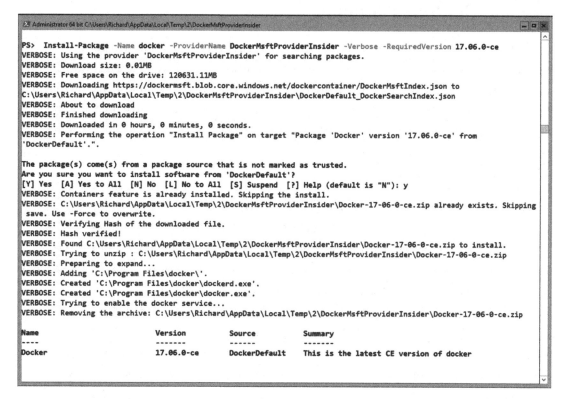

Figure 17-2. *Installing the Docker package*

Restart the VM to finish the installation and start the Docker service.

You've spent a lot of time covering the installation options, but given the differences in procedure between the various options, it's important that you get the installation correct. Now that installation is out of the way, it's time to create your first container.

Your First Container

To create your first container, you need to do three things:

- Find a container image.

- Download a container image.

- Create the container.

First things first. How do you find a container image?

Finding Container Images

Earlier in the chapter, we said that the same OS kernel version and configuration are required for the host and its Windows Server containers. If you try to run a container with a kernel that doesn't match the host, you'll get an error. For example, trying to run a Windows Server 1709 Nano server container on a Windows Server 2019 host will result in the following error:

```
PS> docker run microsoft/nanoserver:1709 cmd /C echo Hello World
C:\Program Files\Docker\docker.exe: Error response from daemon: container
8f405dd893a7a06420211e81ca011f320da852b8d703057f4b933e7bf988fb2a
encountered an error during CreateContainer: failure in a Windows system
call: The container operating system does not match the host operating
system. (0xc0370101) extra info: {"SystemType":"Container","Name":"8f405dd8
93a7a06420211e81ca011f320da852b8d703057f4b933e7bf988fb2a",
"Owner":"docker","VolumePath":"\\\\?\\Volume{fa5bd6a2-697d-4869-bbd1-
029b09c1212f}","IgnoreFlushesDuringBoot":true,"LayerFolderPath":"C:\\
ProgramData\\docker\\windowsfilter\\8f405dd893a7a06420211e81ca011f320da8
52b8d703057f4b933e7bf988fb2a","Layers":[{"ID":"14866e0f-664e-5cf2-addd-
f72ac965a324","Path":"C:\\ProgramData\\docker\\windowsfilter\\7f8cc761ef5db
9475434bfd16b1e15bbcc6d5c703240de8520c9414ea00009eb"},{"ID":"f70855d9-c01f-
5743-a674-12b1f1b85d27","Path":"C:\\ProgramData\\docker\\windowsfilter\\8d
5844dd3bcde0ca32bd65f79c7359508a338f15950d8bfe3773b56e7fc2fabf"}],"HostNam
e":"8f405dd893a7","HvPartition":false,"EndpointList":["ABCA108E-710A-4ECF-
8634-1D51DC3D9FBC"],"AllowUnqualifiedDNSQuery":true}.
```

If you need to run a container that doesn't match the host, you must use Hyper-V isolation. There is an additional restriction that the host must be a later version of the kernel than the container. You can't run a container based on a Windows Server 1709 kernel on a Windows Server 2016 host, even in Hyper-V isolation mode. Windows 10 can run any flavor of the container OS image as Hyper-V containers. Tables 17-2 and 17-3 list the supported container OS versions on the various host OSs that are available.

Table 17-2. *Supported Host and Container Operating System versions—Windows Server Host*

Container Operating System	Host Operating System			
	Windows Server 2016	Windows Server 1709	Windows Server 1803	Windows Server 2019
Windows Server 2016	Supported Windows Server or Hyper-V isolation	Supported Hyper-V isolation only	Supported Hyper-V isolation only	Supported Hyper-V isolation only
Windows Server 1709	Not supported	Supported. Windows Server or Hyper-V isolation	Not supported	Not supported
Windows Server 1803	Not supported	Not supported	Supported Windows Server or Hyper-V isolation	Supported Hyper-V isolation only
Windows Server 2019	Not supported	Not supported	Not supported	Supported Windows Server or Hyper-V isolation

Table 17-3. *Supported Host and Container OS Versions—Windows 10 Host*

Container Operating System	Host Operating System		
	Windows 10 1609 or 1703	Windows 10 1709	Windows 10 1803
Windows Server 2016	Supported Hyper-V isolation only	Supported Hyper-V isolation only	Supported Hyper-V isolation only
Windows Server 1709	Not supported	Supported Hyper-V isolation only	Supported Hyper-V isolation only
Windows Server 1803	Not supported	Not supported	Supported Hyper-V isolation only
Windows Server 2019	Not supported	Not supported	Not supported

The matrices presented in Tables 17-2 and 17-3 will continue to change for two reasons:

- New versions of Windows 10 and Windows Server are released approximately every six months. This will add an additional column to the tables.

- SAC releases have an 18-month life cycle. As older versions are withdrawn, columns will be removed from the tables.

You must remember the following rules regarding host and container OS versions:

- Windows Server can run a container as a Windows container if, and only if, the container OS image version matches the host version. As an example, Windows Server 1803 can only run container images with a Windows Server 1803 OS as Windows containers.

- Windows server can run *earlier* versions of a container OS image as Hyper-V containers. Windows Server 1803 can run Windows Server 1709 and Windows Server 2016 container images as Hyper-V containers, for example.

- A Windows Server host can't run a container using an OS image from a later version container OS image, for example, Windows Server 1709 can't run a Windows 1803 container image.

- Windows 10 can only run Hyper-V containers that match or predate the Windows 10 version number. For example, Windows 10 1709 can run Windows Server 2016 and Windows Server 1709 containers but not Windows Server 1803.

In addition, there are some restrictions on the types of containers that can be used, depending on the host OS. These are detailed in Table 17-4.

Table 17-4. *Type Container Available, Based on Host Operating System*

Host Operating System	Windows Server Container	Hyper-V Container
Windows Server 2016 (Standard or Datacenter)	Server Core or Nano server	Server Core or Nano server
Windows Server 1709 (Standard or Datacenter)	Server Core or Nano server	Server Core or Nano server
Windows Server 1709 (Standard or Datacenter)	Server Core or Nano server	Server Core or Nano server
Windows Server 2019 (Standard or Datacenter)	Server Core or Nano server	Server Core or Nano server
Nano server (Windows 2016 ONLY)	Nano server	Server Core or Nano server
Windows 10 Pro or Enterprise	Not available	Server Core or Nano server

Note   We expect that these rules will continue to work beyond Windows Server 2019.

With the background information out of the way, you'll need to know where to look to find your container OS images.

The answer is the Docker Hub. Microsoft has embraced the Docker ecosystem and made their container images available through Docker's portal: `https://hub.docker.com/`. The Docker Hub directs you to the Docker Store as the new place to find container images, but at the time of writing, the Docker Hub was still the primary point for finding container images.

Note   You'll need to create an account on the Docker Hub to get the most from it.

If you click on Explore of the Docker Hub home page, you'll find a list of vendor repositories to browse through. The URL for the Microsoft repository is `https://hub.docker.com/r/microsoft/`, if you want to shortcut the process. On the first page of the Microsoft repository, you'll find the `nanoserver` and `windowsservercore` images. The Server Core images are shown in Figure 17-3.

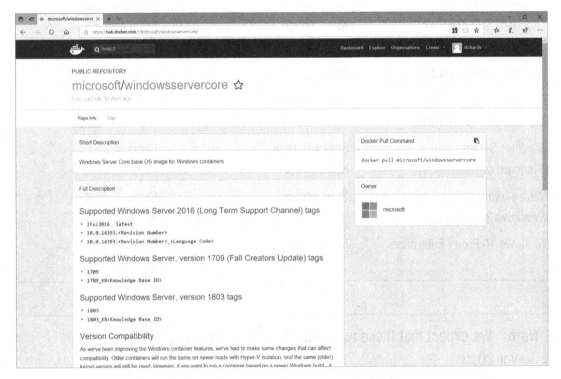

Figure 17-3. *Microsoft Server Core repository on the Docker Hub*

The page shown in Figure 17-3 lists versions of the Server Core container images for Windows Server 2016, Windows Server 1709, and Windows Server 1803. The Windows Insider Preview images are treated separately. The command to download the images is supplied at the right-hand side of the page. The required container image is stated as

```
<container repository>:<tag>
```

As examples, the following commands will pull different versions of the Server Core container images:

```
PS>  docker pull microsoft/windowsservercore
PS>  docker pull microsoft/windowsservercore:1709
PS>  docker pull microsoft/windowsservercore:1803
```

The commands will pull a Windows Server 2016, Windows Server 1709, and Windows Server 1803 image respectively. The repository is Microsoft/windowsservercore and the optional tags are 1709 and 1803. You can view the available options for a container image in the Docker Hub. Navigate to the appropriate repository and click Tags.

If you want to use the Insider Preview images, use the following command:

```
PS>  docker pull microsoft/windowsservercore-insider
```

You're pulling the previews from a different repository.

Note   The Insider images should be used only for development and testing. They are part of the Insider program and, therefore, subject to change.

One thing to think carefully about when pulling base images is the purpose of the container. Nano server images are smaller but have less functionality than a Server Core image. The following have been removed from Nano server images:

- Servicing stack

- .NET core

- PowerShell and WMI

- Administrator accounts

Windows Server Core will provide the full .NET framework. The size of the images is shown in Table 17-5.

Table 17-5. *Indicative Sizes of Container Operating System Images*

Operating System	Nano Server Container Image	Server Core Container Image
Windows Server 2019	236MB	3.42GB
Windows Server 1803	337MB	4.76GB
Windows Server 1709	329MB	5.58GB
Windows 2016	1.1GB	10.4GB

As you can see from Table 17-5, Microsoft is working to decrease the size of the base OS container image with each release.

ABOVE AND BEYOND

Microsoft has stated that a new type of container image will be introduced with Windows Server 2019: `https://blogs.technet.microsoft.com/virtualization/2018/06/27/insider-preview-windows-container-image/`.

The new image option will contain API dependencies that aren't in the Server Core or Nano server images. This means the option will have more functionality, including proofing support and graphics support, but will be bigger.

We'll be using the Server Core and Nano server images in the rest of the book.

You can also search for images from the command line, as follows:

```
PS> docker search microsoft/nanoserver
NAME                                DESCRIPTION
microsoft/dotnet                    Official images for .NET Core
microsoft/mssql-server-linux        Official images for
Microsoft microsoft/aspnet          ASP.NET is an open source
microsoft/aspnetcore                Official images for running
microsoft/windowsservercore         Windows Server Core base OS
microsoft/nanoserver                Windows Server Nano Server base
```

```
mono                              Mono is an open source
microsoft/iis                     Internet Information Services
microsoft/aspnetcore-build        Official images for building
```

`<output truncated>`

You get 25 images returned by default. If you need more, or less, images try the limit parameter (we're not going to show the output of every search to conserve space in the book).

```
PS> docker search microsoft/nanoserver --limit 100
```

The number of images you ask for must be in the range 1–100. Some of the images returned will be from Microsoft, and others from individuals.

Note   Trust is an issue when using images from the Docker Hub, as with any online repository. Any container image you use from the Docker Hub should be rigorously tested in your environment before use.

You could filter for "official" images.

```
PS> docker search --filter "is-official=true" microsoft/nanoserver
```

In reality, the `search` option in the Docker command-line utility doesn't appear to have evolved to match the growth of the Docker ecosystem. In reality, it's not useful for any practical searches, and you're better off using the browser.

Now that you know how to find your container images, it's time to download them.

Downloading Container Images

You saw examples of the commands used to pull container images from the Docker Hub in the previous section. When you issue the command, you'll see progress bars as the download proceeds. When the download completes, you should see a message something like this:

```
PS> docker pull microsoft/nanoserver-insider
Using default tag: latest
latest: Pulling from microsoft/nanoserver-insider
```

```
4a33601959f6: Pull complete
Digest: sha256:4218849128c348b5f5aebcc615c9081fb0b05bc349cdcbdb8ef2267d0ba516fa
Status: Downloaded newer image for microsoft/nanoserver-insider:latest
```

Based on what you've learned so far, you'll see that the following commands pull three images, based on Windows Server 1803:

```
PS> docker pull microsoft/nanoserver:1803
PS> docker pull microsoft/windowsservercore:1803
PS> docker pull microsoft/iis: windowsservercore-1803
```

Note   The preceding 1803 tagged images will be used in the rest of the book. If you're using Windows Server 2016 or Windows Server 1709, substitute the appropriate image names.

When your downloads are complete, you can inspect the images you have installed on the host.

```
PS> docker images
REPOSITORY                        TAG                         SIZE
microsoft/iis                     windowsservercore-1803      4.98GB
microsoft/windowsservercore       1803                        4.76GB
microsoft/nanoserver              1803                        337MB

<Image Id and Created columns removed for brevity>
```

Note the tag for the microsoft/iis image. When you download the IIS image, you'll only download about 94MB, if you have the Server Core image already downloaded.

```
PS> docker pull microsoft/iis:windowsservercore-1803
windowsservercore-1803: Pulling from microsoft/iis
d9e8b01179bf: Already exists
e30fefc566f7: Already exists
e35a364bea7e: Downloading [============================>  ]  76.09MB/93.8MB
e3f2dc22a332: Download complete
e94ecb3c49e7: Download complete
```

The IIS specifics will be merged with the base image, to produce the final image.

When downloading, if you get an error such as `Error response from daemon: Get https://registry-1.docker.io/v2/: dial tcp: lookup registry-1.docker.io: no such host` or an indication of a time-out, then try stopping and restarting the Docker service. Attempt the download again in a new instance of PowerShell or cmd.

You've found your images and downloaded them. It's time to create a container.

Creating a Container

One thing that confuses many people when they start using containers is that when running a container, if the application in the container stops, so does the container. That also means that you can't just start a container as you would a VM. The container has to do something! So, let's fall back on a developer favorite—Hello World.

```
PS> docker run microsoft/nanoserver:1803 cmd /C echo Hello World!
Hello World!
```

```
PS> docker run microsoft/nanoserver-insider cmd /C echo Hello World!
Hello World!
```

In both cases, you're starting a container, based on the stated image, and telling the container to run `cmd.exe` and echo `Hello World!` The output is automatically returned to your console, and the container stops. These containers are running as Windows Server containers.

Note   On Windows Server 2019 Insider Preview, we had to install Hyper-V, after enabling nested virtualization on the VM, to enable containers to run.

You'll be using the `docker run` command extensively. It's worth reading the full documentation at `https://docs.docker.com/engine/reference/commandline/run/`.

You can view the existing containers on your system (the `-a` is needed to view stopped containers).

```
PS> docker ps -a
CONTAINER ID    IMAGE                               COMMAND
CREATED              STATUS                             PORTS     NAMES

d1f85fa76eff    microsoft/windowsservercore:1803    "cmd /C echo Hello W..."
5 minutes ago        Exited (0) 4 minutes ago                sharp_booth

3424ae74d52e    microsoft/nanoserver:1803           "cmd /C echo Hello W..."
6 minutes ago        Exited (0) 5 minutes ago                eager_tesla
```

The display is wrapped, unfortunately, but you should be able to follow it. Docker will automatically assign the container ID and the name. The container ID is the shortened version, as you'll see later. The name is random!

There isn't an easy way to rerun a container that specifically runs a command and stops. You'll have to manually remove the containers.

```
PS> docker rm d1f85fa76eff
d1f85fa76eff
PS> docker rm 3424ae74d52e
3424ae74d52e
```

Later in the chapter, you'll be running containers that don't automatically exit. You'll learn then how to stop and restart them.

If your container will just run a command and then exit, it'll save you time, if you automatically clean up the container by using the –rm flag.

```
PS> docker run --rm  microsoft/nanoserver:1803 cmd /C echo Hello World
Hello World
```

The containers you've run so far have all been Windows containers. It's time to investigate Hyper-V containers.

Running Hyper-V Containers

You learned earlier that you could run containers as Windows containers (share OS kernels with host) or Hyper-V containers (have their own isolated kernel). There are three practical reasons for running Hyper-V containers.

- They ensure application and OS isolation.

- They can run a container image version that predates the host OS version.

- The host is Windows 10.

You might think that using Windows 10 as a host isn't a good idea, but in reality, you can develop and test the container on your workstation and then move the container to a production host, where it could run as a Windows or Hyper-V container, depending on the scenario.

A container is run in Hyper-V isolation mode by using the `--isolation=hyperv` parameter.

```
PS> docker run --rm  --isolation=hyperv  microsoft/nanoserver:1803 cmd
/C echo Hello World!
Hello World!
```

```
PS> docker run --rm  --isolation=hyperv  microsoft/windowsservercore:1803
cmd /C echo Hello World!
Hello World!
```

Note that in these examples, you're also removing the container after execution. One way to illustrate the difference between running a container as a Windows Server container and a Hyper-V isolation container is to view the processes at work when a container is run. Let's start by running a long-running process in a Windows Server container.

```
PS>  docker run -d microsoft/windowsservercore:1803 ping localhost -t
b04fc7cdfe98a34f6687e0b4cf65a0013aa170e074b98093a5e088542057969c
```

This starts a continuous ping process. The `-d` (`-detach`) parameter runs the container in the background and prints the container ID to the screen. Note that you get the long version of the container id.

You can view the processes in the container.

```
PS>  docker top
b04fc7cdfe98a34f6687e0b4cf65a0013aa170e074b98093a5e088542057969c
Name                    PID             CPU                Private Working
Set
smss.exe                3268            00:00:00.125       274.4kB
csrss.exe               3892            00:00:00.265       1.008MB
wininit.exe             1404            00:00:00.109       1.04MB
services.exe            1280            00:00:00.421       1.987MB
lsass.exe               2592            00:00:00.234       2.359MB
fontdrvhost.exe         3264            00:00:00.046       942.1kB
svchost.exe             3584            00:00:00.078       1.184MB
svchost.exe             3384            00:00:00.140       1.372MB
svchost.exe             3220            00:00:00.093       1.032MB
svchost.exe             2764            00:00:00.343       4.854MB
svchost.exe             3672            00:00:00.843       3.002MB
svchost.exe             1980            00:00:00.031       1.745MB
svchost.exe             3692            00:00:02.671       2.142MB
svchost.exe             3404            00:00:00.015       385kB
CExecSvc.exe            3980            00:00:00.015       782.3kB
svchost.exe             3480            00:00:00.453       4.465MB
PING.EXE                2844            00:00:00.015       565.2kB
```

Note PING.EXE with a PID of 2844. You can also see that from the host.

```
PS>  Get-Process pi*

Handles  NPM(K)    PM(K)     WS(K)      CPU(s)      Id  SI ProcessName
-------  ------    -----     -----      ------      --  -- -----------
     79       6      852      3560        0.02    2844   3 PING
```

If you've got this far, you'll notice that there is nothing visible to indicate that a
container is running on the host. To view your container, use the following code:

```
PS>  docker container ls
CONTAINER ID IMAGE                       COMMAND              NAMES
b04fc7cdfe98 microsoft/wind…ore:1803 "ping localhost -t" admiring_bohr
```

We've removed the middle part of the output, so that the display fits on the page. The name is created, at random, by Docker. You can stop a running container by using its ID.

```
PS> docker container stop b04fc7cdfe98
b04fc7cdfe98
```

Now let's repeat this exercise with a Hyper-V isolation container.

```
PS> docker run -d  --isolation=hyperv  microsoft/windowsservercore:1803
ping localhost -t
09195cc8ed2ecb27abe68228cad2e013e4ddb41d127393c3ff1074dbfa61678a
```

Let's view the container processes.

```
PS> docker top
09195cc8ed2ecb27abe68228cad2e013e4ddb41d127393c3ff1074dbfa61678a
```

Name	PID	CPU	Private Working Set
smss.exe	904	00:00:02.375	270.3kB
csrss.exe	940	00:00:00.640	1.061MB
wininit.exe	996	00:00:00.187	1.09MB
services.exe	244	00:00:00.593	2.068MB
lsass.exe	300	00:00:00.578	3.379MB
svchost.exe	620	00:00:06.468	1.442MB
svchost.exe	1040	00:00:00.156	1.155MB
fontdrvhost.exe	1060	00:00:00.109	946.2kB
svchost.exe	1176	00:00:00.359	1.049MB
svchost.exe	1200	00:00:00.531	4.989MB
svchost.exe	1248	00:00:01.046	3.117MB
svchost.exe	1268	00:00:00.109	1.753MB
svchost.exe	1356	00:00:00.468	1.954MB
svchost.exe	1488	00:00:00.953	6.111MB
CExecSvc.exe	1516	00:00:00.046	774.1kB
svchost.exe	1572	00:00:00.078	401.4kB
PING.EXE	1872	00:00:00.031	593.9kB

The ping process is visible inside the container but isn't visible to the host.

```
PS> Get-Process PI*
PS>
```

What you will find is that an instance of the virtual machine worker process (VMWP) is started for the container. Before the container started, this was the situation:

```
PS> Get-Process vmwp | select Id, Starttime

   Id StartTime
   -- ---------
 7420 24/07/2018 14:30:38
 7548 24/07/2018 20:53:38
 7604 24/07/2018 14:21:37
 7832 24/07/2018 20:54:06
 8340 24/07/2018 14:27:38
12944 24/07/2018 14:24:37
```

After the container started, a new instance—Id 10648—is visible.

```
PS> Get-Process vmwp | select Id, Starttime

   Id StartTime
   -- ---------
 7420 24/07/2018 14:30:38
 7548 24/07/2018 20:53:38
 7604 24/07/2018 14:21:37
 7832 24/07/2018 20:54:06
 8340 24/07/2018 14:27:38
10648 24/07/2018 21:17:11
12944 24/07/2018 14:24:37
```

There'll be one instance of VMWP per running VM on your Hyper-V host. Starting a container in Hyper-V isolation mode will also spawn a new instance of the VMWP.

You started the containers in this section in detached mode. You must explicitly stop and then remove them.

```
PS> docker stop 09195cc8ed2e
09195cc8ed2e
PS> docker rm 09195cc8ed2e
09195cc8ed2e
```

You've learned how to create containers, but you've only connected to them from the host. You must learn how to attach a container to your network, so that the application can be accessed from any client.

Container Networking

Docker makes changes to your networking configuration when you install it on a Windows machine (physical or VM) that'll become a container host. We'll start by explaining those changes, what they mean, and how to use and then examine the options you have for networking containers.

Default Container Network

Docker adds a virtual network adapter (NIC) to the machine on which its installed.

```
PS> Get-NetAdapter | select Name, InterfaceDescription, ifIndex, LinkSpeed

Name                InterfaceDescription                    ifIndex LinkSpeed
----                --------------------                    ------- ---------
Wifi                Microsoft Hyper-V Network Adapter #2          9 130 Mbps
vEthernet (nat)     Hyper-V Virtual Ethernet Adapter              7 10 Gbps
LAN                 Microsoft Hyper-V Network Adapter             4 100 Mbps
```

In this case, the adapter vEthernet (nat) is added to the machine. Note the description of the interface and the Link Speed compared to the standard NICs. An address is assigned.

```
PS> Get-NetIPAddress -InterfaceIndex 7

IPAddress       : 172.21.128.1
InterfaceIndex  : 7
InterfaceAlias  : vEthernet (nat)
AddressFamily   : IPv4
Type            : Unicast
PrefixLength    : 20
PrefixOrigin    : Manual
SuffixOrigin    : Manual
```

```
AddressState       : Preferred
ValidLifetime      : Infinite ([TimeSpan]::MaxValue)
PreferredLifetime  : Infinite ([TimeSpan]::MaxValue)
SkipAsSource       : False
PolicyStore        : ActiveStore
```

We're only showing the IPv4 data, for brevity. An IPv6 address and configuration is also assigned. The prefix length of 20 translates to a subnet mask of 255.255.240.0, if you prefer that approach. Table 17-6 lists the prefixes you'll be likely to see and the number of containers you could theoretically run on the resultant network.

Table 17-6. *Network Prefix, Subnet Mask, and Number of Containers per Network*

Prefix	Subnet Mask	IP Addresses	Containers
20	255.255.240.0	4096	4094
21	255.255.248.0	2048	2046
22	255.255.252.0	1024	1022
23	255.255.254.0	512	510
24	255.255.255.0	256	254

The address 172.22.80.1 is part of the 172.16.0.0/12 private address space (see https://technet.microsoft.com/en-us/library/cc958825.aspx).

You can also use view the container-related network information, by using the following PowerShell commands. On Windows Server 2016 or Windows 10 (1603 or 1703), they are

```
PS>  Get-ContainerNetwork | Format-List *

Name              : nat
SubnetPrefix      : {172.24.240.0/20}
Gateways          : {172.24.240.1}
Id                : a1a1084c-3de6-4cd3-ab9a-f2cc8852866a
Mode              : NAT
NetworkAdapterName :
SourceMac         :
```

```
DNSServers        :
DNSSuffix         :
IsDeleted         : False
```

Get-ContainerNetwork is in the Containers module, which has four cmdlets for working with container networks.

On Windows Server 1709 and Windows 10 (1709) or later versions, use the HostNetworkingService module:

```
PS> Get-HnsNetwork

ActivityId              : cde5c3a5-9554-4c0a-ab33-c6559bb7f158
AutomaticDNS            : True
CurrentEndpointCount    : 0
Extensions              : {@{Id=e7c3b2f0-f3c5-48df-af2b-10fed6d72e7a;
                          IsEnabled=False;
                          Name=Microsoft Windows Filtering Platform},
                          @{Id=e9b59cfa-2be1-4b21-828f-b6fbdbddc017;
                          IsEnabled=False; Name=Microsoft Azure
                          VFP Switch Extension},
                          @{Id=ea24cd6c-d17a-4348-9190-09f0d5be83dd;
                          IsEnabled=False;
                          Name=Microsoft NDIS Capture}}
ID                      : a1e00523-7cff-4522-b3a5-03d17aecbd47
LayeredOn               : e449a1e3-e658-4edc-81c2-97945a97f52b
MacPools                : {@{EndMacAddress=00-15-5D-E2-DF-FF;
                          StartMacAddress=00-15-5D-E2-D0-00}}
MaxConcurrentEndpoints  : 1
Name                    : nat
Policies                : {}
Resources               : @{AllocationOrder=2; Allocators=System.Object[];
                          ID=cde5c3a5-9554-4c0a-ab33-c6559bb7f158;
                          PortOperationTime=0; State=1;
                          SwitchOperationTime=0; VfpOperationTime=0;
                          parentId=40037bd3-3e8d-4384-89ef-ccbccf47482a}
State                   : 1
Subnets                 : {@{AddressPrefix=172.21.128.0/20;
                          GatewayAddress=172.21.128.1}}
```

```
TotalEndpoints      : 8
Type                : nat
Version             : 30064771074
```

Before we go any further, we'd better explain the term *NAT*, which is used in the name of the adapter and as the network type or mode. *NAT* stands for "Network Address Translation." It's a technique in networking wherein an internal address, in this case, in the 172.22.80.0/20 range, is mapped to an address and port on the machine's network adapter, so that the container can communicate with machines external to the host. We'll explain this further with an example.

When you run a container, an IP address is automatically assigned from the range defined in the container network.

```
PS> docker run --rm microsoft/nanoserver:1803 ipconfig

Windows IP Configuration

Ethernet adapter vEthernet (Ethernet):

   Connection-specific DNS Suffix  . : manticore.org
   Link-local IPv6 Address . . . . . : fe80::c1c6:9e8a:d547:5d89%21
   IPv4 Address. . . . . . . . . . . : 172.21.134.91
   Subnet Mask . . . . . . . . . . . : 255.255.240.0
   Default Gateway . . . . . . . . . : 172.21.128.1
```

You'll recognize that the IP address of the default gateway is the same as the network adapter Docker automatically installs.

Now let's investigate inside the container, using the IIS container, for a change:

```
PS> $cid = docker run -d microsoft/iis:windowsservercore-1803
```

You've captured the container ID in a PowerShell variable, to make life easier. You can use the variable to complete Docker commands, for example:

```
PS> docker top $cid
```

Name	PID	CPU	Private Working Set
smss.exe	2400	00:00:00.296	266.2kB
csrss.exe	2308	00:00:00.328	1.008MB
wininit.exe	2860	00:00:00.078	1.016MB

```
services.exe          2616      00:00:00.421        2.142MB
lsass.exe             2548      00:00:00.234        2.511MB
svchost.exe           2068      00:00:00.203        2.183MB
fontdrvhost.exe       2848      00:00:00.031        942.1kB
CExecSvc.exe          3156      00:00:00.031        794.6kB
svchost.exe           3212      00:00:02.421        3.654MB
ServiceMonitor.exe    3588      00:00:00.031        626.7kB
<truncated for bevity>
```

You can create a PowerShell remoting session in the container (we'll cover using PowerShell with containers in more detail later in the chapter).

```
PS>  $s = New-PSSession -ContainerId $cid
PS>  $s | Format-List

ComputerType          : Container
ComputerName          : 592448b31023dbcbd1abcfd8dc97a9e3aa402661c
                        8455a7bf077cb4d10ebebfe
ContainerId           : 592448b31023dbcbd1abcfd8dc97a9e3aa402661c8455a7b
                        f077cb4d10ebebfe
VMName                :
VMId                  :
ConfigurationName     :
InstanceId            : 9c600ec8-9d48-4fa6-9533-4cf9a8ecd993
Id                    : 1
Name                  : WinRM1
Availability          : Available
ApplicationPrivateData : {DebugMode, DebugStop, UnhandledBreakpointMode,
                        PSVersionTable...}
Runspace              : System.Management.Automation.RemoteRunspace
State                 : Opened
IdleTimeout           : -1
OutputBufferingMode   :
DisconnectedOn        :
ExpiresOn             :
```

The computer name is set to the container ID. Note that the computer type is set to Container.

You'll notice that we haven't given any credentials when creating the PowerShell remoting session. Don't let that fool you into thinking that the container is part of your AD. It isn't. Containers don't create AD objects and aren't part of your AD.

Once you have a remoting session, you can find the container's IP address.

```
PS> Invoke-Command -Session $s -ScriptBlock {Get-NetIPAddress
-AddressFamily IPv4}
```

```
IPAddress          : 172.21.142.23
InterfaceIndex     : 21
InterfaceAlias     : vEthernet (Ethernet)
AddressFamily      : IPv4
Type               : Unicast
PrefixLength       : 20
PrefixOrigin       : Manual
SuffixOrigin       : Manual
AddressState       : Preferred
ValidLifetime      : Infinite ([TimeSpan]::MaxValue)
PreferredLifetime  : Infinite ([TimeSpan]::MaxValue)
SkipAsSource       : False
PolicyStore        : ActiveStore
PSComputerName     : 592448b31023dbcbd1abcfd8dc97a9e3aa402661c8455a7b
                     f077cb4d10ebebfe
```

There is also a loop back adapter: 127.0.0.1.

You can test that the container's IP address is reachable from the container host.

```
PS> Test-Connection -ComputerName 172.21.142.23 -Count 1
```

```
Source     Destination    IPV4Address    IPV6Address   Bytes   Time(ms)
------     -----------    -----------    -----------   -----   --------
W1803CN01  172.21.142.23  92.242.132.16                32      0
```

The container's C:\ drive shows the presence of the inetpub folder—home of the web site information.

```
PS> Invoke-Command -Session $s -ScriptBlock {Get-ChildItem -Path c:\}
```

```
   Directory: C:\

Mode                LastWriteTime         Length Name
----                -------------         ------ ----
d-----        10/07/2018     23:49               inetpub
d-r---        07/07/2018     23:49               Program Files
d-----        07/07/2018     23:42               Program Files (x86)
d-r---        07/07/2018     23:50               Users
d-----        10/07/2018     23:49               Windows
-a----        12/04/2018     11:27          1894 License.txt
-a----        10/07/2018     23:49        171712 ServiceMonitor.exe
```

The IIS service is running.

```
PS>   Invoke-Command -Session $s -ScriptBlock {Get-Service -Name w3*}

Status    Name              DisplayName
------    ----              -----------
Stopped   W32Time           Windows Time
Stopped   w3logsvc          W3C Logging Service
Running   W3SVC             World Wide Web Publishing Service
```

You can also view information about the container IP address configuration, using

```
PS>   Get-HnsEndpoint

ActivityId                    : b0d098d0-d2c7-4ad2-af5e-2e25b860892e
CreateProcessingStartTime     : 131769865993844250
DNSServerList                 : 172.21.128.1,10.10.54.10
DNSSuffix                     : manticore.org
EnableInternalDNS             : True
EnableLowInterfaceMetric      : True
GatewayAddress                : 172.21.128.1
ID                            : 0cd8966f-b161-4930-ba2f-f1be37afcd1d
IPAddress                     : 172.21.142.23
MacAddress                    : 00-15-5D-E2-DF-F0
Name                          : Ethernet
Policies                      : {}
```

```
PrefixLength            : 20
Resources               : @{AllocationOrder=2;
                            Allocators=System.Object[];
                            ID=b0d098d0-d2c7-4ad2-af5e-2e25b860892e;
                            PortOperationTime=0; State=1;
                            SwitchOperationTime=0; VfpOperationTime=0;
                            parentId=cde5c3a5-9554-4c0a-ab33-c6559bb7f158}
SharedContainers        : {592448b31023dbcbd1abcfd8dc97a9e3aa402661c8455
                            a7bf077cb4d10ebebfe}
StartTime               : 131769866001296692
State                   : 2
Type                    : nat
Version                 : 30064771074
VirtualNetwork          : a1e00523-7cff-4522-b3a5-03d17aecbd47
VirtualNetworkName      : nat
```

If your container host has a GUI and, therefore, a browser, you'll be able to connect to http:// 172.21.142.23/ and view the default web site. You won't be able to ping the container or connect to the web site from another host, as the 172.21.142.23 address is only visible on the container host. You must create a mapping from the 172.21.142.23 address to the external IP address of the host, to make the web site visible on the external network.

Creating an NAT Mapping

The easiest way to create an NAT mapping is to do it when you create the container.

```
PS>  docker run -d -p 80:80  microsoft/iis:windowsservercore-1803
2bafcd69907cbd31cd1c05b8e1cc6a1ae0b9b24161d4681fbf6e2a2bd2b265fe
```

This maps port 80 (HTTP) on the container to port 80 on the external NIC. If you have to define multiple mappings, you can repeat the use of the -p parameter.

```
PS>  docker run -d -p 80:80  -p 443:443 microsoft/iis:windowsservercore-1803
810515cb1bc3956fda66e5e496b8cd69a9526076e9d8ca4fdaeabcbf9e238142
```

In this case, you're mapping port 80 (HTTP) and port 443 (HTTPS) to the corresponding port number on the external NIC. The order in which you define the ports is important. It should be -p <external port>:<container port>.

You can access the container as you would any web site, because you've mapped the HHTP port from the container directly to the external NIC. Figure 17-4 shows the container's web site being accessed from an external machine.

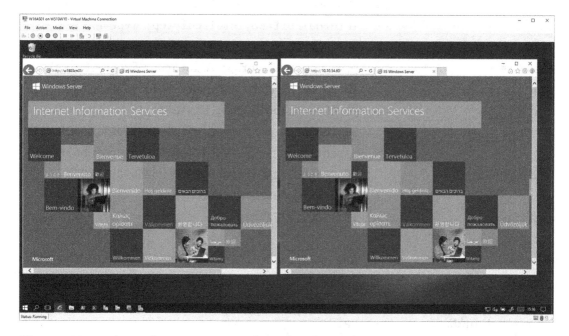

Figure 17-4. *Accessing a container-based web site from an external machine*

The instance of the browser on the left accesses the web site, using the server name http://W1803CN01, and that on the right uses the IP address http://10.10.54.60, which is the IP address of the container host.

You can view the NAT policy from the container host.

```
PS> Get-HnsEndpoint

ActivityId               : 2ec1667d-2bd1-4007-aa6c-b08df5dfc696
CreateProcessingStartTime : 131770025712630306
DNSServerList            : 172.21.128.1,10.10.54.10
DNSSuffix                : manticore.org
EnableInternalDNS        : True
EnableLowInterfaceMetric : True
```

```
GatewayAddress            : 172.21.128.1
ID                        : 77921f2b-2e1c-4cfc-89ef-0be7481380d8
IPAddress                 : 172.21.129.185
MacAddress                : 00-15-5D-E2-D5-A8
Name                      : Ethernet
Policies                  : {@{ExternalPort=443; InternalPort=443;
                            Protocol=tcp; Type=NAT}, @{ExternalPort=80;
                            InternalPort=80; Protocol=tcp; Type=NAT}}
PrefixLength              : 20
Resources                 : @{AllocationOrder=3; Allocators=System.Object[];
                            ID=2ec1667d-2bd1-4007-aa6c-b08df5dfc696;
                            PortOperationTime=0; State=1;
                            SwitchOperationTime=0; VfpOperationTime=0;
                            parentId=cde5c3a5-9554-4c0a-ab33-c6559bb7f158}
SharedContainers          : {810515cb1bc3956fda66e5e496b8cd69a9526076
                            e9d8ca4fdaeabcbf9e238142}
StartTime                 : 131770025717124293
State                     : 2
Type                      : nat
Version                   : 30064771074
VirtualNetwork            : a1e00523-7cff-4522-b3a5-03d17aecbd47
VirtualNetworkName        : nat
```

The Policies parameter shows the port mappings between the container and the external NIC.

An alternative is to use

```
PS>  docker container ls
CONTAINER ID                      IMAGE
COMMAND         CREATED                                STATUS
                      PORTS              NAMES
810515cb1bc3   microsoft/iis:windowsservercore-1803   "C:\\ServiceMonitor.e..."
16 minutes ago       Up 16 minutes      0.0.0.0:80->80/tcp, 0.0.0.0:443-
                                        >443/tcp   agitated_wright
```

The display is wrapped, because of the width of the page, but you can see the PORTS information at the beginning of the last line.

But what if you have multiple containers on the host for which you must map the same port on the external NIC, for instance, multiple containers running IIS. The answer is that you'll have to use a different port on the external NIC.

```
PS>  docker run -d -p 8080:80  -p 8043:443 microsoft/iis:windows
servercore-1803
b4e2046f85eba987a92e1b47919f176c1b7251573cf8408802e64270b0b1061b
```

In this case, you're mapping port 80 on the container to port 8080 on the external NIC. You can connect to the web site in the container, from an external machine, by using `http://W1803CN01:8080/` or `http://10.10.54.60:8080/`. You can use the same techniques as earlier to view the port mappings.

Using NAT works for a small number of containers—ideal for a development environment. NAT breaks down when you have to run many containers on a host, especially if you have to remember the port mappings to connect to the container from an external machine.

Other Network Options

By default, containers use the NAT network that's created when you install the containers feature. Other network options are available, as shown in Table 17-7.

The latest information on container networking is available at `https://docs.microsoft.com/en-us/virtualization/windowscontainers/container-networking/architecture` and subsequent pages. Surprisingly, it doesn't contain clear instructions on setting up container networks.

Table 17-7. *Container Networking Options*

Network Type	Description
Network AddressTranslation (NAT) (default)	Containers receive an IP address from the range defined when the NAT network is created. Multiple NAT networks per host are support in Windows 1709 and later versions. Port mapping is supported.
Transparent	Containers are directly connected to the physical network. IP addresses are assigned statically or via DHCP.
Overlay	For use with Docker Swarm. Containers can communicate with other containers on the same network, across multiple hosts.
L2Bridge	Container is on same IP subnet as host. Container IP addresses are assigned statically. All container end points have the same Mac address (layer-2 address translation [Mac rewrite occurs]).
L2Tunnel	This is for the Microsoft cloud stack only.

Transparent Networks

As an example of another network option, we'll show how to create a transparent network for your containers.

The first step is to identify the network adapter you'll use as the link from the host to the outside world. Then you can create the network, as follows:

```
PS> docker network create -d transparent
-o com.docker.network.windowsshim.interface="LAN"
--subnet=10.10.54.0/24 --gateway=10.10.54.1 Transparent1803
48d9c40457e0e1c64f3537b77d3076d79a0a563fdbb5ec6d914b8e1828d601c5
```

This command creates a transparent container network attached to the network adapter, named LAN. The subnet and default gateway are set. This is required if you're going to set IP addresses transparently. The final argument is the network name.

A new virtual adapter is created.

```
PS> Get-NetAdapter | Format-List Name, InterfaceDescription, ifIndex,
MacAddress, LinkSpeed

Name                 : Wifi
InterfaceDescription : Microsoft Hyper-V Network Adapter #2
ifIndex              : 9
MacAddress           : 00-15-5D-36-C9-70
LinkSpeed            : 144.5 Mbps

Name                 : vEthernet (nat)
InterfaceDescription : Hyper-V Virtual Ethernet Adapter
ifIndex              : 7
MacAddress           : 00-15-5D-E2-D6-80
LinkSpeed            : 10 Gbps

Name                 : LAN
InterfaceDescription : Microsoft Hyper-V Network Adapter
ifIndex              : 4
MacAddress           : 00-15-5D-36-C9-6F
LinkSpeed            : 100 Mbps

Name                 : vEthernet (LAN)
InterfaceDescription : Hyper-V Virtual Ethernet Adapter #4
ifIndex              : 15
MacAddress           : 00-15-5D-36-C9-6F
LinkSpeed            : 100 Mbps
```

Notice that it has the same Mac Address as the LAN adapter from which it was created. You'll have to enable Mac spoofing on the adapter in the container host. Run this on the Hyper-V host.

```
PS> Get-VMNetworkAdapter -VMName W1803CN01 |
where SwitchName -eq 'LAN' |
Set-VMNetworkAdapter -MacAddressSpoofing On
```

Now let's create a container on the new network.

```
PS> docker run -d --network Transparent1803
--ip 10.10.54.200 microsoft/iis:windowsservercore-1803
de9fc9c9c8e3b8aa5bf2b057af4e567aa6656c9c136986250a49319b932efb54
```

Your container is now on the external network with a pingable IP address. You'll be able to connect to your container from an external host using http://10.10.54.200. If you create a static DNS entry, you could connect using that name too.

Working with Containers

So far, you've learned to install the containers feature, download base images, and configure networking for containers. In this section, you'll discover how to manage containers in practice. Containers, as all objects in IT, have a defined life cycle. The ephemeral nature of containers means that they have a limited life cycle. You don't do much to modify containers, once they're running, so the life cycle becomes

- Create container.

- Run container—possibly stop and start a container.

- Remove container.

This doesn't cover all the options, though. You also must be able to modify your container images. You saw how to use PowerShell remoting to connect to a container, earlier in the chapter.

Let's start by looking a bit more at how to create and connect to your container.

Creating Containers

So far, you've created and run containers using commands such as this:

```
PS> docker run microsoft/nanoserver:1803 cmd /C echo Hello World!
Hello World!
```

This will create the container, run the command, return the results, and shut down the container.

The docker run command has the following syntax:

```
docker run [OPTIONS] IMAGE [COMMAND] [ARG...]
```

You can view the full syntax and options at `https://docs.docker.com/engine/reference/commandline/run/`.

You'll usually run in the background, but you can run containers interactively.

Interactive Containers

If you run a container interactively (by using the `-it` option), you are immediately connected to the container, as shown in Figure 17-5.

The first line in Figure 17-5 shows the process ID (PID) of the current PowerShell session as 2928. A Windows Server Core container is started. The container is started in an interactive mode by using the `-it` parameter.

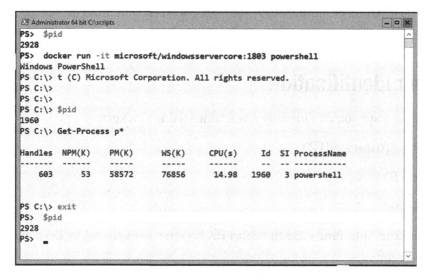

Figure 17-5. Running a container interactively

A new PowerShell session is generated within the container, and your current session is connected to it. You'll see the PowerShell start banner and a new (and different) prompt, as in Figure 17-5. The console overwriting itself seems to be a console artifact.

If you repeat the exercise of retrieving the PowerShell PID, you'll get a different result—1960, in this case. You can run PowerShell commands, and they execute within the container. Getting the PowerShell process only shows the process within the container—isolated environment—though there are four instances of PowerShell running on the host at that time, including the one in the container.

You can use the exit command to close the container instance of PowerShell, which will also shut down the container. Check the PID, and you'll see that you're back in your original PowerShell session.

TRY IT YOURSELF

Experiment with running containers interactively. What would stop you from accessing a container interactively?

This approach works when you want to work interactively with a container, but what about a situation in which you have multiple containers on a host? You must be able to pick and choose which containers to work with, meaning you must be able to identify your containers.

Container Identification

There are three ways you can identify a container using Docker:

- Short (truncated) ID

- Full ID

- Name

Many Docker commands use the short ID. It's what's displayed by Docker.

```
PS> docker ps --format "{{.ID}} {{.Names}}"
6e788f4d6876 IIS2
```

If you need the full ID, use

```
PS> docker ps --format "{{.ID}} {{.Names}}" --no-trunc
6e788f4d68764c03b25827ff550bd67dc5a94bb00cd3c7455a4fb119f6ff9118 IIS2
```

The short ID is the first 12 characters of the full ID.

You can use the name parameter to give the container a meaningful name, rather than the random (and sometimes rather silly) name that Docker generates.

```
PS> docker run -d microsoft/iis:windowsservercore-1803
661d48c6acd417ed89af8ee11f394a0ed99f5a771cb907e5143aca128aef8016
```

```
PS> docker run -d --name IIStest microsoft/iis:windowsservercore-1803
31278e91cdc05901d3ada053d74be868ddfb1df742af0dbf7ad6be9b0816053e
```

```
PS> docker ps --format "{{.ID}} {{.Names}}"
661d48c6acd4 inspiring_hoover
31278e91cdc0 IIStest
```

It's worth assigning names to your containers, even though some Docker commands expect to work with IDs (usually the short ID), rather than container names. Container names must be unique.

TRY IT YOURSELF

Identify the containers on your machine. Which containers are stopped and which are running?

The commands you've seen so far have been to create and immediately run a container. You have the option of creating the container and running it as two separate actions.

Pre-creating Containers

The docker run command is used to create and run a container. If your container may be stopped and started a number of times, you'd be better off by pre-creating the container.

```
PS> docker create  --name IIStestC  microsoft/iis:windowsservercore-1803
88e5a2a9a3ac358fcb6c0d1583b46c7f92cd67fc22dab0a102bde28325738f6a
```

```
PS> docker ps -a --format "table {{.ID}}\t{{.Names}}\t{{.Status}}"
CONTAINER ID        NAMES                STATUS
88e5a2a9a3ac        IIStestC             Created
661d48c6acd4        inspiring_hoover     Up 45 minutes
31278e91cdc0        IIStest              Up 45 minutes
```

In this example, you're creating another instance of the IIS container but not starting it. The docker ps command uses the table option to display a header for each column. The columns are spaces using tabs (\t). Note that the long ID is supplied when the container is created, but the short ID is usually used in subsequent commands.

The newly created container can be started.

```
PS>  docker start 88e5a2a9a3ac
88e5a2a9a3ac
```

```
PS>  docker ps -a --format "table {{.ID}}\t{{.Names}}\t{{.Status}}"
CONTAINER ID        NAMES               STATUS
88e5a2a9a3ac        IIStestC            Up About a minute
661d48c6acd4        inspiring_hoover    Up About an hour
31278e91cdc0        IIStest             Up About an hour
```

TRY IT YOURSELF

Pre-create a container and then start it.

You now have three instances of your container running. The next step is to stop the containers or remove them from the host.

Stopping and Removing Containers

You can stop an individual container.

```
PS>  docker stop 88e5a2a9a3ac
88e5a2a9a3ac
```

If you need to stop all running containers, use the following:

```
PS>  docker stop $(docker ps -q)
661d48c6acd4
31278e91cdc0
```

This is the type of scenario in which PowerShell, with its ability to filter and pipe objects, would be of real benefit. Use the Docker commands you need, to quietly get the running containers to use as the input to docker stop.

Once you've stopped the containers, you can remove them.

Note   Attempting to remove a running container will generate an error.

Removing a single container relies on the container ID or name.

```
PS>  docker rm IIStestC
IIStestC
```

You can also clean up all containers.

```
PS>  docker rm $(docker ps -a -q)
661d48c6acd4
31278e91cdc0
```

You need the -a parameter on docker ps, to view non-running containers.

TRY IT YOURSELF

Stop the running containers on your system. Remove all existing containers on your system.

You've installed the container feature, downloaded container images, and created containers from those images. At some stage, you'll have to modify a container image and roll that changed image into production.

Modifying and Using Container Images

Containers are very lightweight objects and, therefore, easy to move around your environment. They are a great component to include in your DevOps procedures. In earlier sessions, you've seen containers running IIS. Modifying the web site is a common occurrence in application development.

The process we're going to follow is

- Create an IIS container on a development machine.

- Modify the web site.

- Create a container image from the modified container.

- Move the new image to our production system.

- Create a container in production from the new image.

The first step is to create the container.

Create Development Container

You can use a Windows 10 system as your development machine (using Hyper-V isolation to run your containers) or a Windows Server instance. We'll use `microsoft/iis` image as our starting point. The first step is to create a container.

```
PS>  docker run --name IISdev -d -p 80:80 microsoft/iis:windowsservercore-1803
b2585f81aa6e8585ac9f16df13605eaf6046477c55655543efb0d0c5152c5480
```

Ensure that you can connect to the web site.

Note   In reality, at this stage, you'd complete a test sequence on your web site or application.

Now that you have a working container, it's time to modify the web site.

Modify Web Site

As a quick change to your web site (we're just demonstrating concepts), modify the `iisstart.png` file (the default web site start page) to look like Figure 17-6.

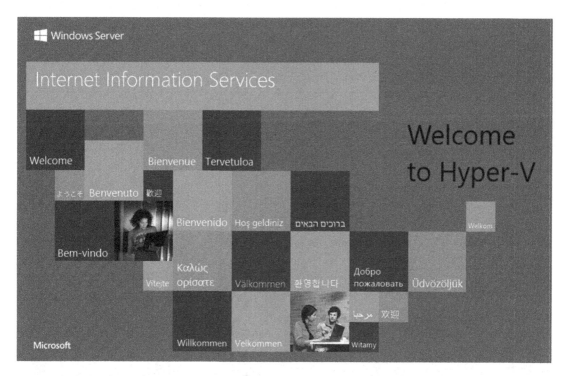

Figure 17-6. *New* `iisstart.png` *file*

Copy the replacement `iisstart.png` file into the container, using a PowerShell remoting session.

```
PS> $sc = New-PSSession -ContainerId ` b2585f81aa6e8585ac9f16df13605eaf
        6046477c55655543efb0d0c5152c5480 `
-RunAsAdministrator

PS> Copy-Item -Path C:\Source\iisstart.png `
-Destination c:\inetpub\wwwroot\ -ToSession $sc -Force

PS> Remove-PSSession $sc
```

Create a remoting session to the container, copy the file, and then remove the session. You'll have to restart IIS in the container, so the new file is used.

```
PS> docker restart IISdev
IISdev
```

Connect to the container's web site, and you should see the changed page, as shown in Figure 17-7.

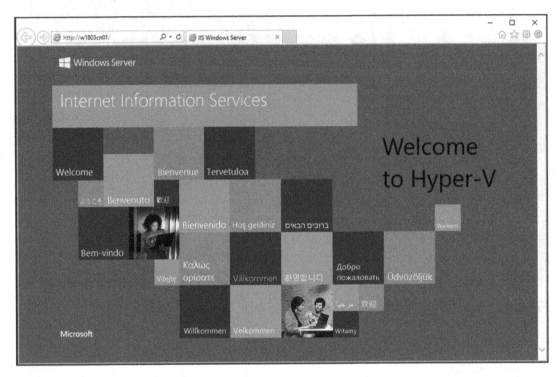

Figure 17-7. *Changed web site running in container*

The change in file survives stopping and starting the container. After the web site changes have been tested, it's time to move the change into production.

Create Container Image

Changes to containers are propagated through the organization by the use of container images. You've already seen a number of container images in use that you downloaded from the Docker Hub. In this section, you'll create an image from the IISdev container you used in the previous section.

Note   Windows doesn't support the commit of a running container. If you try, you'll get an error message!

You must to stop the container before creating an image.

```
PS> docker stop IISdev
IISdev
```

Create the image.

```
PS> docker commit IISdev prohyperv/iis:version1
sha256:c1f924e4e43435546f7e0c443d9425d71929ff0037062b3c84fbc47a5b10b0bd
```

Then check the images.

```
PS> docker images
REPOSITORY             TAG            IMAGE ID       CREATED        SIZE
prohyperv/iis          version1       c1f924e4e434   6 minutes ago  5.16GB
microsoft/iis          win..ore-1803  248afbbe0fd1   4 weeks ago    4.98GB
microsoft/win..ore     1803           fc9cd8b52f1a   4 weeks ago    4.76GB
microsoft/nanoserver   1803           3ba4e30fed90   4 weeks ago    337MB
```

Note   Windowsservercore is abbreviated to win..ore, to make the text
fit the page.

One last step is required. You have to export the image, so that it can be copied to
other machines.

```
PS> docker save prohyperv/iis:version1 --output c:\source\prohyperv_iis_
version1.tar
```

You can then copy the image to one or more production hosts. One of the easiest
ways to perform the copy is to use a PowerShell remoting session, as you've seen earlier.

Once your container image has been copied, you can use it to create new containers.

Using the New Container Image

Before you can use the new image, you must import the image.

```
PS> docker load --input c:\source\prohyperv_iis_version1.tar
b88f82691d05: Loading layer
[=====================================================>]  184.4MB/184.4MB
Loaded image: prohyperv/iis:version1
```

Once the image is imported, you can create containers. Create a container from the original IIS image and the new one.

```
PS>  docker run --name IIS1 -d -p 80:80 microsoft/
iis:windowsservercore-1803
8b18255fc3150068a25e999e3a29c284348d2dc7d8a0cb1a886574e690b88592
```

```
PS>  docker run --name IIS2 -d -p 81:80 prohyperv/iis:version1
f455230201acd26a3153d191c9bda8bcc0265ccb577224acc4dfce230a564ac1
```

The container using the original image is mapped to external port 80, and the container from the new image is mapped using port 81. This means that you can view both the original web site and the new web site, as shown in Figure 17-8.

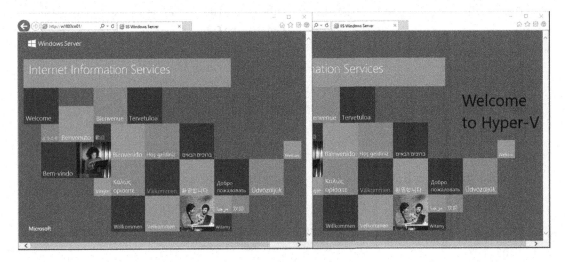

Figure 17-8. *Original and new versions of the web site*

The ability to modify running containers and create an image from that container that can be exported to other machines gives you a very fast, safe way to deploy applications in your environment. If your organization is embracing the DevOps principles, you'll find that containers can play a significant role in your application deployment strategies.

TRY IT YOURSELF

Follow the steps in this section to modify a container, create a new image, copy the image to a new machine, and create a container from the new image.

The steps involved in modifying a container and creating an image that can be used throughout the organization are manually intensive. The container images can be several gigabytes in size, leading to slow copy times. It would be useful if there were a way to automate the production of new images and reduce the size of data that had to be copied around the environment.

Automating Image Creation

The tasks you used in the previous section involved a lot of manual effort. You can use Docker files to automate the image creation process, including

- Effectively storing images as code

- Easily and accurately creating and re-creating container images

- Enabling continuous integration between container images and the development cycle

A Docker file is a text file that contains the instructions to create a new container image—using an existing base image—the commands to be run when the image is created, and the commands to be run when containers are created from the image. The Microsoft documentation for Docker files is located at `https://docs.microsoft.com/en-us/virtualization/windowscontainers/manage-docker/manage-windows-dockerfile`.

As an example, let's rework the modification of the web site that was performed manually in the previous section.

First, we must create a new IIS start image (Figure 17-9).

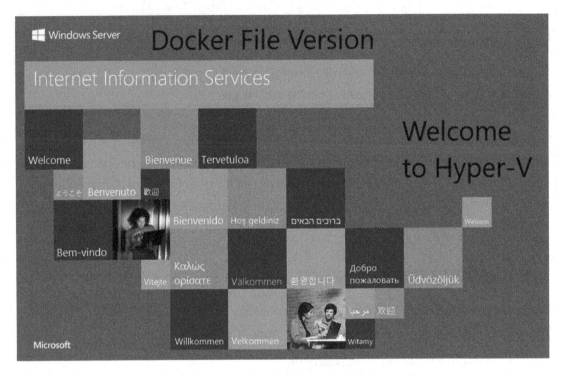

Figure 17-9. *New start image for use with Docker file*

In this version, we've added the fact that we're using a Docker file to make the differences obvious. The next task is to create a Docker file. Visual Studio Code (the recommended editor for PowerShell v6 and later versions—https://code.visualstudio.com/) works with PowerShell and many other languages, including Docker files.

The Docker file looks like this:

```
## docker file to change IIS start page
##

##  base image
FROM microsoft/iis:windowsservercore-1803

COPY iisstart.png C:/inetpub/wwwroot
```

The FROM directive instructs Docker to use the microsoft/iis:windowsservercore-1803 image as the basis of the build. The COPY command instructs the build process to copy the new version of iisstart.png into the image.

Many other tasks can be accomplished using Docker files. The Docker file reference can be found at https://docs.docker.com/engine/reference/builder/#usage.

VSCode automatically adds a .dockerfile extension to the file when you save it. The file is used to build the new image.

```
PS> docker build -f IIS2.dockerfile -t prohyperv/iis:version2.
Sending build context to Docker daemon  107.5kB
Step 1/2 : FROM  microsoft/iis:windowsservercore-1803
 ---> 248afbbe0fd1
Step 2/2 : COPY iisstart.png C:/inetpub/wwwroot
 ---> 1cb8593fb79f
Successfully built 1cb8593fb79f
Successfully tagged prohyperv/iis:version2
```

In this case, you're using a Docker file IIS2.dockerfile to build a new image called prohyperv/iis:version2. The dot at the end of the command line instructs Docker that all of the required files are in the current directory. It's recommended that you keep the Docker file and other required files together, for simplicity.

The build process is verbose, so you can see what happens. It's also quick. We recommend that you view the images as a check. The last test is to create a container from the new image.

```
PS> docker run --name IIS3 -d -p 82:80 prohyperv/iis:version2
e38a44d34b324e6c43c54f3d28f3fa434f6b3f5ac26d298d11ccffaed66ce3f9
```

Figure 17-10 shows the latest version of the web site, with the original and the version you created in the previous section.

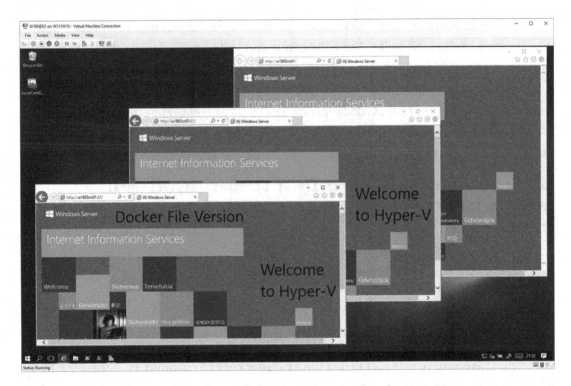

Figure 17-10. *Three generations of the containerized web site*

Once you've tested the new web site, you can copy the Docker file and any other required files to your production machine(s). This is much less data than a full image, so it is much quicker. Re-create the image, using the same docker build command. You can then create containers from the new image.

Using Docker files is a quicker and easier way to modify your container images and get the new image into production.

TRY IT YOURSELF

Follow the steps in this section to create a new image using a Docker file. Create a container from the new image. Copy the Docker file and data to another system and re-create the image and container.

The containers you've been working with throughout the book use the Windows OS. You can also run containers based on Linux.

Linux Containers on Windows

The Windows 10 Fall Creators Update and Windows Server 1709 introduced the capability of running Linux containers on Windows (see `https://docs.microsoft.com/en-us/virtualization/windowscontainers/deploy-containers/linux-containers`).

The posts in various online forums indicate that this is still an experimental technology. People are experiencing varying degrees of success. You should also note that the documentation is very poor at the time of writing. The tutorials are contradictory, and a number of them have broken links.

If you want to experiment with Linux containers on Windows, you'll have to

- Run Windows 10 Fall Creators Update or Windows Server 1709, as a minimum. We used Windows 10 1803. We recommend that you use the latest version possible of the Windows OS, as Linux containers on Windows are still an experimental feature.

- Use the latest version of Docker—18.03 or later versions.

- Enable experimental features. Open Docker Settings ➤ Daemon and check the Experimental features box.

- Switch Docker to running Linux containers (see installation section earlier in this chapter) or use `PS> & $env:ProgramFiles\Docker\Docker\dockercli.exe -SwitchDaemon`.

- Have Hyper-V installed. You'll be running the containers in Hyper-V isolation mode. If you check Hyper-V Manager, you'll find that a VM called MobyLinuxVM is running. It's used to support the containers.

There are some Linux-based containers available from Microsoft on the Docker Hub. You should be able to use `mcr.microsoft.com/powershell` or `microsoft/mssql-server-linux`. You can pull the container image as normal (see Figure 17-11).

```
PS>  docker pull mcr.microsoft.com/powershell
```

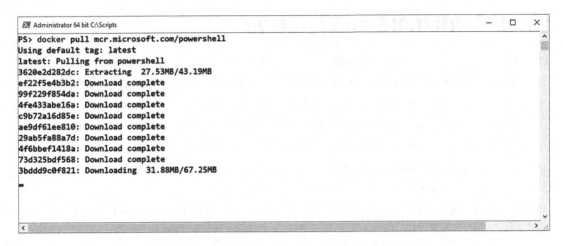

Figure 17-11. *Downloading a Linux container to Windows*

Check the image.

```
PS> docker images
REPOSITORY                        TAG              IMAGE ID
         CREATED                     SIZE
mcr.microsoft.com/powershell   latest              b761a4b9aa92
         6 days ago              320MB
```

Note the size of the image. Let's create an interactive container from the image.

```
PS> docker run --name PSTest -it mcr.microsoft.com/powershell pwsh
PowerShell v6.0.3
Copyright (c) Microsoft Corporation. All rights reserved.

https://aka.ms/pscore6-docs
Type 'help' to get help.
```

You're running the latest version of PowerShell 6.0 in a Linux container on Windows 10!

Note   If you start a Linux container, then switch back to Windows containers, your Linux container will continue to run *but* you won't be able to manage it until you switch back to Linux containers. The same is true for running Windows containers, if you switch to Linux containers. You can run Linux and Windows containers side by side, but you can only manage one or the other at a time, if you use the switching mechanism. See later in the section for an alternative approach.

View the PowerShell version information.

```
PS /> $PSVersionTable

Name                        Value
----                        -----
PSVersion                   6.0.3
PSEdition                   Core
GitCommitId                 v6.0.3
OS                          Linux 4.9.93-linuxkit-aufs #1 SMP Wed Jun 6
                            16:55:56 UTC 2018
Platform                    Unix
PSCompatibleVersions        {1.0, 2.0, 3.0, 4.0...}
PSRemotingProtocolVersion   2.3
SerializationVersion        1.1.0.1
WSManStackVersion           3.0
```

Check the Linux information.

```
PS /> uname -a
Linux 2054dae884f4 4.9.93-linuxkit-aufs #1 SMP Wed Jun 6 16:55:56 UTC 2018
x86_64 x86_64 x86_64 GNU/Linux
```

One last point with the Linux container: you can install other Linux functionality into the container.

```
PS /> apt-get install net-tools
```

```
PS /> ifconfig
eth0      Link encap:Ethernet  HWaddr 02:42:ac:11:00:02
          inet addr:172.17.0.2  Bcast:172.17.255.255  Mask:255.255.0.0
          UP BROADCAST RUNNING MULTICAST  MTU:1500  Metric:1
          RX packets:20256 errors:0 dropped:0 overruns:0 frame:0
          TX packets:10389 errors:0 dropped:0 overruns:0 carrier:0
          collisions:0 txqueuelen:0
          RX bytes:26717565 (26.7 MB)  TX bytes:571826 (571.8 KB)

lo        Link encap:Local Loopback
          inet addr:127.0.0.1  Mask:255.0.0.0
          UP LOOPBACK RUNNING  MTU:65536  Metric:1
          RX packets:0 errors:0 dropped:0 overruns:0 frame:0
          TX packets:0 errors:0 dropped:0 overruns:0 carrier:0
          collisions:0 txqueuelen:1
          RX bytes:0 (0.0 B)  TX bytes:0 (0.0 B)
```

Once the container is shut down, you'll lose these changes, so remember to create an image from the container, so that you can still access the tools you've downloaded.

If you want to experiment with the latest PowerShell preview versions, or with other Linux distributions, you'll find them available as containers at `https://hub.docker.com/r/microsoft/powershell/`.

We stated earlier that the switching mechanism allows you to manage Windows or Linux containers but not both simultaneously. The latest versions of Docker for Windows enable you to run and manage both Windows and Linux containers simultaneously, without using the switching mechanism. You set Docker for Windows to run Windows containers and then start Linux containers, using the `platform` parameter.

```
PS> docker run –platform=linux --name PSTest -it mcr.microsoft.com/
powershell pwsh
```

You'll also have to use the `platform` parameter when pulling the container image from Docker Hub.

To run containers in this manner, you'll have to use Docker 18.03-ce-win59 as a minimum version and have the experimental features enabled.

TRY IT YOURSELF

Experiment with Linux containers on your Windows system. Can you find other Linux-based containers that will run on Windows?

Our recommendation, for now, is to experiment, if this is a feature you require, but be very aware that it's a rapidly changing technology. Keep a close watch on future Windows and Docker releases, for further advances and enhancements.

Recommendations

We currently make the following recommendations regarding the use of containers:

- Use containers, where appropriate. They're not suitable for all scenarios but do provide a valuable option for virtualizing applications.

- Pick a version of Windows Server and stick with it, but be aware that the SAC releases only have an 18-month life cycle. If you do decide to upgrade, remember that your existing containers can be run on newer versions of the OS, using Hyper-V isolation. You can upgrade the hosts and containers as a two-step process.

- We recommend Windows Server 1803, as a minimum, for your container host, because it has the latest enhancements to run containers on Windows.

- Use Docker files for building images. They are much smaller and quicker to move between machines than full images.

- Learn Docker syntax. PowerShell is the automation tool of choice, but there isn't a module for managing containers. Wrapping Docker commands in PowerShell functions could be a viable alternative, if you're going to be heavily invested in using containers.

Before the chapter closes, we'd like to offer you a few ideas for some next steps in learning about containers.

Next Steps

We haven't space in this book to cover all aspects of containers. It's a rapidly changing field, and you'll have to keep checking the links in this chapter for changes. As next steps, we recommend that you investigate which applications in your organization would benefit from using containers. Remember that big-bang projects generally fail, so plan a gradual introduction.

In this chapter, we've shown you how to perform manual actions to manage your container environment. When you get to the point of having a large number of containers, you should start to think about orchestration.

An orchestrator is used to perform a number of tasks, including scheduling, health monitoring, failover, scaling, networking, and application upgrades. There are two orchestrators you should investigate first.

The first is Docker Swarm, which provides orchestration capabilities, native clustering of Docker hosts, and scheduling of container workloads. An introduction is available at `https://docs.microsoft.com/en-us/virtualization/windowscontainers/manage-containers/swarm-mode`. It has the advantage of being from Docker and has been the leading orchestrator.

Kubernetes can be used with Windows Server 1709 and later versions. Kubernetes is used to manage containerized workloads and services, including declarative configuration, load balancing, and automation. Kubernetes has taken over from Docker Swarm as the de facto orchestrator `https://docs.microsoft.com/en-us/virtualization/windowscontainers/kubernetes/getting-started-kubernetes-windows` and `https://kubernetes.io/docs/home/?path=users&persona=app-developer&level=foundational`.

One drawback to both orchestrators is that they use a Linux system as the control server.

Lab Work

This has been a very long chapter. Rather than supply specific exercises, we recommend that you complete all of the Try It Yourself sections. The preceding "Next Steps" section provides some ideas for further investigation of containers.

CHAPTER 18

Managing VMs with System Center Virtual Machine Manager

So, here we are near the end! Hard to believe that just 17 short chapters ago we were talking about the basics of Hyper-V, and now you're quite comfortable with the technology. We've covered nearly everything from host and virtual machine (VM) configuration to clustering and Hyper-V Replica. Throughout, you likely found the various management utilities, such as Hyper-V Manager and Failover Cluster Manager, to be sufficient, yet a bit lacking at times. A lot of new Hyper-V administrators find the disparate management experience in the multitude of utilities that Microsoft provides for Hyper-V to be a bit hard to grasp at times. This is because for some items, you need Hyper-V Manager, and for others, you need Failover Cluster Manager. Wouldn't it help if you had a unified management utility? Well, there is indeed such a utility: System Center Virtual Machine Manager, or SCVMM, for short.

In This Chapter and Beyond

This is really the last full chapter of our book. Chapter 19 is designed to point you in the direction of where to go next. This chapter starts you on that journey. SCVMM (part of the huge System Center suite) is a massive software package with numerous functions and features. Entire series of books could, and have, been written about System Center, so our goal here is to teach you how to add Hyper-V hosts into SCVMM for management and then give you an overview of VM management using VMM. SCVMM fills out your Hyper-V management experience, by getting your hands on the fourth and final Hyper-V management utility (alongside Hyper-V Manager, Failover Cluster Manager, and PowerShell.)

© Andy Syrewicze, Richard Siddaway 2018
A. Syrewicze and R. Siddaway, *Pro Microsoft Hyper-V 2019*, https://doi.org/10.1007/978-1-4842-4116-5_18

What Is SCVMM and Where Does It Fit?

As you've seen throughout the book, you've had to jump back and forth between multiple utilities to manage the holistic Hyper-V solution. This can be time-consuming and frustrating, but SCVMM makes it simpler. Think of SCVMM as the enterprise-grade, gold-level management utility. It allows you to manage Hyper-V hosts and clusters and the associated fabric. The fabric in your infrastructure consists of such things as your storage and networking. Additionally, SCVMM has the cool ability to carve out "clouds" from your infrastructure. A cloud is essentially a collection of resources that you can then allocate to Active Directory (AD) groups and users for delegated control. This is really useful for departmental scenarios in which you may want to give a large accounting department with their own IT, for example, X amounts of resources, and a sales team with their own IT, X amounts of resources. Finally, some of the more advanced Hyper-V features, such as network virtualization and service templates, require SCVMM. (While both of these features are nice, only the large enterprises of the world will use them.)

Knowing exactly what SCVMM is, is one thing, but knowing where it fits is entirely another. SCVMM isn't for the faint of heart. Not only is System Center expensive, it can be downright unwieldly to manage, if you let it sprawl out of control. An SQL Server instance is required and is recommended to be running on a server separate from the machine running VMM. Additionally, the VMM server itself must be fairly large, with a fair amount of disk space, if you plan to use a SCVMM library share (Image and ISO Repository) to any degree. Needless to say, it's a pretty significant investment to place any of the System Center products within your environment, and you should really ask yourself if you *need* the functionality, before moving forward. If you want a quick and dirty recommendation on environment size, we always tell people that unless you're running 40 to 50 or more Hyper-V hosts, you don't need network virtualization and, therefore, don't need SCVMM. The other management tools are sufficient, and a high level of automation can be achieved with a moderate understanding of PowerShell.

SCVMM isn't hard to use (assuming proper configuration) and is fairly easy to pick up, as you already know much of the terminology from working through this book. However, some of the tasks that you've done throughout the book are done a bit differently when SCVMM is in play. If you recall earlier in the book, we destroyed the failover cluster that we set up. In this chapter, before we get to VM management with SCVMM, we're going to use it to re-create the cluster and then make sure that cluster is present within VMM. Let's get started on that now.

Note on SCVMM Installation   The following instructions and exercises assume that you have SCVMM installed within your environment. Installation of SCVMM can be quite complex, depending on the configuration. As covering the installation would consume many pages, you can find more information on planning and installing SCVMM here: `https://docs.microsoft.com/en-us/system-center/vmm/install?view=sc-vmm-1807`.

Creating a Cluster with SCVMM

As mentioned, we must re-create the cluster that we destroyed in the previous chapter. We'll do this using SCVMM, so that you can see some of the differences. After the installation, you can launch the VMM utility, either from the server running SCVMM or remotely, from a workstation that has the VMM client utility installed on it. When you launch the utility, you'll be greeted with a screen such as that shown in Figure 18-1. Start by logging in.

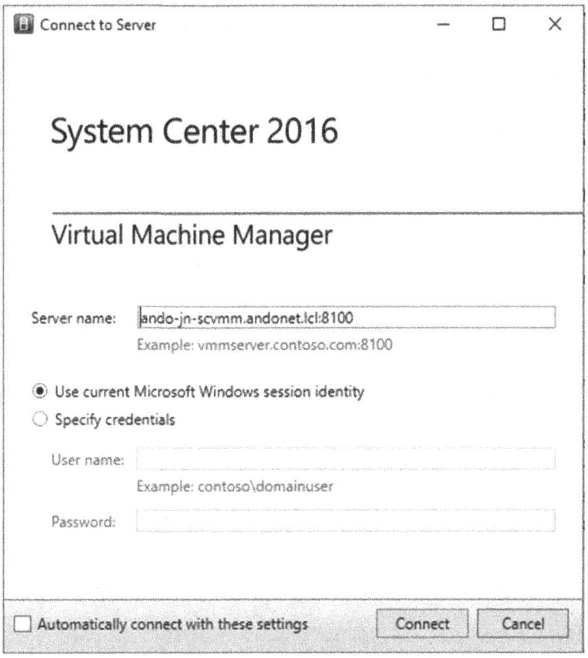

Figure 18-1. *SCVMM sign-in screen*

Note on SCVMM Versions   This chapter uses SCVMM 2016 for the demo, as the 2019 LTSC version is slated for release in Q1 of 2019. While there have been two preview editions released (Builds 1801 and 1807), nothing has changed in regard to the procedures and best practices laid out following. If you're curious about the changes that have been announced to date, follow this link: `https://docs.microsoft.com/en-us/system-center/vmm/whats-new-in-vmm?view=sc-vmm-1807`.

1. Launch the VMM client either on the server running SCVMM or remotely, from a workstation that has network connectivity to the SCVMM server.

2. Enter the Server FQDN, followed by the port number that was defined during the installation. The default port is 8100.

3. Choose the credentials to be used for the connection to the SCVMM server. By default, it will use the currently signed-in credentials.

The client will connect to the back end SCVMM management service and connect you to the running instance. You will be greeted by a screen very similar to that shown in Figure 18-2.

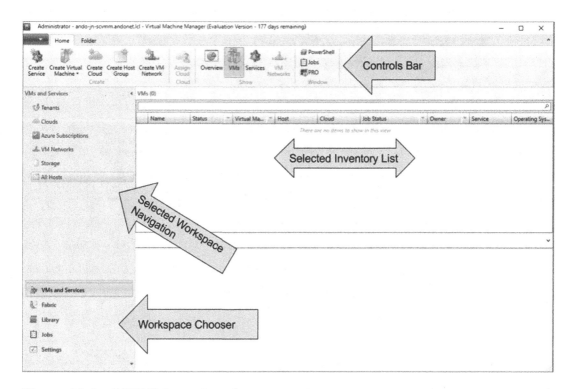

Figure 18-2. *SCVMM user interface*

We won't be covering the UI in its entirety, but as you can see, it's fairly easy to navigate. The left-hand pane contains the Workspace Chooser and the navigation for the selected workspace. The top of the UI contains the Controls Bar, and the middle of the UI contains the inventory for the selected workspace and subsection. These general UI principles are the same throughout all sections of the application. Now that we're logged in, let's re-create that cluster.

The steps to re-create the cluster are

1. Select the Fabric workspace in the left-hand pane and then click the server subsection above the Workspace Chooser.

2. In the Controls Bar, click Add Resources, then click Hyper-V Hosts and Clusters.

3. You'll be greeted with the wizard shown in Figure 18-3. Select the Windows Server computers in a trusted Active Directory domain radio button and then click Next.

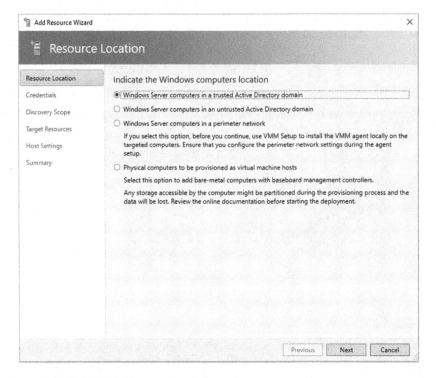

Figure 18-3. SCVMM Add Resource Wizard

4. Select the Use an existing Run As account radio button and then click Browse.

5. In the Select a Run As account dialog, click the Create Run As account button.

Note on Run As Accounts   A Run As account is a saved set of credentials within an SCVMM instance that can be used for various operations. For the purposes of this demo, you can use an existing AD user account for this, but in production situations, you'll want to create dedicated AD objects for this purpose, for maximum security. For more information on Run As accounts in SCVMM, see the following link: `https://docs.microsoft.com/en-us/ previous-versions/system-center/system-center-2012-R2/ gg675096(v=sc.12)`.

---

6. Fill out the form to create a new Run As account and then click Finish.

7. On the Select a Run As account dialog, select your newly created account and click Next.

8. Make sure the Specify Windows Server computers by names radio button is selected and then enter the hostnames for each Hyper-V host in your environment into the Computer names field, one hostname per line, and click Next.

9. Click the check boxes for each host in the Discovered computers list and then click Next.

10. Make sure the Host Group "All Hosts" is selected in the drop-down and that the Reassociate this host with this VMM environment check box is unchecked. Then click Next.

11. On the Summary screen, verify the settings, then click Finish.

12. Monitor the job progress in the jobs UI pop-up, until the job status shows as "Completed" for both Hyper-V hosts. Close the Jobs window, then verify that the Hyper-V hosts show in the All Hosts group.

13. In the Controls Bar, click Create, then click Hyper-V Cluster.

14. Define a cluster name, make sure the check box for enabling storage spaces direct is unchecked, and click Next.

15. Click Browse to select the Run As account that was created in the previous steps; make sure the Existing servers running a Windows Server operating system radio button is selected; uncheck Skip cluster validation; and then click Next.

16. Select both hosts in the Available hosts list and then click Next.

17. On the block storage screen, take note of the storage names, size, partition styles, and filesystem. Using the storage size as a guide, label the volumes for shared storage and quorum. Select quick format and CSV for the storage that will be housing VMs and click Next.

> **Caution**   This process is destructive for any data that is on any of the volumes shown in this list. If any VMs remain on these volumes from previous chapters, and you have not yet moved the VMs off this storage, as mentioned in the previous chapter, do so now, before continuing, or they will be lost.

18. On the IP Address screen, click the check box for all networks to be used and define a cluster IP address, then click Next.

19. On the Summary screen, verify all defined settings and then click Finish.

20. On the Jobs screen, select the Install Cluster Job and monitor it to completion.

21. Once completed, close the Jobs window and then verify that the new Cluster is now showing underneath the All Hosts group.

See how we just used a single utility for multiple tasks that would have required both Hyper-V Manager and Failover Cluster Manager? Plus, you likely noticed how SCVMM has improved log viewing and task notifications. Additionally, you can access the Hyper-V host settings that you've been used to seeing throughout this book, by selecting a host from the list, clicking the host tab in the Controls Bar, and then clicking Properties. Looks familiar, doesn't it?

TRY IT YOURSELF—CONFIGURE A VM FOR REPLICATION

If you haven't already, using the preceding steps, use SCVMM to re-create your Hyper-V cluster. Once complete, connect to that cluster, using Failover Cluster Manager, just as a verification step, to show that Failover Cluster Manager can still manage a cluster that is created by SCVMM.

Managing Virtual Machine with SCVMM

Now that we've added our hosts and re-created the cluster, let's first take a look at the VMs with SCVMM, and then we'll move them back to the clustered storage, so we can make them highly available once again.

1. Using the VMM client, make sure you're connected to the applicable SCVMM instance.

2. Expand All hosts in the left-hand tree and expand your cluster view. Then select one of the hosts in your cluster.

3. If no VMs are showing in the list, click the Host tab in the Controls Bar, then click Refresh Virtual Machines.

4. Select a VM from the list. Once selected, make sure the Virtual Machine tab in the Controls Bar is selected and click Properties.

5. Click Hardware Configuration in the left-hand pane. This will show a nearly identical view to what you're used to seeing with VM settings in Hyper-V Manager. An example of this is shown in Figure 18-4.

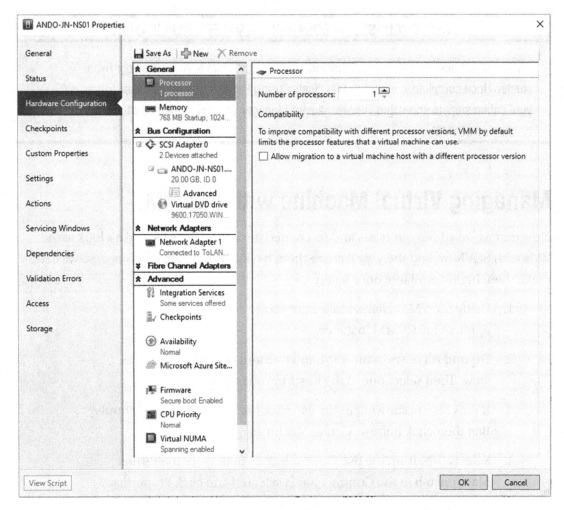

Figure 18-4. *VM Hardware Configuration UI in SCVMM*

6. Select the VM's disk object and take note of the path. If you moved the VM back to local storage, as instructed in the previous chapters, this should be a path other than `C:\ClusterStorage\...`

7. Navigate through the other sections within the Properties UI and take note that several of the various VM settings are present here. When done, close the VM Properties UI.

8. Pick a VM to move back to cluster storage and select it. Click the Virtual Machine tab in the Control Bar and click Migrate Storage.

9. Make sure the Storage Location has defaulted to cluster storage, usually designated by a path such as `C:\ClusterStorage\...`

10. Make sure the Automatically place all VHDs with the configuration radio button is selected and then click Next.

11. Review the Summary for accuracy and then click Move.

12. Monitor the completion of the job.

13. Once complete, open the properties of the VM once again and take note of the new path for the virtual VM's disk in the hardware configuration section of the VM's settings.

14. With the VM's Hardware Configuration settings still open, click Availability, under Advanced, and make sure the check box for Make this virtual machine highly available is checked.

15. Open Failover Cluster Manager, locate the VM under Roles, and take note that it is showing here as a clustered role.

16. Back in SCVMM, select the VM we just configured for high availability and select the Virtual Machine tab on the Control Bar. Click Power On. Wait for the VM to start, then Click Connect or View, and then click Connect via Console.

17. Test VM control through this VM console and take note of the same functionality as Hyper-V Manager.

18. Close the console window when finished.

As you can see, all the same controls that are present in Hyper-V Manager and Failover Cluster Manager are here in SCVMM, but in slightly different areas and contexts. With a little practice and review, you'll be able to manage the solution in a much easier fashion and from a single pane of glass.

TRY IT YOURSELF—VM MANAGEMENT WITH SCVMM

Using the preceding steps, repeat this process for each VM that you would like to be highly available. Additionally, now that you know how to access a VM's hardware properties via SCVMM, use them to modify the memory and CPU settings for a selected VM.

Looking for More on SCVMM?

What we covered in this chapter was just a tiny fraction of what you can accomplish with SCVMM in your Hyper-V environment, but it's likely been enough to show you its value and why you may want to include it in your deployment. If you're interested in further information on this subject, there is a vast array of documentation on `docs.microsoft.com`. The link to that material is `https://docs.microsoft.com/en-us/system-center/index?f=255&MSPPError=-2147217396`.

Lab Work

For additional practice, use SCVMM to create some new VMs and take note of how the process is the same. Once these new VMs are created, review the various controls in the Control Bar, with the Virtual Machine tab selected, and attempt to manipulate the VM in different ways. For example, conduct a live migration or take some snapshots. Put together everything you have learned and do some experimentation!

CHAPTER 19

Continue Learning

Congratulations on reaching the end of the book! The skills and knowledge you've acquired in the previous chapters enable you to confidently—and safely—administer your production Hyper-V environment. We designed this book to allow you to start applying your new skills and knowledge as soon as possible, so that you, and your organization, can reap the benefits immediately.

This isn't the end of your learning journey, though. As an IT professional, there is always something extra to learn—a new technology, a new version of Windows, or something to expand your basic knowledge set.

Many professions enforce the concept of continuing professional development (CPD), both to enhance their skill set and keep it up to date. The majority of IT professionals doesn't seem to have embraced this concept. How many times have you heard "We've always done it this way." IT is one of the fastest changing arenas in which to work. If you don't keep up to date and broaden your skills, you'll stagnate and, ultimately, adversely affect your career.

The dictum "you are responsible for your career" has never been truer, and in IT, the way to improve your professional prospects is to ensure that your skills are current. You know what you want to learn next and in which direction you want your working life to move. Organizations seem very reluctant to pay for training these days, so it's up to you to learn the skills you need.

In this chapter, we're going to suggest some ideas that you can use to build on what you've learned in this book and help take you to that next level, at which you become the "go-to person" in your organization. These aren't mandatory, or meant to be exclusive, just a set of ideas about what else you should be thinking about.

Automation

We've yet to meet an administrator who has enough time to complete all the tasks that he or she is asked to perform. It's more likely that your to-do list grows faster than you can reduce it. This is where automation enters the picture.

375

© Andy Syrewicze, Richard Siddaway 2018
A. Syrewicze and R. Siddaway, *Pro Microsoft Hyper-V 2019*, https://doi.org/10.1007/978-1-4842-4116-5_19

Automating repetitive and tedious tasks will free more of your time, allowing you to concentrate on those tasks that require you to think, for example, capacity planning (but automate the data-gathering process), upgrades, and the implementation of other new capabilities in your organization. When you start automating, pick a single process that takes a lot of your time and create the code to automate it. The code doesn't have to be perfect, as long as it delivers the results you require and runs in a reasonable time frame. Once you're happy with that code, move on and solve another problem. You can always revisit earlier projects as requirements or knowledge changes. Aim for automating as much as you can, rather than for the perfect piece of code.

PowerShell is the default automation engine and scripting language for the Windows platform. We've already introduced PowerShell as a way to perform Hyper-V administration tasks. The Hyper-V PowerShell cmdlets provide a command-line tool for administering Hyper-V and virtual machines (VMs). Nearly every Windows Server feature and role has a set of PowerShell cmdlets. Microsoft's major products, such as Exchange, SharePoint, and SQL Server, together with products from many other vendors, also have PowerShell cmdlets available. This means that you can use one tool to manage your whole environment.

If you want to learn more about PowerShell, we recommend *PowerShell in Depth,* 2nd ed., by Don Jones, Jeffery Hicks, and Richard Siddaway (Shelter Island, NY: Manning Publications, 2014), which provides an excellent view across the breadth of PowerShell functionality. *PowerShell in Action,* 3rd ed., by Bruce Payette and Richard Siddaway (Shelter Island, NY: Manning Publications, 2017), provides a deeper view into how PowerShell works under the covers, and why it works the way it does.

Microsoft has a number of web sites related to PowerShell.

- *PowerShell Documentation page*: `https://msdn.microsoft.com/en-us/powershell`

- *Windows PowerShell documentation and help files*: PowerShell v5.1, at `https://docs.microsoft.com/en-gb/powershell/scripting/powershell-scripting?view=powershell-5.1`, PowerShell v6, at `https://docs.microsoft.com/en-gb/powershell/scripting/powershell-scripting?view=powershell-6&viewFallbackFrom=powershell%3D5.1`, and PowerShell Team Blog, at `https://blogs.msdn.microsoft.com/powershell/`

If you require answers to get PowerShell-related questions, the forums at `PowerShell.org` are a good place to start. The PowerShell Summit, `https://powershell.org/summit/`, is an annual conference (and more) dedicated to PowerShell and DevOps. The recordings of many of the summit's technical sessions are available through the preceding summit URL.

Windows Server Insider Previews

Windows 10 has had an Insider Preview program for a number of years. Under this program, you gain access to new builds during the process of developing the next semiannual update of Windows 10. The Insider Preview builds are a good way to test new functionality.

In 2017, Windows Server joined the Insider Preview program. You can test the latest functionality coming in a Semi-Annual Channel (SAC) or Long-Term Servicing Channel (LTSC) release. SAC releases are Server Core only; LTSC releases are Server Core and Server with Desktop Experience (GUI).

You can sign up for the program at `https://insider.windows.com`. The server builds and associated software can be downloaded from `www.microsoft.com/en-us/software-download/windowsinsiderpreviewserver`.

Testing the latest builds in your lab will put you ahead of the curve in understanding the functionality in the next releases of Windows Server.

Windows Server Roles and Features

Hyper-V is a part of Windows Server, but it's just one part. Windows Server supplies many other parts of your environment, for example:

- Active Directory and DNS

- IIS

- File servers

- Windows Server Update Services (WSUS)

You should look for references that contain information on automating the respective features, as well as providing technical information. A good starting place to learn more about the other components of Windows Server is `https://docs.microsoft.com/en-gb/windows-server/windows-server`.

In this book, we've concentrated on Hyper-V as a feature of Windows Server. You can also get a "hypervisor only" version at `https://technet.microsoft.com/en-us/library/hh833684(v=ws.11).aspx`. This is worth investigating as a component of your Hyper-V environment. The management tools you learned about in this book can be used to manage Hyper-V Server also.

Microsoft also has a virtual academy that contains free online courses on many aspects of Windows Server: `https://mva.microsoft.com/`.

The Cloud

Many organizations are moving some, or all, of their infrastructure to the cloud. The cloud is essentially having your infrastructure—servers, storage, and networking—hosted on the Internet, rather than in your own datacenter. Combinations of on-premise and cloud-based hybrid infrastructures are continually being developed and released by the major vendors.

Cloud-based infrastructure suppliers include

- Microsoft's Azure platform

- Amazon Web Services

- Rackspace

Other services, such as storage and databases, are available, in addition to infrastructure.

The hybrid solutions allow for the possibility of moving VMs from your datacenter to the cloud and vice versa, depending on the most cost-effective solution.

Cloud computing is rapidly evolving, and rather than supplying out-of-date information, we recommend that you investigate the current situation with one or more suppliers.

DevOps

DevOps is the merging of development and operations, to enable swift and painless delivery of applications. Hyper-V can be used as a foundation for using infrastructure as code (IaC), one of the basic principles of DevOps.

IaC takes the creation of infrastructure (VMs, storage, and networking) through automated processes (see the "Automation" section at the beginning of this chapter) and adds development activities, such as source control, versioning, and formalized testing, to the process. The goal is to be able to re-create your infrastructure and deploy the latest version of your application at the press of a button—up to several times a day, if required.

Many organizations don't need that level of agility, and not all workloads are suitable for rebuilding multiple times per day. (We'd certainly NOT like to perform a Hyper-V or Exchange migration on a daily basis!) Even if you don't adopt a full DevOps approach, there are certain aspects, such as configuration management, that could be useful to you and your organization. For example, configuration management tools can be used to automate the creation of new servers. Need a new domain controller? Then create a configuration that can be applied every time you create a domain controller, so you *know* that they are built automatically. You can also get your configuration-management tool to report on the configuration of the servers it controls, then correct configuration drift, if required.

Various configuration-management tools are available, including

- *PowerShell Desired State Configuration*: `https://msdn.microsoft.com/en-us/PowerShell/dsc/overview`

- *Chef*: `www.chef.io/`

- *Puppet*: `https://puppet.com`

A DevOps approach is not required by every organization, or even every application in the organization, but it is the way the industry is currently progressing.

A number of good sites are available for DevOps-related material, including

- `http://devops.com/`

- `http://dev2ops.org/`

- `https://devopscollective.org/`

DevOps is another rapidly evolving field for which we encourage you to research, adapt, adopt, and use to benefit your organization.

Index

© Andy Syrewicze, Richard Siddaway 2018
A. Syrewicze and R. Siddaway, *Pro Microsoft Hyper-V 2019*, https://doi.org/10.1007/978-1-4842-4116-5

W, X, Y, Z

Printed in the United States
By Bookmasters